R
writte
CW00468513
CVIVS PRINCIPATVS
SVPER·HVMERVM·EIVS

www.purpleguide.com

The Purple Guide: Rome

Credits

Writer: Hope Caton
Editor: Robin Bell
Design: Sharon Platt
Cartography: Anderson Geographics Ltd
Sub-editor: Jon Stanhope
Contributors:
Catherine McCormack, Bruce Gordon-Smith, Sharon Platt, Silvia Nacamulli
Website design: Mark Parker at Escape Media www.escape-media.com
Photography: All photographs by Hope Caton, except:
Bridgeman Art Library: 66,173; Scala Archives: 57, 61, 145, 148, 153, 164, 174; Robin Bell: 20; Sharon Platt: 40, 50, 68, 84, 85, 100, 161, 166, 187, 226, 241, 242, 254; Bruce Gordon-Smith: 44, 144, 177, 211; scans by Bobbett Creative

With many thanks to ...

The Italian Tourist Board in London and their associates in Rome. Our team of advisors includes Angela Lopez and Cristiana Pazienti at APT, and the lovely and talented Roman actor, Carmen Sorrenti. *Mille grazie!*

Publishing Information

Published in the United Kingdom in September 2005 by:
The Purple Guide Ltd
Teddington Studios
Broom Road
Teddington Middlesex
TW11 9NT

ISBN 0-9547234-2-2
Printed in The Netherlands by Chevalier

Sales and PR

For information, telephone our sales department on 020 8614 2277
or email: **sales@purpleguide.com**
Public Relations: Sue Ockwell at Travel PR: 020 8891 4440
Distibuted in the UK and EU by NBN International: 01752 202327

Write to us

We welcome the views and suggestions of our readers. If we include your contribution in our next edition, we will send you a copy of the book, or any other Purple Guide that you would prefer.
Please write to us at the address above or email: **feedback@purpleguide.com**

thepurpleguide

the inside story

'a winning formula' The Sunday Times

Every city has a story and Rome has one of the greatest stories of all time. The Purple Guide presents artists, emperors, kings and popes as characters in the tale. To set the scene, read the brief history at the front of the book. Then browse through and find the sights you want to visit, using our colourful introductory pages as a guide. You will find more in-depth information and biographies right where you need them: close to the sight most associated with a famous – or infamous – character.

Our favourite places are covered extensively in the main body of the book. For information on other sights, look in our *Churches, Monuments, Museums and Galleries* section at the back. Everything is cross-referenced to our detailed maps. We don't review accomodation, so we devote more care and attention to our *Food & Drink* and *Shopping* sections. All of our listings are personally researched and we do not accept any favours in return.

Updates We constantly update our website with useful information to support each guidebook we publish. Before you leave for Rome, be sure to visit our *Updates* page for new information on restaurants, shopping and special events. You can also find out about other titles and buy your guidebooks online. **www.purpleguide.com**

A word about GPS This is the first city guidebook to include GPS data for key sights. Traditionally, latitude and longitude has been expressed in degrees, minutes and seconds. Today the decimal format is frequently used, and it is the one you will see in this book (eg. 41.90623, 12.48151). You may need to change the units option on your GPS locator. Be aware that some locators are more accurate than others and atmospheric conditions can affect GPS accuracy.

CONTENTS

Introducing Rome

'Roma: una vita non basta'

Rome: a lifetime is not enough

Every traveller has Rome on a list of cities to visit. In that sense, all roads do lead here, to the city that was once *caput mundi*, the capital of the world. No other city has had more influence on Western culture than Rome. The longest-running empire in history had its centre here. Ancient Rome gave the world running water, indoor plumbing, paved roads, the arch, the dome, and concrete that sets under water. Roman literature, architecture, art and language have permeated every area of our civilisation. The physical remains of this culture are waiting for the visitor in Rome.

There is another Rome that is immediately visible: the great city of the Renaissance and Baroque popes. The art treasures in the Vatican alone would make any nation proud, but in Rome this is just the beginning. Step inside one of the many churches or galleries, and works by Michelangelo, Raphael, Titian and Caravaggio are there to be admired. Because so much art is incorporated into the buildings themselves, a visit to Rome is essential.

These layers exist side-by-side with modern Rome, the city that is alive and buzzing with people and the constant sound of traffic. Nowhere else will you find the daily parade of human interaction that you see in Rome: perfectly-coiffed policewomen in well-fitting uniforms, wearing designer sunglasses; impossibly handsome waiters; clerics walking with robes flapping at their heels; and squadrons of motor scooters performing death-defying manoeuvres. With a population of 2.5 million (3.3 million in the metropolitan area) Rome is the capital of Italy, a nation of 58 million people, a member of the European Union and the G8.

There is a saying, *'Roma: una vita non basta,'* which means a lifetime is not enough for the city. You can stick to a brisk agenda and try to see everything in a week, but you won't succeed. It really is better to plan on returning. That way you can take the time to soak up the atmosphere in a tranquil piazza, listen to the music of water splashing in the fountains, watch the play of sunlight on the buildings and enjoy a cool *frullato*. You don't need to plan every step in advance. After seeing some of the main sights, copy the young English aristocrat who came to Rome on his Grand Tour in 1780 and *'decided to straggle and wander about as the spirit pleases'*.

The Romans

Your first encounter with a Roman may leave you feeling somewhat intimidated. They have a lot of bluster and it can come across as arrogance. Romans feel the weight of their history and they exude confidence. They seem to think whatever is Roman is best. There is a sense of megalomania – mine is bigger, *better* than yours. This is the public face, especially of someone in an official capacity. It is usually a front. If you get to know a Roman better you will likely find a warm and generous person who likes nothing better than to tease and have fun. Romans are very social people – they love to talk and laugh out loud. Sometimes the volume and the passion of their conversations can overwhelm a tourist who is used to quieter behaviour.

It's not easy living in Rome. Since the introduction of the euro in 2002, prices and rents have risen for the average person. A Roman's social skills are essential for survival. Jobs and apartments are found through personal contacts and without a large network of friends and associates nothing is possible. Life in the city revolves around people getting together, forming connections and helping each other – sometimes for money, often out of friendship.

Romulus and Remus

The founding of Rome is attributed to Romulus and Remus: twin boys borne to Rhea Silva, daughter of King Numitor, ruler of Alba Longa. Numitor's evil brother had stolen the crown of the thriving kingdom located on Lake Albano near modern-day Castel Gandolfo. The King was imprisoned and Rhea was forced to enter the service of the goddess Vesta, whose priestesses either remained virgins for life – or faced death. When Rhea became pregnant, the god Mars was attributed as the father. When mother and babies were condemned to death by drowning, Rhea bundled Romulus and Remus into a reed basket and cast it into the river Tiber.

The basket floated downstream and was caught in the branches of a fig tree, where it was discovered by a She-Wolf who suckled the boys and protected them. Later, a herdsman named Faustulus found the boys and took them home to his wife. When Romulus and Remus were told the story of their origins, the brothers returned to Alba Longa and restored King Numitor to his throne. Romulus then decided to have his own kingdom. In 753 BC, he returned to the fig tree and founded *Roma Quadrata*. Remus challenged him but was quickly assassinated. King Romulus needed an influx of women to help populate his kingdom of male peasants so he invited the neighbouring tribe of Sabines to a celebration. At the feast – held in the field that would later become the Circus

Maximus – Romulus' soldiers abducted the wives and daughters of his guests at swordpoint. In all, 600 Sabine women were kidnapped. The notorious incident became known as the *Rape of the Sabine*.

Kings and Emperors

Romulus was the first of seven kings who ruled Rome from 753-509 BC. During this time, an infrastructure was created for what would later become the Empire. Four kings were Etruscan with knowledge of how to form an arch – the basis for building aqueducts, bridges and walls. Roman builders also knew about concrete and how to make it set under water. Roman society was divided into two groups: Patricians and Plebeians, rich and poor. Patricians who supported the king with money became his advisors, a select group of men that would evolve into the Senate, an organisation that grew in power as kings became more corrupt and distrusted by Romans. The last of the seven, King Superbus, was exiled in 509 BC.

In 390 BC, Gallic barbarians sacked Rome and the surrounding area of *Latium* (modern Lazio). Roman guards were warned of the attack by the cackling of geese at the temple of Juno on the

THE PALATINE

BC	
753	Romulus founds Rome
600	Circus Maximus built
560	Servian wall begun
509	Roman Republic founded
390	Gauls sack Rome
312	first aqueduct
44	Julius Caesar assassinated
27	Augustus declared Emperor
0	Birth of Christ
AD	
67	Saints Peter and Paul martyred
313	Edict of Milan
410	Goths sack Rome
476	Western Roman Empire ends
1096	first Crusade
1300	first Jubilee year
1454	printing press invented
1517	Protestant Reformation begins
1533	Henry VIII excommunicated
1545	Council of Trent
1789	French revolution begins
1804	Napoleon crowned Emperor
1815	Napoleon at Waterloo
1861	Kingdom of Italy founded
1870	Rome made Italian capital
1914-18	World War I
1922	Mussolini ascends to power
1929	Lateran Treaty
1939-45	World War II
1946	Republic declared, King exiled
1989	Berlin wall removed
2000	Jubilee year

Capitoline Hill. The Gauls were swift. They poured into Rome, looted the city, raped the women and departed, allowing themselves just a brief moment to appreciate the beauty and majesty of the Roman Senate, before killing all the Senators.

Roman building knowledge meant it was able to rebuild more quickly than other cities. Rome became the centre of power in the region.

Carthage was defeated in the Punic Wars, its territories – including Iberia (Spain and Portugal) – passed to Rome. Warring Greek armies, who appealed to Rome for help, later found themselves subjects of the Romans – as did the people of Alexandria and Judea. Rome now ruled the entire Mediterannean and its citizens became very wealthy. The vast empire traded in every kind of commodity, including huge numbers of slaves. Roman soldiers sold their captives to slave traders who followed the armies, with money changing hands directly after a battle.

Julius Caesar used his talents as a military commander to secure himself the title

Dictator for Life. Caesar was not, as many believe, the first emperor – rather, he was the last dictator. Caesar's assassination in 44 BC put an end to his ambition and to the Republic. A leadership struggle ensued between Caesar's anointed heir Gaius Octavius (Augustus) and his bastard son Caesarian, who was represented by Marc Antony and Cleopatra. Octavius emerged victorious with the added bounty of a conquered Egypt.

Octavius was declared Emperor Augustus in 27 BC, the first of 93 emperors. The last Emperor took the name of Rome's first king: Romulus. The decline and fall of the Roman Empire was a gradual process that officially ended with the abdication of Romulus on 4 September AD 476. Rome then fell to the Goths. Theoderic, who named himself Emperor, could only sign his name with the help of a stencil. The new ruler may have pretended to love all things Roman, but he moved the capital of his empire to Ravenna. Rome was left to rot.

Decline and rebirth

Roman patricians decamped to the glistening Byzantine court at Constantinople – the new centre of Christendom. Rome was repeatedly plundered and its population declined from 800,000 in AD 400 to 30,000 by 546. Goths cut the aqueducts that fed the baths and fountains and, more importantly, provided drinking water. The city was reduced to using water from the Tiber and the land reverted to marshland. Malaria was rife and the papacy was reduced to begging for clothing and food from bishops in Gaul.

The growing power of Islam began to eat away at Byzantine territories in the eastern Mediterranean. At the same time, marine-based mercantile city-states Venice, Pisa, Amalfi and Genoa were growing in power and wealth. Visigoth armies couldn't compete on water and were kept busy fighting the French. Roman popes needed a means to consolidate political and spiritual power in Christian Europe. Pope Urban II announced the first Crusade in an effort to wrest Jerusalem from the Muslims and unify the European kingdoms under a common cause. During the fourth Crusade in 1204, Christian armies sacked Constantinople. In economic terms, Venice benefited the most but Rome emerged as the undisputed centre of the Christian church. By the beginning of the 13th century, the popes were full of confidence as they effectively became monarchs. For a brief time there were two popes: one in Avignon and one in Rome.

A new Rome

When matters were resolved in 1417, Rome entered a second phase of glory. The city was completely rebuilt during the Renaissance (1400-1600) and Baroque (1600-1750) periods. The new Rome was designed to demonstrate the power and authority of the Catholic church, with the Pope at its head. As well as being the spiritual leader, he was a secular prince, town planner, autocratic warlord and hated tax collector. The supreme ruler in Rome, the Pope was responsible for major building works and minor repairs. (This peculiar political tradition continues today in slightly altered form – Berlusconi is responsible for fixing Roman roads. He is the one Romans curse when they hit a pothole and tumble off their scooters.)

The Renaissance papacy was worldly and corrupt, with an international court numbering in the thousands. The building and decorating of St Peter's and other churches required an enormous amount of money. One method of raising funds was through the sale of 'indulgences', whereby sins were remitted for a cash payment. Then Martin Luther nailed his attacks on papal abuses and the sale of indulgences to a church door in Wittenburg, Germany in 1517. The Reformation had begun.

At the time, Pope Leo X (Medici) ruled over one of the most lavish and ostentatious papal courts in history, one he viewed as his God-given right to enjoy. Leo excommunicated anyone who challenged the papacy. All dissenters were labelled heretics. Leo's cousin Clement VII excommunicated Henry VIII, who then established the Church of England. The battle for souls in Europe was often bloody. The papacy eventually responded with a call for austerity at the Council of Trent. It was too little too late for many people in northern Europe who became Protestants. The resulting confiscation of Catholic lands and property sharply decreased the papal purse. The papacy turned instead to central Italy as its tax base, directing attention towards expanding and maintaining the Papal States.

Napoleon set the wheels in motion for the transformation of the papacy and the rise of Italian nationhood. He removed the papal government and instituted a new constitution in Italy, one that Italians preferred. Citizens rebelled when the French returned the papacy to power in 1815. Turin was the centre of the *Risorgimento*, with men like Cavour, Mazzini and Garibaldi conspiring with King Vittorio Emanuele II against the French-supported papacy. Rome became a battleground until 1870 when the storming of Porta Pia secured the city for the King. The political power of the popes had ended.

Modern Rome

The incompetence of the monarchy led to Mussolini and the fascists coming to power in the early 20th century. Italian families were going hungry and thousands were leaving for North America. Mussolini instituted a food programme and drained the marshes around Rome, but his foreign policy saw Italians march into Ethiopia and make alliances with Hitler. Italy entered World War II on the side of the Germans. Yet Italian armies received little German military support until Italy began negotiations with the Allies. Talks dragged on, giving Hitler time to send German Panzer divisions to occupy Rome. Fighting continued longer than anyone thought possible before Allied troops liberated the city in 1944. At the end of the war, King Umberto II abdicated. Italy declared itself a Republic with both a President and a Prime Minister. Since then the country has experienced political instability, with ongoing conflict between left and right wing factions. Elected in 2001, Silvio Berlusconi has become the longest-sitting Prime Minister.

Rome celebrated the turn of the millennium with a Jubilee declared by Pope John Paul II. When he died in April 2005, over three million people flooded into Rome to pay their last respects. Romans coped with the influx as they have always done. After all, this is Rome – the Eternal City.

ROME

VIA DELLA CONCILIAZIONE AND ST PETER'S

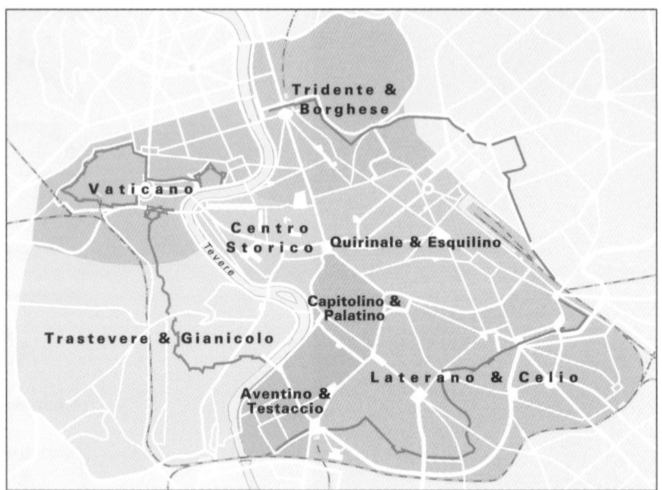

The colours of the districts on this map correspond to chapters in the book. Use the coloured side-bar headings to find your way around. Each chapter has introductory pages with suggestions on what to visit.

Getting Around

Rome is a frenetic, exciting city where cars and scooters hurtle around, honking at anything that happens to be in the way. To the outsider, the aggressiveness of Roman drivers can appear dangerous. It does take some getting used to and even crossing the street can be an ordeal for the beginner. The best solution is to tag along with the locals until you are confident enough to strike out alone, or wait to cross with a nun or a priest. Romans are respectful towards the clergy.

Don't rely on striped crossing zones because if you stand and wait, no one will stop. Pedestrian crossings with lights are the safest bet all around.

When you begin to feel more confident you can attempt to cross as the Romans do: hold out your arm in the direction of ongoing traffic, be sure to make eye contact with the driver of the nearest approaching car and then boldly step forward as you observe the car braking. It takes nerve but it works.

Much of central Rome can be covered on foot but travelling across the city will involve the metro, bus or tram. Taxis are also an option.

Tickets

Rome has an integrated system: tickets are valid for metro, bus and tram journeys and are widely available at tobacconists, metro stations, main bus stops, news kiosks and some bars. Look out for the ATAC symbol. You can also enquire even if there is no symbol displayed. If you know you are going to use many tickets during your stay, try to purchase several at the same time.

Tickets have to be stamped when you start your journey, at the turnstiles on the metro and in ticket machines on the buses and trams. The fine for not having a validated ticket is €52. Regular spot checks are carried out and no excuses are accepted. Children up to ten years old travel free if accompanied by an adult. There are no discounts for senior citizens.

Ticket types

BIT €1
(biglietto integrato a tempo)
A timed ticket that can be used for 75 minutes from the first validation. It is valid for only one metro journey and you can change lines in order to reach your final destination. When changing from bus to metro the ticket must be validated a second time on entering the metro.

BIG €4
(biglietto integrato giornaliero)
A day ticket that can be used up to midnight on the day of purchase.

CIS €16
(carta integrata settimanale)
A seven-day pass that must be shown to the ticket inspector on request. It does not have to be stamped but you need to fill in details on the ticket itself, including your name and the dates when the pass is to be used.

Tickets cannot be used on the tourist buses or the direct service to Fiumicino Airport.

Metro

The metro is a simple two-line affair in the shape of a cross, which intersects at Termini – the only station where you can change lines. It's a quick and mostly efficient way to get from place to place and provides a good cross-city option to avoid inevitable traffic jams. However, it does represent the bare necessities of travel with graffiti-covered cars passing through featureless stations. The metro is also unpredictable. It can be busy at strange times that do not conform to rush hour rules, and can also be subject to sudden strikes with no warning. There have been many attempts to extend the network but digging underground is invariably halted by new archaeological discoveries.

Buses and trams

There is an extensive network of bus routes, which can seem confusing. It is better to concentrate on getting to know a small number of useful cross-city routes (p.310). There is also a range of bus sizes, with the smallest electric buses having only eight seats. Try to get on at the beginning of a route or you will almost certainly be standing.

There are points in the city that are useful transport hubs: Largo Argentina, Piazza Venezia, Termini, and Piazza San Silvestro. Bus stops *(fermata)* have boards that show a list of stops for the different routes. The starting point is at the top and your location on the route is circled. Board at the rear of the bus *(entrata)* where you will find machines for stamping your ticket and leave by the middle doors *(uscita)*. The front doors can be used to enter if you have a validated ticket. These door rules become more flexible during rush hours, so try to follow the Romans.

The trams are very efficient and useful, in particular the number 8 running from Centro Storico down to Trastevere. These are long vehicles with various places that you can board.

Useful bus and tram routes (map p.310)

64 (east-west)
Vatican • Campo de'Fiori • Piazza Navona • Pantheon • Piazza Venezia • Capitoline Museums • Forum • Termini

23 (north-south)
Vatican • Castel S.Angelo • Trastevere
(goes down the west side of the river and returns up the east side)

81 (northwest-southeast)
Vatican • Piazza del Popolo • Trevi Fountain • Piazza Venezia • Forum • Circus Maximus • Colosseum • San Giovanni in Laterano

115 electric (north-south)
Vatican • Parco Gianicolense • Trastevere

116 electric (east-west)
Vatican • Piazza Farnese • Campo de'Fiori • Piazza Navona • Pantheon • Trevi Fountain • Spanish Steps • Piazza Barberini • Borghese Gardens

117 electric (north-south)
Piazza del Popolo • Spanish Steps • Trevi Fountain • Piazza Venezia • Forum • Colosseum • San Giovanni in Laterano

Tram 8
Centro Storico • Trastevere

Tram 3
(south-east-north)
Trastevere • Circus Maximus • Colosseum • University • Borghese Gardens • Museum of Modern Art • Villa Giulia

Taxis

Legal taxis in Rome are white with an identification name and number, and they all have meters. Unregistered operators may approach you at Termini or the airport. If you use them you will almost certainly be taken for a very expensive ride.

It is almost impossible to hail a taxi in Rome. Use one of the taxi ranks marked on our maps or telephone in advance (06 3570, 06 4994 or 06 5551). Please note that you will pay additionally for the time it takes for the taxi to reach you from where your call was first received. In this case the amount on the meter will be higher than the basic starting rate of €2.33 (daytime) or €4.91 (after 10pm). There are surcharges for luggage and for travel to and from the airport. A typical daytime journey in the city centre will range in price from €5 to €20. Try to have the correct change for your driver; most drivers don't like changing large banknotes.

IF IT RAINS YOU CAN EXPECT A VERY LONG WAIT FOR A TAXI. THEY JUST SEEM TO DISAPPEAR WHEN IT IS WET.

Cars

There is a Roman saying: *'To drive in Rome you must have five eyes and be a mind reader.'* Driving in the city centre is not advisable. You will encounter heavy congestion, inconsiderate drivers, restricted access and a lack of adequate parking. Worse, your car may be towed away or broken into. If you find that you do have to drive in Rome, see p.283 for more information.

Motorcycles and scooters

You may be tempted to hire a scooter to get around Rome. Unless you are very experienced this is a dangerous notion and a recipe for disaster. Aside from the madness of Roman traffic, the roads are full of potholes which add to the risk. Leave this one to the Romans.

Manifestation

Broad avenues and town planning notwithstanding, traffic in Rome is barely managed chaos at the best of times. This delicate balance can tip into complete chaos at any time and can affect your holiday plans. Don't be surprised if one day you will want to reach a destination only to be told: '*No, not possible, there is a manifestation.*' Images of a mass sighting of the Virgin might enter your mind, but in this case *manifestation*, or *manifesto*, refers to a political demonstration that disrupts traffic – be it an anti-war protest or a transport workers' strike.

The areas around Via Veneto and Piazza della Repubblica are particularly prone to manifestations because wide streets lead to beautiful *piazze*, which make elegant backdrops for the television cameras. During a demonstration the area is cordoned off and no traffic is allowed in or out, causing absolute chaos on the roads and public transport systems.

State funerals, processions and rallies can disrupt traffic throughout the entire city. Romans have become sanguine about these incidents but they do create havoc for the tourist.

CHECK WITH YOUR HOTEL FOR INFORMATION ABOUT EVENTS OR VISIT www.whatsoninrome.com/strikes.php BEFORE YOU GO.

The Seven Hills

Rome was founded in 753 BC by Romulus. The city included seven hills that overlook the *Fiume Tevere* (Tiber River): *Palatino, Capitolino, Quirinale, Viminale, Esquilino, Celio* and *Aventino.* These are known as the Classical Hills because they were included within the original boundary of the city, enclosed by the Servian Wall. The seven hills can be hard to identify when walking in Rome because there are so many churches, obelisks and monuments dominating the skyline, but an understanding of them helps when finding your way around.

Monte Palatino (Palatine Hill)

This is the sacred birthplace of the Eternal City, the cradle of Rome. Legend has it that Romulus chose to found his new city here; it is from the Palatine that all of the seven kings ruled over Rome. EmperorAugustus was born on the Palatine and he located his imperial residence here. His successors ran the Empire from the Imperial Palace, the ancient ruin that now dominates the hill and overlooks the Circus Maximus and the Forum. Almost all the emperors lived and ruled

from the palace, which was expanded gradually until it incorporated the entire hilltop within its grounds.

The entrance to the Palatine is in the Forum. It is very quiet here and you can easily spend a couple of hours wandering among the ruins. You may want to take a picnic because there aren't many facilities.

Monte Capitolino (Capitoline Hill)

The hill is dominated by the 19th century *Monumento a Vittorio Emmanuele II*, a large white building topped by bronze equestrian statues. Romans call it 'the Wedding Cake'. It has a museum dedicated to the *Risorgimento* and there is a great view from the top. Next to the monument are two sets of stairs: one leads to the church of *Santa Maria in Aracoeli*, and the other to the *Piazza del Campidoglio,* designed by Michelangelo. The artist's grand staircase is called the *Cordonata* and is framed by statues of *Castor and Pollux* taken from the Temple in the Forum. In the centre of the piazza is a bronze equestrian statue of the great Roman emperor and philosopher Marcus Aurelius. Bordering the piazza are the buildings of the *Capitoline Museums*.

SAN GIOVANNI IN LATERANO FROM GIANICOLO

Monte Quirinale

The highest of Rome's seven hills, this is the heart of political Rome and the location of the presidential palace, *Palazzo del Quirinale*. The Palazzo was once the summer palace of the popes, then it became the palace of the Italian kings and it is now the official residence of the President of Italy. A changing of the guard occurs daily at 4pm. The Palazzo is only open to the public on Sunday mornings from September to June. In the Piazza Quirinale are ancient equestrian statues of *Castor and Pollux* and an obelisk removed from the Mausoleum of Augustus. Fine views of St Peter's are available from here.

Monte Viminale

The smallest of the seven hills has good shopping on Via Nazionale. The gardens at Villa Aldobrandini are peaceful and offer good views over the city.

Monte Esquilino (Esquiline Hill)

One of the oldest and most important churches in Rome, *Santa Maria Maggiore,* graces the summit of the Esquiline, the largest of the Classical Hills. From the obelisk behind the church, you can look out over the Viminale and Quirinale hills and see the obelisk at *Trinità dei Monti*. At the front of the church, you can look down the hill to the obelisk at *San Giovanni in Laterano*. On the southernmost slope is the *Parco Oppio,* once the site of Nero's Golden House but now a park with good views across to the Colosseum. One of Rome's best restaurants is located in Esquilino.

Monte Celio

Directly south of the Colosseum, this is Rome's greenest hill. There is a large, walled garden open to the public at the *Villa Celimontana*. The church of *Santi Giovanni e Paolo* is worth a visit. Underneath the church are remains of several Roman houses from different periods. East of Celio is Laterano and two of Rome's most interesting churches: *San Clemente* and *San Giovanni in Laterano*.

Monte Aventino (Aventine Hill)

Bordered by the Circus Maximus, the Tiber and the Viale Aventino, the Aventine is accessed from the Via del Circo Massimo. The crest of the hill overlooks the Tiber and there are three good viewpoints across to St Peters: in the *Giardini degli Aranci* (also known as Parco Savello); the garden at San Alessio; and from the *Piazza Cavalieri di Malta,* which has a door with a keyhole view framed by an arch of ivy. Be prepared to walk or take a taxi to the top; the Aventine is primarily a wealthy residential district and has no public transport, bars or restaurants.

Other Hills

Monte Gianicolo (Janiculum) and Monte Pincio were incorporated into Rome in the 3rd century AD, when the Aurelian Wall was built to enclose the city.

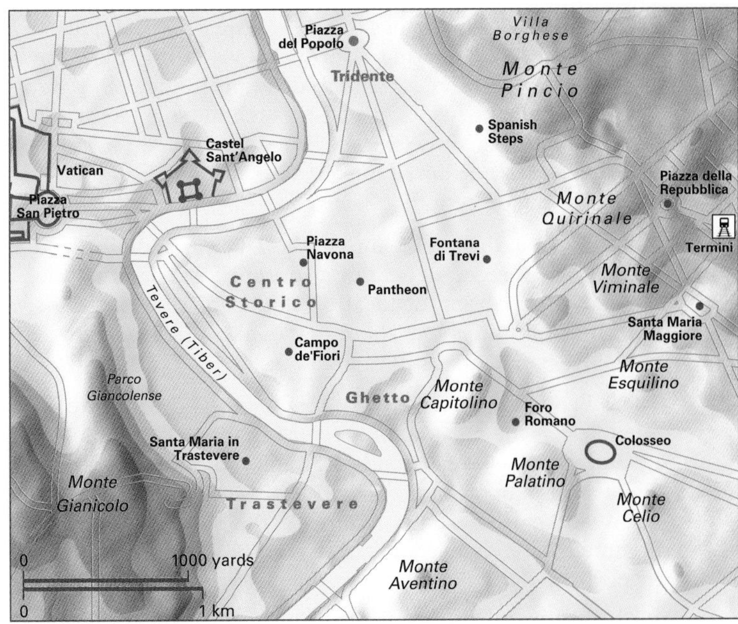

Fiume Tevere (Tiber River)

The river begins its long journey to Rome just south of Bologna in the *Alpe di Serra* near *Monte Fumaiolo* (elevation 1,407 feet). It travels down through the Tibernia valley in Tuscany, passes near Sanselpocro and continues past Perugia in Umbria to flow alongside the A1 motorway from north Lazio to Rome. The Tiber empties into the Tyrrhenian Sea at Ostia, Rome's seaport.

Known as the *Blonde Tiber* because of the yellowish colour of its muddy waters, just how much of this is due to mud and how much to simple pollution is difficult to say. The Romans drank the Tiber's water and that of the local springs until 312 BC, the year in which Appius Claudius built the Appian Aqueduct.

The legendary basket carrying twins Romulus and Remus was caught in the branches of a tree beside the Tiber, just south of the Isola Tibernia. A bridge was built here as early as 179 BC. The strong current, which can still be seen today, caused the bridge to collapse. It was rebuilt so often that it acquired the nickname *Ponte Rotto* (rotten bridge). In true Roman style, a portion of the abandoned stone bridge exists alongside the present day *Ponte Palatino*.

Isola Tiberina, the only island in the Tiber, was dedicated to *Aesculapius,* the god of healing. Appropriately enough, the island has long been the location of a hospital. *Ponte Fabricio,* built in 62 BC, links the island to the mainland. It is the oldest Roman bridge still in use.

The Tiber had its glory days at the height of the Empire when it was the most famous river in the world. Ships loaded with passengers and cargo docked on its shores. Slaves towed barges into the city, carrying obelisks from Egypt and marble from Tuscany. As the Tiber silted up, it became less navigable and subsequently less important. Now its ports are little more than the names of two streets: *Porto di Ripa Grande* near the Ponte Sublico in the south, and *Piazza di Porta Ripetta* near the Ponte Matteotti north of Piazza del Popolo.

Ponte Sant'Angelo

From the bridge there are excellent views of St Peter's, Castel Sant'Angelo and the Tiber.

Regarded as the most beautiful bridge in Rome, it is decorated with ten angels, each one representing an element of Christ's passion.

Commissioned by Pope Alexander VII (Chigi), statues of Saints Peter and Paul, along with the ten angels, were conceived by Gian Lorenzo Bernini (p.51) to welcome pilgrims on their way to St Peter's. The statues were completed by Bernini, his pupils and other artists, and placed on the bridge in 1670.

Originally called *Pons Aelius*, the bridge was built

West side

St Peter School of Lorenzetto
Scourge Lazzaro Morelli
Crown of Thorns GL Bernini
Dice Paolo Naldini
Derogatory Inscription GL Bernini
Offer of Vinegar Antonio Giorgetti

POOR VESTMENT

by Hadrian in 134 AD to connect Castel Sant'Angelo with central Rome. It has a violent history. In medieval times convicted criminals were hung, drawn and quartered on the bridge.

During the Jubilee of 1450 a large crowd of pilgrims were crossing when a bucking mule provoked a panic. More than 200 pilgrims fell into the Tiber and were drowned. In 1455 Pope Nicholas V (Parentucelli) had the bridge structurally renovated and cleared of shops. Three central arches survive from this period; the two outer arches were added in 1892 in a bid to regulate the flow of the Tiber.

TODAY THE BRIDGE IS POPULAR WITH STREET TRADERS.

East side

St Paul
School of Paolo Taccone

Throne Antonio Raggi

Poor Vestment
Cosimo Fancelli

Nails Girolamo Lucenti

Cross Ercole Ferrata

Lance Domenico Guidi

NAILS

Water and Fountains

Both the Empire and the city depended on a constant supply of pure, fresh water. Roman aqueducts were capable of delivering 200 million gallons per day to the thirsty city, from the surrounding hills. The longevity of an emperor depended on his ability to control and manage the water supply to a myriad of public fountains, baths and private villas. In ancient Rome there were over 1,000 fountains.

A 260 mile-long network of tunnels and aqueducts channels fresh water to the modern city. Water passes through several purification tanks before entering the aqueducts. Impurities and sediment hit the side of the tanks and sink while the fresh, clear water flows over the top.

The only ancient Roman service in constant use today, aqueducts still carry water to Rome's most famous fountains. The Trevi Fountain is the termination point of the *Acqua Vergine* aqueduct. Completed in 19 BC, it also supplies water to the fountains at the Spanish Steps and the shops of the Via Condotti, so named because part of the *Acqua Vergine* channel, or *conduit*, is buried under the street. The *Acqua Felice* flows into the *Fontana Acqua Felice* at Piazza San Bernardo near Termini, and the *Fontana dell'Acqua Paola* on Janiculum Hill is the end point for the *Acqua Paola* aqueduct.

Bottled water today is marketed by taste and purity. In ancient times Romans would also distinguish where the water came from by the taste: *Acqua Marcia* was the sweetest tasting, drawn from three clear springs of the River Anio; the *Acqua Alsietina* was gritty lakewater, only good for irrigation; *Acqua Giulia* was sparkling; *Acqua Tepula* was always tepid. Today many Romans still consider that water from the *Acqua Vergine* makes the best coffee, which may explain why a cappuccino tastes better near the Spanish Steps and the Trevi Fountain.

There are 2,000 *nasoni* fountains in Rome. These are roadside taps where water continuously flows out of a curved pipe, which resembles a large nose protruding from a hydrant. The water is drinkable and can be used to refill water bottles.

To use a *nasone*, place your thumb over the nozzle and water will flow upwards through a hole in the top of the pipe, making a drinking fountain.

Churches

Rome's status as the centre of the Catholic church is based upon the fact that the Apostles Peter and Paul preached and were martyred in the city. It was only natural that they should come to Rome to spread the gospel. In their time, it was the capital of the Empire, the most important city in the world. Pilgrims came to Rome to visit the graves of the Apostles and many early Christians wanted to be buried near them.

In 313, Emperor Constantine declared Christianity legal. A building boom started, with the result that there are now more than 900 churches in Rome. Churches were built on the site of homes used for services (Santa Maria in Trastevere), on the site of martyrdom (St Peter's), in the middle of an ancient bath (Santa Maria degli Angeli), above a pagan temple (San Clemente) and on the site of miraculous weather (Santa Maria Maggiore). These buildings are artistic treasure troves.

According to Catholic theology, when a pilgrim visited a holy relic and prayed in a pilgrimage church, a portion of the 'debt' of his sin was paid for and heaven became that much closer. Called an 'indulgence', this could also be earned on behalf of a loved one who was unable to make the journey. There were seven churches a pilgrim had to visit in order to be granted indulgence: **Basilica di San Pietro** (St Peter's), **San Paolo Fuori le Mura** (St Paul's Outside the Walls), **Santa Maria Maggiore**, **San Giovanni in Laterano**, **San Sebastiano**, **San Lorenzo Fiore le Mura** and **Santa Croce in Gerusalemme** (Basilica of the Holy Cross). The first four are known as the main basilicas of Rome and each has a Holy Door, only opened during a Jubilee year.

In the Bible, Jubilee was a time when the ground was left fallow and debts were forgiven. Pope Boniface VIII revived the practice and proclaimed a Jubilee in 1300, when he named the seven churches. In the Jubilee of 2000, John Paul II declared that the faithful only had to pray at the altar of one of the seven churches to receive an indulgence.

RESTITVIT A. MDCCC
CELLAM

Obelisks

Rome came into contact with Egypt after conquering Sicily in 241 BC. Initially, the relationship was of mutual benefit and the Egyptian pharaohs did not confront Rome. That all changed when Ptolemy XIII assassinated Pompey, a former son-in-law of Julius Caesar, in a misguided attempt to gain a closer friendship with the dictator. Caesar attacked and defeated the Egyptian armies and set Cleopatra upon the throne.

Caesar fell famously in love with Ptolemy's ambitious sister. She was crowned Queen of Egypt in 47 BC. As Caesar loved Cleopatra, so did Romans adopt all things Egyptian. No other culture except Greece had more influence over ancient Roman civilisation and religion. Egyptian gods became key members of the Roman pantheon. Later, Emperor Augustus celebrated his victory over Antony and Cleopatra in 30 BC by removing the obelisks dedicated to Rameses II and Psammetichus II from the

OBELISK, PIAZZA DEL POPOLO

Heliopolis and shipping them to Rome. The giant granite carvings were put on display in important public spaces – the two largest were placed in the centre of the Circus Maximus.

Because obelisks represented the glory of Rome, the invading Goths made sure to topple them. After the sacking of the city in AD 410, they lay broken and buried until they were rediscovered during building works carried out in the 16th century under Pope Sixtus V (Felice Peretti). One obelisk was not toppled because it was built into the south wall of Basilica di San Pietro (St Peter's) – marking the spot where the saint was martyred. The papal architect Domenico Fontana moved this obelisk to the centre of Piazza San Pietro in 1586. It was a challenge of huge proportions: the monument is 836 feet tall and weighs 360 tonnes.

In an effort to directly connect the church of the day with the power of ancient Rome, Sixtus V christianised the Egyptian obelisks by placing a cross at the top and an inscription at the base, linking the pope – as Christ's authority on earth – with Augustus and Constantine. Sixtus V established the tradition, followed by subsequent popes, of placing family heraldic symbols at the top of the obelisk, just below the cross. The Peretti family coat of arms, for instance, was a complex design incorporating four symbols: a rampant lion holding pears (for Peretti) and three mountains topped by a star. Through subsequent centuries, many popes adopted the mountain and star symbol. The number of mountains would vary from three to nine but there would always be just one star.

Sixtus V placed the obelisks at the end of broad avenues to guide pilgrims to the basilicas of San Pietro, Santa Maria Maggiore and San Giovanni in Laterano. He also placed one in the Piazza del Popolo to greet pilgrims entering the city from the north. There are 13 obelisks in Rome: eight were brought from Egypt and five are copies made in the city.

Passeggiata Romana

To get acquainted with Rome on your first day, take a leisurely walk from the Spanish Steps to Piazza Navona, with stops at the Trevi Fountain and the Pantheon, following a route that some call the *Passeggiata Romana*. Traditionally, a Roman *passeggiata* takes place on weekends in the late afternoon and early evening. Roman women will dress smart and wear high heels for the walk because it is more about being seen and greeting friends than taking exercise.

Begin at Piazza di Spagna (top right of the map) and the Spanish Steps (p.156), a gathering place for both tourists and locals. Climb up for a good view across to St Peter's from Piazza dei Monti. At the foot of the steps is the *Fontana della Barcaccia* (literally 'the fountain of the worthless boat').

Stroll west along Via Condotti and you will pass designer shops for Armani, Prada, Gucci, Bulgari and Ferragamo. When you see Via Belsiana on your right, turn left at the corner to walk down the pedestrianised Via del Gambero, a cobbled street lined with potted plants and interesting shops. Heading southwards, you will soon reach Piazza San Silvestro, a central bus station worth remembering. There is a post office on the north side of the piazza.

Leave the piazza from the south and walk through Piazza di San Claudio to Via del Tritone. Cross the street and jog left to find the Piazza Poli. Before you arrive at the Trevi Fountain you will hear the sound of people talking as noise reverberates around the tiny piazza, hidden behind Palazzo Poli.Try to make a return visit at night when lights illuminate the fountain.

TRADITION SAYS IF YOU THROW A COIN OVER YOUR SHOULDER WITH YOUR BACK TOWARDS THE FOUNTAIN YOU WILL BE ASSURED A RETURN TO ROME.

To continue your walk, pick up the Via delle Muratte and head west to the Via del Corso. Cross the street to the Via di Pietra and stroll past the remains of Hadrian's Temple, which now forms the façade of the stock exchange. Walk west along Via dei Pastini to the

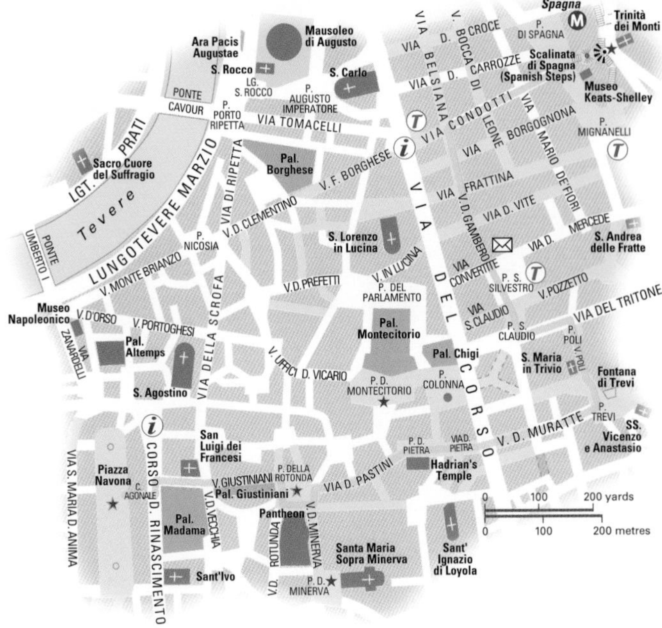

Piazza della Rotunda and the Pantheon.

The best-preserved monument of ancient Rome, the Pantheon (p.44) remains the most magnificent symbol of the Empire. It is open Monday to Saturday from 9am-4.30pm and on Sunday 9am-1pm. The maze of narrow streets around the Pantheon has a mixture of lively restaurants and cafés. Here you will also find bespoke tailors for popes, bishops and cardinals, along with other shops selling ecclesiastical goods.

From the northwest corner of the piazza, locate the Via Giustiniani. Continue west and cross the Via Dogana Vecchia to Via del Salvatore. Jog left at Corso del Rinascimento and take the first right. This leads directly to the middle of Piazza Navona (p.49) where you will see the glorious Bernini centrepiece, *Fontana dei Quattro Fiumi* (Fountain of Four Rivers). There are fountains at either end and the piazza is ringed with cafés. Reward yourself with a *Tartufo* ice cream from Tre Scalini, on the west side.

CENTRO STORICO

IN PIAZZA DELLA ROTONDA

This is the heart of Rome, an area densely packed with many of the city's most famous sights.

Bordered by the Tiber on the west and Via del Corso on the east, this area is also known as *Campo Marzio*, after the temple dedicated to Mars that was located here in the 1st century.

Wander through the narrow streets to find the Pantheon, with a dome that is wider than St Peter's. Have a coffee in Piazza della Rotonda before you strike out for the Bernini fountains in nearby Piazza Navona. Stop along the way to see the Caravaggio paintings in San Luigi dei Francesi.

Michelangelo, Raphael, Titian and Rubens lived and painted here. Their works can be seen in many museums and churches in the area.

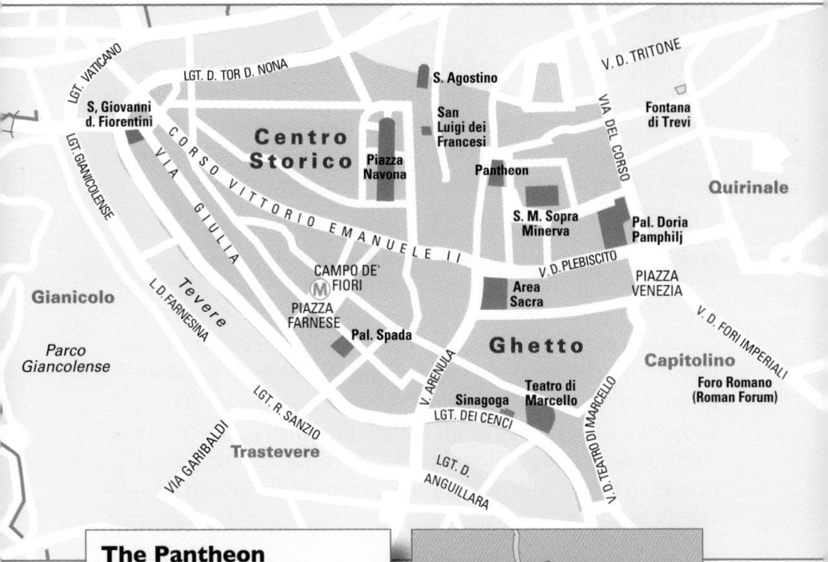

LGT. VATICANO
LGT. D. TOR D. NONA
S. Agostino
V. D. TRITONE
S, Giovanni d. Fiorentini
San Luigi dei Francesi
Fontana di Trevi
Centro Storico
Piazza Navona
Pantheon
VIA DEL CORSO
LGT. GIANICOLENSE
CORSO VITTORIO EMANUELE II
VIA GIULIA
Quirinale
S. M. Sopra Minerva
Pal. Doria Pamphilj
V. D. PLEBISCITO
CAMPO DE' FIORI
PIAZZA VENEZIA
Gianicolo
Tevere
L.D. FARNESINA
Area Sacra
PIAZZA FARNESE
Pal. Spada
Ghetto
V. D. FORI IMPERIALI
Parco Giancolense
Capitolino
V. ARENULA
Teatro di Marcello
Foro Romano (Roman Forum)
LGT. R. SANZIO
Sinagoga
LGT. DEI CENCI
VIA GARIBALDI
Trastevere
LGT. D. ANGUILLARA
V. D. TEATRO DI MARCELLO

The Pantheon
- architectural marvel

Piazza Navona
- Bernini's fountains

Galleria Doria Pamphilj
- Renaissance paintings

San Luigi dei Francesi
- Caravaggio's masterpieces

Ghetto
- Roman Jewish food

Sant'Agostino
- stunning interior

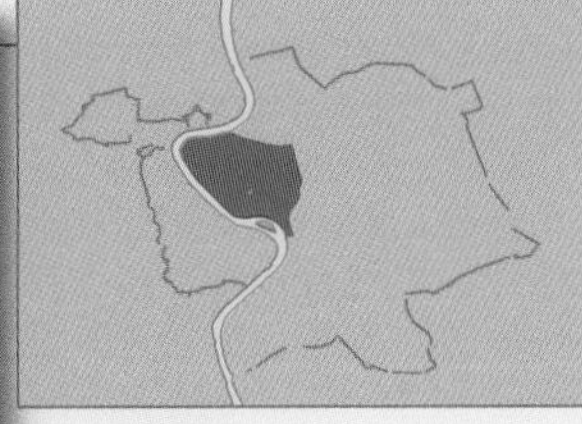

CENTRO STORICO

Via Giulia

A quiet street with interesting antique shops.

Campo de'Fiori

Lively square with a daily market.

Caffè della Pace

Enjoy an *aperitivo* and watch the world go by.

restaurants p.231
shopping p.259
nightlife p.235

Did you know that..?
The Pope's ceremonial robes are made in a tiny shop behind the Pantheon.

An overview

Although the area has kept some of its medieval streets, the Centro Storico district was almost completely rebuilt during the Renaissance. Throughout this time the wealthy families of Rome, who made up the papal court, had huge palaces constructed and commissioned several churches.

A constant flow of pilgrims would pass through on their way to St Peter's. People of many nationalities required churches to provide spiritual and physical care for them. Churches for Spaniards (San Giacomo degli Spagnoli), Germans (Santa Maria dell'Anima) and the French (San Luigi dei Francesi) were established or expanded in the narrow streets around the Piazza Navona. To show the superiority of all things Florentine, the Medici commissioned San Giovanni de'Fiorentini, with its tall dome, to be built directly across from St Peter's in a high-status location.

Churches in Centro Storico often contain a special chapel endowed by a rich family. These can display priceless works of art. For instance, Sant'Agostino has a Caravaggio painting, a Raphael fresco and a sculpture by Jacopo Sansovino, *Madonna with Child*. San Luigi dei Francesi is known as 'the Caravaggio church' for its three paintings on the life of St Matthew. Santa Maria della Pace has a beautiful lintel fresco, *Sibyls and the Angel*, by Raphael.

Bernini's *Elephant obelisk* is easy to miss, tucked away in the small Piazza della Minerva behind the Pantheon. It stands in front of Santa Maria Sopra Minerva, Rome's only Gothic church, which is worth a visit not only for Michelangelo's *Redeemer*, but also for the beautiful blue ceiling.

Today, some of the grand palaces are public museums like Palazzo Doria Pamphilj. Some are buildings of state such as Palazzo Madama, which houses the Italian Senate. The Palazzo Firenze was once the home of the Medici, who established the north-east corner of Centro Storico as a Florentine centre.

Near to the Piazza Firenze is the narrow lane, Vicolo del Divino Amore, where Caravaggio lived. The prison was close by in the Tor di Nona and this is where public executions were held.

Campo de'Fiori was once a marketplace for selling flowers. Markets are still held here in the mornings. The campo is a good place to come in the early evening for an *aperitivo.* Nearby is the elegant Piazza Farnese whose matching fountains are made from old tubs removed from a Roman bath. The Palazzo Farnese is now the French Embassy but it was once the residence of the Farnese family. Pope Alexander VI (Roderigo Borgia) regularly visited his teenage mistress Giulia Farnese in the palazzo.

The Via Giulia is named after Julius II (della Rovere) who planned it to be the most important avenue in Rome. It connects the Vatican to Ponte Sisto and was intended to include the Palazzo dei Tribunale as a centrepiece. Construction of the palazzo never progressed beyond the foundations but the road became a fashionable address. Raphael lived here and the street was known for its week-long parties. Apparently, during one debauched event, the *Fontana Mascherone* flowed with wine for three days. In another unfinished building project, the now vine-covered arch over Via Giulia was designed by Michelangelo as part of a private walkway to connect the Palazzo Farnese with the Villa Farnesina, just across the Tiber.

Today the Via Giulia is a pleasant tree-lined walkway with exclusive antique shops and art galleries. Bus 116 travels part way along the Via Guilia from Ponte Sisto to the Vatican.

South of Via Giulia and across the Via Arenula is the Ghetto, the oldest Jewish district in Europe. As well as the synagogue, there are quite a few good restaurants and bars in the area.

In the centre of Piazza Mattei is the charming *Fontana delle Tartarughe,* by Taddeo Landini.

Pantheon

Piazza della Rotonda
06 683 00230
admission free
map 12, F2
GPS 41.89914, 12.47693

08.30-19.30 Mon-Sat
09.00-18.00 Sun
mass Sat 19.30
Sun 10.30 and 16.30

Built between AD 118-125 by the Emperor Hadrian, the structure of the Pantheon has remained virtually intact for nearly two thousand years. From the piazza, the ground slopes down to a portico with 16 Egyptian granite columns. The giant bronze doors are original and the largest to survive from ancient Rome. The interior is astounding, with the dome that inspired Brunelleschi's *Duomo* in Florence and Michelangelo's dome of St Peter's. At 43.3 metres across, the dome is wider than that of St Peter's. Sunlight streaming through the opening in the apex (the *oculus*) creates a pool of light that illuminates the interior beautifully. It is also wonderful to see rain (and sometimes snow) gently falling inside the building.

THE FLOOR CAN BE SLIPPERY WHEN WET.

When Hadrian began construction, there was no precedent for this type of building. The key challenge was how to support the interior concrete dome and prevent it from collapsing under its own weight. The walls are 6 metres (20 feet) thick, with a series of imbedded arches designed to reduce the weight on the supporting piers (similar to the construction of the Colosseum). The arches are visible from the exterior but hidden from view are eight supporting columns with hollow inspection shafts.

To reduce the weight of the dome itself, and to make it progressively lighter as it rises, three different types of concrete were used, each with a different aggregate. The heaviest bottom ring contains basalt, the middle has tufa and the lightest top ring uses pumice. With no weight the oculus (9 metres across) reduces the point of maximum stress in the centre of the dome.

There is a story that Hadrian showed his plans for the Pantheon to his imperial architect Appolodorus, the man responsible for Hadrian's Villa in Tivoli. The architect dismissed the Emperor's ideas as impossible and may even have been so foolish as to laugh. The Emperor had him executed and became even more determined to see his vision completed. This impatience is the reason the portico seems too small for the overall building. In fact, it is ten feet shorter than originally planned. Hadrian settled for 40-foot columns when the Egyptian suppliers couldn't deliver 50-foot blocks of granite within the required time.

The dedication on the portico (M AGRIPPA) refers to Marcus Agrippa, the son-in-law of Augustus. Agrippa erected the first building on the site in AD 27, one that was dedicated to the worship of the Olympian gods. Hadrian's purpose for the Pantheon remains something of an enigma. In 609 it was converted into a Christian church, Santa Maria ad Martyres, and dedicated to the martyrs whose bones were brought here from the catacombs.

The Pantheon also contains the tombs of Raphael and the kings Vittorio Emmanuele II and Umberto I.

Elephant Obelisk

Piazza della Minerva

Temples to Isis and Serapis once covered a large area in Centro Storico and were embellished with several small Egyptian obelisks. This one originates from Sais in lower Egypt, dates from the 6th century BC and was dedicated to the Pharaoh Hophra. In 1665 it was rediscovered in the garden of a nearby convent and erected here. The obelisk was tiny and, in an ironic gesture, it was decided to place it on a large elephant, a popular animal in Rome at the time. The elephant was a symbol of the strength of mind required to hold the Divine Wisdom of the ages.

For centuries the design has been attributed to Bernini and his colleague, Ercole Ferrata, who carved the elephant. The Dominicans of Santa Maria Sopra Minerva however, credit the design to Fra Giuseppe Paglia. The heraldic symbols of Pope Alexander VII (Chigi), six mountains and a star, can be seen at the top as well as on his family crest on the base.

Santa Maria Sopra Minerva

Piazza della Minerva 42
06 679 3926
map 12, F3
GPS 41.89799, 12.47753

07.00-19.00 daily
(occasionally closed Sun pm)
cloister: 09.00-12.30
16.00-18.30 Mon-Sat

A temple to Minerva was located here next to a tiny Christian church, known as Santa Maria in Minerva. As Christianity grew, the church and temple were absorbed into a convent of Benedictine nuns who cared for *'repented women'*. The nuns moved to San Pancrazio near Campo de'Fiori, and the land was granted to the Dominican order.

In 1280, two architects responsible for Santa Maria Novella in Florence, Sisto Fiorentino and Ristorio da Campi, were commissioned to build a grand Gothic church. Pope Boniface VIII (Caetani) bestowed money, but funding slowed when the Papal court moved to Avignon. Hence, it took two hundred years to complete the building, which has a lower ceiling than most Gothic churches due to the ensuing financial compromises.

The church contains the tomb of Catherine of Siena, the patron saint of Italy and Europe. The shade of blue used in the ceiling was discovered in Siena and many Tuscan artists contributed to the decoration of the church. The Medici popes Leo X and Clement VII are entombed behind the main altar. Beato Angelico, beatified by Pope John Paul II, is entombed in a chapel to the left of the altar.

Michelangelo's *Redeemer* is on the left of the altar and his *Saint Sebastian* is in the Aldobrandini Chapel along the right side of the church. Michelangelo completed the faces but then rejected both sculptures because of flaws in the marble. Other artists went on to finish the works later. In the vestibule, to the left of the main altar, is a riot of sculpture by Bernini and Ercole Ferrata, decorating the tombs of Cardinals Pimentel and Bonelli. To the right of the main altar, in the Carafa chapel, is a brilliant fresco *Assumption of Mary* by the Tuscan painter Filippino Lippi. In the chapel next to Saint Sebastian is a delicate *Annunciation of the Angel* showing the Virgin bestowing dowries to poor girls.

MARTINI

Piazza Navona

map 11, D2; GPS 41.8995, 12.4728

The piazza preserves the outline of a stadium erected by Emperor Domitian in AD 86 after a fire destroyed much of the district. Jousting tournaments took place here in the Middle Ages and, between the 17th and 19th centuries, this was the location for spectacular water pageants. The fountains overflowed until the piazza was flooded and members of the aristocracy drove through the water in their gilded coaches to the sound of bands playing.

There are three fountains in the Piazza. Bernini's centrepiece *Fontana dei Quattro Fiumi* (Fountain of the Four Rivers) is an allegory symbolising the four great rivers of the world: the Nile, the Ganges, the Danube and the Rio de la Plata. Each river is personified: Danube has raised arms, Ganges holds an oar, Nile covers his head (symbolic of the difficulty locating the source). Rio de la Plata is rendered as a negro, with coins representing America's riches beside him on the rock. The obelisk is Roman and originated in *Campus Martius* before it was moved to the Circus of Romulus along Via Appia in AD 309. It was discovered in 1648, broken in five pieces. Pope Innocent X (Pamphilj) had it placed in the centre of the fountain. The obelisk is topped with the Pamphilj symbol: a dove with an olive branch in its beak.

The other two fountains have more complicated histories. They were both commissioned to Giacomo della Porta in 1574, during the reign of Gregory XIII (Boncampagni). The southern *Fontana del Moro* had the four Tritons and masks carved at this time. In 1654 Giovanni Mari sculpted the central figure riding a dolphin, working from a design by Bernini. It was called *il Moro,* the Moor, because of its facial features. All of the figures in this fountain are substitute copies made in 1874 by Luigi Amici; the originals are at Villa Borghese.

Fontana del Nettuno, the northern fountain, was originally designed to resemble *Fontana del Moro*. The work was

FONTANA DEI QUATTRO FIUMI: GANGES

never completed. The basin was installed, but the fountain remained without figures for three hundred years. Since it had no identity, residents named it *Fontana dei Calderai* (Fountain of the Coppersmiths) after the tradesmen who lived in the area. In 1878, the fountain got its present name after Antonio della Bitta carved the central figure of Neptune slaying an octopus and Gregorio Zapalà carved the group of eight sea creatures playing in the basin.

On the west side of the piazza is Sant'Agnese in Agone, a Baroque church begun by the Rainaldi and completed by Bernini's rival Borromini. On the piazza's south side, in Palazzo Braschi, is the Museo di Roma (p.274), which documents the history and life of Rome from the Middle Ages to the first half of the 20th century. The museum displays an interesting painting of a papal coronation in Piazza San Pietro before the addition of Bernini's colonnades. It is surprising to find such a beautiful collection of early photographs of 19th century Japan.

The piazza is a lively social centre thronged with tourists and surrounded by restaurants and cafés. The famous gelateria Tre Scalini is on the west side.

ROMANS ARE OFTEN FOUND BUYING THEIR GELATO AT *MARIOTTI*, ON VIA AGONALE 5-7, JUST OFF THE NORTHERN END OF THE PIAZZA.

Gian Lorenzo Bernini (1598-1680)

To walk in central Rome is to experience the influence of the artist Gian Lorenzo Bernini and his followers. Whether gazing in wonder at the angels on Ponte Sant'Angelo, relaxing by a fountain in the Piazza Navona, or worshipping at the altar of St Peter's, Bernini's talent permeates Rome.

Gian Lorenzo was born in Naples and moved to Rome at a young age. Like many great artists, he learned from his father. Pietro Bernini (1562-1629) was a respected sculptor and architect who designed the *Fontana Barcaccia* at the base of the Spanish Steps. The fountain's sunken boat design was an imaginative and elegant solution to the engineering challenge caused by the elevation of the Piazza Spagna and the consequent lack of water pressure from the source aqueduct, the *Acqua Vergine*.

Pietro had such excellent connections at the papal court that he was able to secure a valuable commission for his son. When Gian Lorenzo was 21 he started work on four sculptural groups for Cardinal Scipione Borghese, the nephew of Pope Paul V (Camillo Borghese). On display in the Borghese Gallery, these are the sculptures that established the artist as a great talent: *David; Apollo & Daphne*; *Rape of Proserpina*; and *Aeneas, Anchises and Ascanius Fleeing Troy*. Gian Lorenzo's ability to express sensuality and exuberance broke with convention; he made stone look like skin and imbued inanimate objects with intense energy.

The young Bernini soon became a favourite of Rome's elite and those who revolved around the papal court, while Scipione Borghese remained his patron. The energetic Bernini worked quickly and boasted that he could complete a bust in just one night. To prove his point he created a rather haphazard bust of Scipione, one that he was required to do again because his patron was not pleased with the likeness.

Bernini was 26 when Maffeo Barberini was elected Pope Urban VIII. At a time when a long papacy was ten years,

Urban served for 21 years. The Barberini were great patrons of Bernini, making him the top artist in Rome with unrestricted access to the Pope. Soon Bernini was involved in the ongoing beautification of St Peter's. He designed the colonnade around Piazza San Pietro in the shape of two arms, symbolic of the church, welcoming and protecting the faithful. Urban also encouraged Bernini to marry and in 1639 the artist wed Caterina Tezio. They had 11 children.

Urban VIII died in 1644. His successor Innocent X (Pamphilj) resented Bernini's elevated status and his close connection to the papal court. Innocent diverted the finest water from *Acqua Vergine* to the Piazza Navona and invited many artists to submit designs for the central fountain. Not only was Bernini excluded, Innocent refused to allow the artist to bid for any new commissions. One story has it that the sculptor smuggled in his designs and, once the Pope had seen the drawings, Bernini won easily. Another claims that he obtained the commission by 'corrupting' Dame Olimpia Maidalchini, the Pope's sister-in-law. Bernini gave her a model of the project cast in silver and she was so impressed that she persuaded the Pope to award him the work. Innocent then promptly raised the tax on bread to compensate for the additional expense.

In 1669 Alexander VII (Chigi) succeeded Innocent X. He commissioned Bernini to decorate Ponte Sant'Angelo with two saints and ten angels, to greet pilgrims on their way to St Peter's. Bernini carved two statues: *Angel of the Cross* and *Angel with the Crown of Thorns*. Other artists completed the remainder. Fifty-nine years after Bernini's death, Clement IX (Rospigliosi) ordered copies of the two Bernini originals. He claimed the statues on the bridge needed protection from the elements. In reality he wanted them for his own palace in Pistoia. The copies were made but Bernini's nephew held on to the originals until after the Pope died. They were then immediately donated to Sant'Andrea delle Fratte, Bernini's parish church. From 1641 to his death, Bernini lived nearby at 11 and 12 Via delle Mercede where there is an inscription and bust of the artist. The Bernini family tomb is at Santa Maria Maggiore.

Bernini in Rome

Basilica San Pietro
Baldacchino 1624-33
Throne of St Peter 1657-66
Chapel of the Sacrament 1675
St Longinus 1638
Tomb of Urban VIII 1647
Tomb of Alexander VII 1678

Piazza San Pietro
Colonnade of St Peter's 1657-65

Piazza Navona
Fontana d. Quattro Fiumi 1648

Piazza Barberini
Fontana del Tritone 1643
Fontanella delle Api 1644

Piazza della Minerva
Elephant Obelisk 1667

S. Maria Sopra Minerva
Giovanni Vigevano 1631
Maria Raggi Memorial 1647

Ponte Sant'Angelo
Designs for angels and saints

Sant'Andrea delle Fratte
Crown of Thorns 1668-71
Derogatory Inscription 1668-71

Santa Maria della Vittoria
Cornaro Chapel
Ecstasy of St Theresa 1647-52

Santa Maria del Popolo
Chigi Chapel
Daniel in the Lion's Den 1667
Habakkuk & the Angel 1661

San Francesco a Ripa
Ludovica Albertoni 1674

San Pietro in Montorio
Raimondi Chapel
Tomb of Maria Raggi 1642-48

Santa Bibiana
Santa Bibiana 1626

Galleria Borghese
David 1624
Apollo & Daphne 1625
Rape of Proserpina 1622
Aeneas, Anchises & Ascanius Fleeing Troy 1619
Self-Portrait 1622
Paul V 1618
Scipione Borghese 1632
Scipione Borghese (2) 1632
Truth Unveiled by Time 1652

Galleria Doria Pamphilj
Innocent X 1650

Musei Capitolini
Urban VIII 1635
Head of Medusa 1630

San Lorenzo in Lucina
Bust of Gabriele Fonseca 1668

S. Giovanni de'Fiorentini
Antonio Coppola 1612 (with Pietro)
Antonio Cepparelli 1624

Il Gesu
Cardinal Bellarmino 1622

Projects as architect:

Rome
Sant'Andrea al Quirinale 1658-70
Palazzo Barberini 1630

Castel Gandolfo
San Tommaso 1658-61

Ariccia
Santa Maria dell'Assunzione 1662-64

San Luigi dei Francesi

Piazza di San Luigi dei Francesi 5
06 688 271
map 11, E2
GPS 41.89973, 12.47453

08.30-12.30, 15.30-19.00 daily
closed Thurs pm

Located between the Pantheon and Piazza Navona, this is the French church in Rome. It is also known as the *Chiesa Caravaggio* because there are three of the artist's paintings here: *Calling of St Matthew, Martyrdom of St Matthew* and *St Matthew and the Angel*. These are the works that really established Caravaggio as a painter of rare talent and a master of light. His gift for capturing human expression and gesture introduced an earthy naturalism to Roman religious painting; an innovation both popular and controversial. The paintings are in the **Contarelli Chapel**, to the left of the altar.

Caravaggio received the San Luigi commission because the first artist to be chosen, Giuseppe Cesari (also known as Cavaliere d'Arpino) was too busy. The year was 1599 and the next year was a Holy Year. Rome's churches were in the grip of Jubilee fever and artists were much in demand. After years of dithering, it was now imperative to secure a painter for the Contarelli Chapel. Caravaggio was living across the road in Palazzo Madama, the residence of Cardinal Del Monte, who was well-respected by the clergy in San Luigi dei Francesi. They decided to take a risk and on 23 July 1599, Caravaggio promised in writing to complete two paintings for the start of Jubilee on 1 January 1600. Formally d'Arpino's apprentice, Caravaggio had no experience with this type of commission.

Calling of St Matthew

Caravaggio created a beautiful shaft of light to illuminate the scene from the right. As if from a divine source above Christ's head, the light follows the line of Christ's arm to the face of Matthew. In true tax collector fashion, Matthew keeps one hand on the coins and with the other points to himself in a 'Who, me?' gesture. Christ and St Peter are barefoot, symbolising the rejection of worldly goods required to follow Jesus. In this painting Caravaggio perfected a way of capturing reality at the key psychological moment, in a style that appears cinematic to the modern viewer.

Martyrdom of St Matthew

Completing this painting was a struggle for Caravaggio. He was unhappy with the composition in his first attempt; the one on display is the second painting. The artist included himself in the painting as an onlooker (on the left) wearing a black cloak, one which was later recognised and used in a legal case against Caravaggio (p.63). A witness found the cloak in Piazza Navona, where Caravaggio dropped it during an altercation with a notary.

St Matthew and the Angel

In February 1602, Caravaggio was commissioned to paint the altarpiece for the Contarelli Chapel. His first effort stuck very closely to the demands of the contract, but was rejected because Caravaggio portrayed Matthew as a peasant with a worker's large hands and dirty feet, seated next to an angel guiding his hand. Clerics determined that Matthew wasn't saintly enough and the angel, with feet on the ground, was not considered angelic. This painting once hung in Berlin at the Kaiser-Friedrich museum but was destroyed in World War II. The second version, currently hanging in the chapel, depicts Matthew as much more saintly in his red robe and the angel is shown descending from heaven rather than standing on earth.

BRING COINS FOR THE ILLUMINATO, LOCATED ON THE RIGHT WALL AS YOU FACE THE CHAPEL.

Across the nave in **Chapel 12** there is an altarpiece by Guido Reni, a popular Roman artist who first copied and idolised Caravaggio, but then later turned against him and allied himself with d'Arpino. The painting is a copy of Raphael's *Santa Cecilia*.

Caravaggio (1571-1610)

Michelangelo Merisi, the artist known as Caravaggio, was born on 29 September 1571 in Caravaggio – a small town near Milan. Caravaggio was the son of a household steward to Costanza Colonna, a member of one of Italy's noble families and the daughter of Marcantonio Colonna, a hero in the Battle of Lepanto. Caravaggio's father and grandfather both died of plague when he was six years old and Costanza assumed a lifelong interest in his welfare.

Caravaggio arrived in Rome in 1592 at the age of 20. Clement VIII (Aldobrandini) was the newly elected Pope. With a Jubilee year set for 1600, there were plenty of opportunities for ambitious young artists among the cardinals, princes and diplomats surrounding the papal court. Many artists found themselves a rich patron who would provide a studio and a residence, in addition to a regular supply of commissions. Costanza's brother Cardinal Ascanio Colonna was close friends with Frederico Borromeo who, as head of the painters' guild Accademia di San Luca, was able to grant Caravaggio the required guild membership. Caravaggio had a lavish residence in which to live, the Palazzo Colonna, but his station was modest: steward to Camilla Peretti, a sister of the preceding pope and a resident in the palazzo.

Caravaggio soon got a position in the studio of Antiveduto Grammatica, a Sienese artist who specialised in portraiture. Although he was only allowed to paint the flowers and fruits in the background, it was here that Caravaggio was able to meet many of Rome's powerful elite as they sat for portraits. The relationship ended when Antiveduto began to copy his student. Artists of the day often imitated each other but Caravaggio would not tolerate this. Throughout his life he would become enraged if another painter attempted to duplicate his style.

In 1593 Caravaggio obtained another position in the studio of Giuseppe Cesari (d'Arpino) a popular Roman painter. He had befriended Bernardino, d'Arpino's lead apprentice and wild younger brother, recently exiled in Naples for consorting with criminals. Caravaggio worked at the studio for two years but left after a dispute over painting styles, one that engulfed Rome's young artists. Painters began to divide themselves into rival camps: those favouring the studied elegance of d'Arpino versus those embracing the earthy naturalism of Caravaggio. Poems insulting rival

painters were printed in the local papers and several artists were arrested for slander and libel.

Caravaggio entered the service of Cardinal del Monte and his stature as a painter grew. Unfortunately, so did his swagger. In 1598 he was arrested near Piazza Navona for carrying weapons without a licence. He was released without charge because he was the painter to Cardinal del Monte and had lodgings in the Palazzo Madama. Police records of the time indicate that Caravaggio and his associates were often arrested for violent incidents involving members of the Tomassoni family.

In those days whenever the papal throne stood empty, normal government was suspended. As bells rang out to signal the death of a pope, Rome's prisons were emptied and the last man out took with him the *corda*, the torturer's rope. Lay officials in each district, known as *caporioni*, would then administer justice. Giovan Francesco Tomassoni was *caporione* of Campo Marzio. Together with his brothers Ranuccio and Alessandro, he ran a group of local vigilantes. They lived in Piazza di San Lorenzo in Lucina, and dispensed their brand of local justice in the taverns and brothels around the Augustus Mausoleum. Ranuccio Tomassoni's sexual affairs with local whores aroused violent passions and he suffered more than one stab wound as a result. One story has it that he shared a woman with Caravaggio.

In March 1605, Caravaggio moved into his own house on what is now Vicolo del Divino Amore, a tiny lane off Via dei Prefetti near Piazza Firenze. No longer under the protection of Cardinal del Monte, he was soon homeless when his landlady locked him out for non-payment of rent. He was arrested again for carrying a weapon without a permit and was frequently incarcerated for fighting. Caravaggio's life was spiralling out of control.

On 28 May 1606, two rival gangs met to sort out their differences in Piazza di San Lorenzo in Lucina. Caravaggio had three associates, all wearing swords. Three armed companions also backed up Ranuccio Tomassoni: a brother and two brothers-in-law. Spectators reported that Caravaggio and Ranuccio fought each other fiercely with swords. They said the final blow was delivered by Caravaggio, who was also seriously wounded. In the event, Ranuccio died and Caravaggio became a murderer.

He fled south, to the protection of the Colonna in the Alban Hills, where he recovered and waited. Crimes of passion rarely invoked a strong sentence and there was hope Caravaggio would be pardoned. But news soon came that Pope Paul V (Borghese) had imposed a capital death sentence, meaning that anyone could kill him at any time. Caravaggio went to Naples, then under Spanish rule. Private and clerical patrons, eager for his work, welcomed him and the exiled artist was able to complete many pieces, including an altarpiece *The Flagellation of Christ* for San Domenico Maggiore (now in the Capodimonte Museum). Caravaggio's paintings became much darker in this period; the gestures of his subjects less theatrical. An old woman began to appear in his work. She is found in many paintings after the murder, her sad wrinkled face representing death or regret.

Still on the run, Caravaggio travelled to Malta in 1607 and found the protection of the Knights of Malta, who were thrilled to have such a genius in their midst. Caravaggio served a 12 month novitiate and completed several paintings. He was made a Knight of Justice, a highly prestigious honour, one usually requiring 200 years of nobility on both sides of the knight's parentage. But Caravaggio's temper soon got the better of him and after insulting another knight, he was imprisoned below ground in a shaft sunk into rock. Caravaggio engineered a miraculous escape, boarded a waiting ship and set sail for Sicily.

On landing in Syracuse, Caravaggio travelled to Messina in 1608 and then found his way back to Naples. He was constantly on the move, fearing both papal assassins and the Knights of Malta. But in Rome, powerful families were lobbying for his return. A rumour began to circulate around Naples that the Pope was willing to grant a pardon. Caravaggio painted furiously, to satisfy the demand of his patrons in Naples and persuade Scipione Borghese to intercede with his uncle, Paul V. One of the paintings *David with the Head of Goliath* (now at the Borghese Gallery) includes an anguished portrait of Caravaggio as the decapitated giant.

In 1610 a pardon was granted. Caravaggio loaded a boat with his paintings and set sail for Rome, but was arrested and imprisoned at Palo, near the mouth of the Tiber river. While the validity of his pardon was checked, the boat, with his paintings still on board, sailed on without him. Caravaggio was released. He was desperate; he needed those paintings to secure his pardon in Rome.

Caravaggio travelled alone through 100 km of mosquito-infested marshes to the next harbour at Port'Ercole, only to find that the boat had sailed on again with his paintings still on board. Caravaggio fell ill with fever and died on the 18 July at the confraternity of San Sebastiano. He was only 39.

Caravaggio in Rome

Galleria Borghese
Ailing Bacchus 1593
Boy with a Basket of Fruit 1594
Madonna and Child with St Anne 1605
St Jerome in his Study 1606
The Infant St John 1609
David with the Head of Goliath 1610

Villa Ludovisi, Casino dell'Aurora
Jupiter, Neptune and Pluto 1597

Santa Maria della Concezione
St Francis in Meditation 1603

Palazzo Barberini
Judith Beheading Holofernes (c.1599)
Narcissus (c.1599)

Santa Maria del Popolo
Crucifixion of St Peter 1601
Conversion of St Paul 1601

Musei Capitolini
St John the Baptist 1599
The Fortune Teller 1595

Galleria Doria Pamphilj
Rest on the Flight into Egypt 1599
Mary Magdalene 1598

San Luigi dei Francesi
Calling of St Matthew 1600
Martyrdom of St Matthew 1600
St Matthew and the Angel 1602

Sant'Agostino
Madonna di Loreto 1604

Palazzo Corsini
St John the Baptist in the Desert 1603

Pinacoteca Vaticana
Entombment of Christ 1604

Sant'Agostino (Basilica of Saint Augustine)

Piazza di Sant'Agostino
06 688 01962
map 11, E1
GPS 41.90065, 12.47442

08.00-12.00, 16.00-19.30 daily

St Augustine (354-430)

Born in Tagaste (Algeria), Augustine lived a wild and dissolute life until his baptism at the age of 38. His radical conversion to Christianity was attributed to the constant prayers of his mother Monica. Augustine became fascinated by the question of man's freedom versus God's grace. In his *Confessions* he wrote about his experiences in everyday language. This was the first of many volumes and letters whereby Augustine described the principles of original sin and the absolute dependence on God for salvation. His writings form the basis of Christian thought; both Catholics and Protestants acknowledge him as the father of modern theological philosophy. The remains of Augustine's mother were brought here from Ostia in 1431 and placed in the Chapel of Santa Monica to the left of the main altar.

The church

In 1286, Egidio Lufredi, a Roman nobleman, donated houses on this street to the Augustinians of Piazza del Popolo. The church took a long time to complete: the first stone was laid in 1296 and the first service was held in 1446. Over the next two hundred years, wealthy patrons commissioned paintings and sculptures for the church. In 1756 further restorations were begun which took until the year 2000 before they were considered finished.

Art is integral to the philosophy at Sant'Agostino. The church brochure includes the *Letter to Artists* written in 1999 by John Paul II: '*Art is a flowering of beauty that draws its vitality from the Incarnation... for believers and nonbelievers alike, art remains a reflection of the fathomless mystery in which the world is wrapped and in which it lives. Beauty is the key to mystery and a call to the transcendent.*'

Madonna di Loreto (Madonna of the Pilgrims)

In the first chapel to the left of the entrance is Caravaggio's *Madonna di Loreto.* The Virgin stands at a simple doorway holding the naked Jesus in her arms. She looks with compassion at the pilgrims kneeling before her, the plump cleanliness of the Christ contrasting starkly with the hard dirt on the pilgrims' feet. Caravaggio won the commission for this important altarpiece in 1603.

A woman named Lena was the model for the Madonna. Lena's mother charged Caravaggio a considerable fee and kept a close eye on the proceedings. A jealous young notary, in love with Lena, misinterpreted the visits. He rebuked the mother, besmirching the name of Caravaggio and slandering Lena in the process. Caravaggio attacked the man with his sword in Piazza Navona and wounded him. He was later identified as the culprit because of a black cloak left behind. Caravaggio had painted himself wearing the same cloak in his *Martyrdom of St Matthew.*

Isaiah

On the third column to the left of the entrance is Raphael's fresco of the prophet *Isaiah.* After sneaking into the Sistine Chapel to see Michelangelo's work in progress, Raphael painted over his original fresco of *Isaiah.* Michelangelo was furious when he learned that Bramante had loaned his special keys to the 'great copier' (as he called Raphael). Raphael's student, Domenico lo Spagnolo, painted the delicate *Our Lady of the Roses* in the Chapel of St Joseph (second on the right).

Madonna and Child

By Jacopo Sansovino, the statue is immediately to the right of the entrance. Mary's shrunken left foot is the result of the many kisses bestowed by women for protection in childbirth. Veneration began in 1820 when Leonardo Bracci's wife was safely delivered of a child after Leonardo left a lamp burning in front of the statue during the difficult birth.

Galleria Doria Pamphilj

Piazza del Collegio Romano 2
06 679 7323
www.doriapamphilj.it
map 12, G3
GPS 41.8981, 12.4809

10.00-17.00 Fri-Wed
admission €8

Housed in an enormous palazzo, this is one of the most important private art collections in Rome and it is presided over by a member of the family. Jonathan Doria Pamphilj is a modern prince and, as the adopted son of Princess Doria Pamphilj, he is joint heir to the family fortune. The first two years of his life he lived in an English orphanage. A recognised art historian, he now resides in the palazzo, which has 150 apartments ranging in size from two to 20 rooms. The family entrance is on the Via del Corso, where you might see Jonathan walking one of his little dogs.

JONATHAN DORIA PAMPHILJ IS THE VOICE ON THE MUSEUM AUDIOGUIDE.

The collection is very much a manifestation of the family's longstanding wealth. When Giambattista Pamphilj became Pope Innocent X, he duly became head of both the Church and one of the ruling patrician families of 17th century Rome. He made his grandson, Prince Camillo, a cardinal with the powers of a secretary of state. In 1647, Cardinal Camillo fell in love and renounced his position. He married Olimpia Aldobrandini and, banished from the Church, came back to live in the palazzo.

Art is displayed in the original 17th and 18th century style. At that time paintings were not exhibited as objects in their own right but as part of a decorative scheme: pictures were hung like wallpaper to cover every available space on the walls. For this reason most of the paintings do not have a label explaining the artist and date of the work, instead they are numbered.

BE SURE TO PICK UP A LIST OF PAINTINGS AT THE GALLERY ENTRANCE TO MATCH THE NUMBER WITH THE ARTIST AND TITLE.

The **ballroom** is lavishly decorated and is the newest part of the palazzo. When the building was recently rewired, electricians found parts of the original circuitry for the chandeliers. These were so old that they were donated to a museum of electricity. In the corner is a harp where the orchestra would have sat. The Doria Pamphilj were great patrons and once played host to Handel, who wrote his first oratorio while staying in the palazzo.

The rather eerie **chapel** is testimony to another popular 17th century pastime: the collecting of holy relics. In the glass case are the remains of St Theodora and St Justin salvaged from the Roman catacombs during the 17th century. Remains of holy saints were held in high regard and the fact that the family were in possession of such valuable relics is further evidence of their status and importance.

In the **picture gallery** is Andrea Pudestà's *Amor Sacro e Profano.* At first sight this painting looks like a tussle among some infants. Closer inspection reveals some of the infants have wings and are in fact *putti* (cherubs). Representing *amor sacro* (sacred or divine love), they are being overpowered and wrestled to the ground by characters with devilish grins, who represent *amor profano* (profane or base love).

On the opposite wall is a work by an unknown French painter, showing a woman engaged in the rather humble act of removing a flea from her bodice. This intimate moment is rendered lyrical by the play of candlelight on the female form. Consequently, the unknown artist was named 'Master of the Candle'. There are five other works by him in the collection.

Velasquez's portrait of Giambattista Pamphilj as *Pope Innocent X* is one of the most important works in the collection. The intensity and realism of the portrait has inspired artists since it was completed in 1650. When Innocent saw the finished painting for the first time it left him feeling unsettled for he found it to be too true a representation.

VELASQUEZ: *POPE INNOCENT X*

Displayed alongside the portrait is Bernini's equally realistic bust of Innocent X. Note the character and vitality in the details of his misshapen nose, the brow, ears and the folds in the fabric.

The **hall of mirrors is** a spectacular gallery of gilt-framed mirrors, reminiscent of the one at the palace of Versailles. The ceiling was painted by Aurelio Milani and depicts the

Labours of Hercules, who appears here with his club. Part of the Doria Pamphilj classical sculpture collection is on display. The remainder is in the **Aldobrandini Room**, the oldest part of the palace, which houses sculptures originally seen in the gardens of the Villa Doria Pamphilj.

The other rooms have a chronological display of the family's picture collection, showcasing works from the 15th to the 17th century.

17th century *(Seicento)*

Rest On the Flight Into Egypt (1599) is one of Caravaggio's first works, depicting the holy family at rest on their way to sanctuary. Caravaggio has boldly painted the angel with his back to the viewer, changing standard pictorial composition. The texture of fabric and landscape, the eye of the donkey and the crossed feet of Joseph on the left of the painting are all rendered with an earthy naturalism.

Alongside this painting is the *Repentant Mary Magdalene,* also by Caravaggio. This painting provoked scandal, not only because Caravaggio dressed Mary Magdalene in the clothes of a contemporary Roman prostitute but also because he used the same model and pose for the Madonna in *Rest On the Flight Into Egypt*.

16th century *(Cinquecento)*

Titian's *Salome with the Head of John the Baptist* is perhaps the most important in this room. It has been suggested that this is a self-portrait of Titian and the figure of Salome is a lover who spurned him.

15th century *(Quattrocento)*

Hans Memling's *Lament Over the Dead Christ* is arguably one of the best the collection has to offer. Drops of blood and tears, Christ's wounds and the depiction of the crown of thorns and nails that pinned him to the cross intensify the emotions of pity and suffering. The family wisely acquired this work in the 19th century, when northern and medieval art was out of fashion.

Campo de'Fiori

map 11, D4
GPS 41.89580, 12.47190

The square holds one of the longest-running markets in Rome, selling fruit, vegetables and flowers. Late starters will miss out. Merchants set up at dawn and everything is closed and neatly put away by lunchtime (things run a bit later on Saturdays). The trattorie then put out tables for lunch and the bakeries do a brisk business selling takeaway. In the evening the campo fills up with Romans and tourists taking an aperitivo in one of the many bars such as La Vineria, once the haunt of bohemian poets.

The campo's statue is a memorial to Giordano Bruno, a Dominican monk, who advocated the separation of church and state. Bruno also believed the universe was infinite and contained a number of worlds, all inhabited by intelligent beings. His beliefs outraged a faculty at Oxford when he lectured there in 1583. Even Galileo, a liberal-minded contemporary, was not sympathetic to his theories. Bruno was burned at the stake for heresy in 1600. The statue portrays him with hands bound, stoically facing the end.

The area became prime real estate during the 16th century, with wealthy families, like the Orsini, building palazzi nearby. The streets around the campo are named after the artisans who once inhabited them: Via dei Baullari (trunk makers); Via dei Chiavari (locksmiths); Via dei Cappellari (milliners); and Via dei Giubonnari (jacket makers). Via Pellegrino has interesting shops and is a good street for a stroll.

Piazza Farnese

map 11, C4
GPS 41.8951, 12.4709

Alessandro Farnese was elected Pope Paul III in 1534 and he greatly enlarged Palazzo Farnese to suit his new status. Antonio da Sangallo began the building, Michelangelo completed the upper floors and Giacomo della Porta finished the construction. Such was the power of the papacy that houses on three medieval streets were destroyed and the Via dei Baullari was built to lead directly to the main entrance of the palazzo.

In an inspired property deal, following the unification of Italy in 1870, the French swapped the Hotel Galiffet in Paris for the Palazzo Farnese. The building, which they had used on and off since 1635, became the permanent location for the French embassy. It is not open to the public.

The fountains, made of Egyptian granite, were brought here from the Terme di Caracalla (Baths of Caracalla).

Galleria Spada

Piazza Capo di Ferro 13
06 32 810
www.galleriaborghese.it
map 11, C5
GPS 41.8943, 12.4719

08.30-19.30 Tues-Sun
admission €5

Named after Cardinal Benardino Spada, the palazzo was originally the family home of Cardinal Capo di Ferro, who had it built around 1550. When Bernardino and his brother Virginio (also a cardinal) acquired the property in the 17th century, they quickly set to work adjusting the palace to suit their own needs.

Bernardino was a progressive thinker with a special interest in science. His choices in collecting art were bold for the day. He had a fondness for the Bolognese school of painters. Guido Reni's portrait of *Cardinal Spada* (1631) dominates the **Entrance Hall** together with Guercino's huge canvas *The Death of Dido* (1631). This painting was originally intended for Maria de'Medici, who was the queen of France at the time. Titian's *Portrait of a Musician* is found in **Room 2**.

Portraits of scientists are included: *The Botanist* by Bartolomeo Passerotti and Niccolò Tornioli's *The Astronomers*. The latter pays homage to Galileo with a telescope in the foreground. There are also two globes from 17th century Holland in the collection, one representing the Earth's terrain, the second detailing the sky and constellations.

Galleria Prospettiva

Experiments in perspective were popular in the 17th century. This example, built by Borromini in 1653, is the highlight of the gallery. The paving stones gradually slope upwards while the ceiling angles downwards, and the walls gradually converge as the columns on either side decrease in size. The gallery appears to recede much deeper into the distance than the real measurement of nine metres. Be sure to join a guided tour and see the illusion revealed.

Borromini (1599-1667)

Giovanni Domenico Castelli, known as Francesco Borromini, was born at Bissone on Lake Lugano. He took the name Borromini from the Borromean League of Catholic Switzerland. His father was an architect who worked for the Visconti family in Milan. Borromini learned stonecutting as a child and at the age of 15 he travelled to Rome to apprentice with his relative Carlo Maderno, chief architect at St Peter's. When Maderno died in 1629, Bernini took over his workshop. Borromini assisted Bernini with the redesign of Palazzo Barberini.

Borromini had none of Bernini's social advantages and a rivalry soon developed between the two artists, with Borromini cast as the underdog. Bernini was thin and wiry and liked to work quickly; Borromini was portly with a large nose. Bernini tackled sculpture and painting in addition to architecture; Borromini was always an architect. Notoriously finicky with an incredible eye for detail, he had traits that made him an object of caricature and ridicule: the Roman poet Carlo Belli compared Borromini to an industrious beaver.

At one point Bernini was favoured by the Barberini papal court of Urban VIII. But when Giambattista Pamphilj was elected Innocent X in 1644, he banished Bernini from his court. Borromini seized his chance by taking over the reconstruction of San Giovanni in Laterano – the second most important church in Christendom. He gleefully ordered the demolition of a building recently completed by Bernini to build Palazzo di Propaganda Fide. Bernini loudly retorted: *'Borromini has been sent to destroy architecture'*.

Borromini's life did not end well: he became withdrawn and depressed. A few days before his death, he burned all the drawings he had intended to send to the engraver. At the age of 59, in a fit of fever and insomnia, Borromini committed suicide by falling on his sword. He is buried in San Giovanni de'Fiorentini.

Talking statues

Piazza di Pasquino
map 11, D3
GPS 41.8978, 12.4721

In Piazza di Pasquino, just off Piazza Navona, you may find people clustered around a dilapidated statue. They are attracted by pieces of writing fixed on and around a statue, typically satirical comments on the current political scene and the state of the nation. This is *Pasquino*, one of the so-called 'talking statues' of Rome – adopted as a type of civic chatroom.

Pasquino originally had an official government function. Because the statue was on one of the principal papal parade routes, it was often hung with Latin poems to edify the people. In the 16th century, during a succession of repressive papal governments characterised by corruption and high taxes, any opposition was considered heresy. The ever-resourceful Romans began to use *Pasquino* as a vehicle for their own *scritti politti*. This angered those in power who tried to prohibit these *pasquinades* but to no avail.

Pasquino has even been known to correspond with other statues around the city that are used in much the same way. These are: *Marforio* by the Capitoline Museums, *Babuino* in Via del Babuino, *Facchino* in Via Lata, *Madama Lucrezia* in Piazza San Marco and *Abate Luigi* in Piazza Vidoni.

Area Sacra (Torre Argentina Cat Sanctuary)

entrance on the corner of Via Florida and Via Arenula
06 687 2133
daily 12.00-18.00, Sun 15.00-18.00
www.romancats.com
map 12, F4
GPS 41.8961, 12.4764

One of the oldest temples in Rome, the Area Sacra in Torre Argentina is known as the place where, in 44 BC, Julius Caesar was stabbed 23 times. Today it is a busy transport hub, the ruins forming a sunken oasis in the centre. It is famous for another reason – as the home of a cat sanctuary.

Since ancient times cats have been kindly regarded by the Romans as a symbol for freedom. They wander around Rome at their leisure, ambling through ruins and dozing at the feet of ancient statues. This affection is an ongoing one; you can see it in the many feline-inspired books, postcards and calendars on sale.

The Area Sacra was first excavated in 1929. Because it was an enclosed area below street level, it began to attract stray cats. These were fed by a succession of cat lovers (*gattare*), including the Italian film star Anna Magnani. In 1994, Lia Dequel and Silvia Viviani assumed responsibility. A British woman, Molga Salvalaggio, came to their aid and put them in touch with the Anglo-Italian Society for the Protection of Animals. Subsequently, volunteers from various countries helped to create the fully operational cat sanctuary that exists today. Strays are name-tagged, registered, given medical attention and food. There are anywhere between 350 and 500 cats at any one time.

WITH NO PUBLIC FUNDING, THE SANCTUARY RELIES ON DONATIONS.

The Ghetto

In 63 BC the princes of the free state of Judea invited Pompey to intervene in a civil war between two brothers: Hyrcanus and Aristobulus. Pompey had recently established order in Syria after years of chaos and Judea was an ally of Rome. Pompey backed Hyrcanus and, even though Aristobulus accepted the defeat, his followers barricaded themselves in Jerusalem. Pompey besieged the city for three months and Hyrcanus emerged victorious, but Judea was no longer an ally; it had become part of Rome's vast empire.

Jews were welcome in Rome where they were treated as freemen, working as tradesmen and businessmen. But in AD 70, following the Jewish revolt in Judea, Emperor Titus decreed that all Roman Jews were henceforth slaves – many were forced into building the Colosseum.

After the Edict of Milan in AD 313, Rome's Jewish population enjoyed a fluctuating type of freedom under Catholicism – until the Reformation. In 1555 an edict by Pope Paul IV (Giovanni Caraffa) established a walled ghetto. Jews were locked in at night and had to pay for the cost of their Christian wardens. The walls of the district remained in place until they were destroyed in the revolutions of 1848.

Jews were given full citizenship at the unification of Italy in 1870 but were once again in peril during the Italian-German collaboration in World War II.

Today global hostilities mean that some streets immediately around the Synagogue are a strict security area, and these are sealed off during Jewish high holy days. Tourists are allowed in the area after being searched and questioned by perimeter security police.

ONCE INSIDE THE AREA, DO NOT TAKE PHOTOGRAPHS OF THE SYNAGOGUE OR YOU MAY FIND YOURSELF TAKEN AWAY FOR QUESTIONING BY THE POLICE.

The Synagogue and Museum of Jewish Culture

Lungotevere dei Cenci
06 684 0061
Apr-Sept: Mon-Thurs 09.00-19.30, Fri and Sun 09.00-13.30
Oct-March: Mon-Thurs 09.00-16.30, Fri 09.00-13.30
Sun 09.00-12.30, closed Saturday
by guided tour only, ID required.
admission €6
map 12, F6; GPS 41.8927, 12.4774

Consecrated in 1904, the synagogue was built to a height that is visible from the Vatican. On 13 April 1986, John Paul II met here with Rabbi Elio Toaff. This was the first time a pope had been invited to pray in a Jewish synagogue.

Via Portico d'Ottavia

This is a lively street with kosher food shops, bakeries and bars. Near the portico is a Roman institution, Da Gigetto, where you can sit outside and enjoy a plate of *carciofi alla giudia* (deep-fried artichokes). Just north of the street in Piazza Campitelli is the Vecchia Roma, with two Michelin stars.

The houses here date from the medieval period when a fish market and a church – Sant'Angelo in Pescheria – were built in the ruins of the portico. On a pillar near the church is a plaque, stating that the heads of all fish exceeding the length of the plaque must be donated to the *conservatori* (Capitoline magistrates) for the making of fish soup to feed the needy.

THE SYNAGOGUE AT ROSH HASHANAH

Portico d'Ottavia

map 12, F6; GPS 41.8924, 12.4784

In 146 BC this was a colonnaded market with temples and libraries named after its builder Octavius. The portico enclosed temples dedicated to Jupiter and Juno, and the entrance displayed statues of gods newly arrived from Athens – a city that was sacked by the Romans in 86 BC. Greek classic civilisation had an enormous influence: Greek gods were renamed and incorporated into the Roman pantheon. It was fashionable for every Roman patrician to have a sculpture of at least one Olympian god in the courtyard of his villa.

Augustus had the portico rebuilt in 23 BC and kept the name in honour of his sister Octavia; she was the wife abandoned by Mark Antony for Cleopatra.

Teatro di Marcello

Via del Teatro di Marcello
06 671 03819 or 06 871 31580
by appointment only
map 12, F6; GPS 41.8918, 12.4803

This was once a prestigious theatre that could seat 20,000 people. It was planned by Julius Caesar and completed by Augustus, who named it after his nephew and son-in-law, Marcellus. It fell into ruin in the 4th century and was converted into a fortress by the Perleone family in the 12th century. In the 16th century it was made into a palace for the Savelli family whose heirs, the Orsini, still own the property and have partially restored the theatre.

The three Corinthian columns in the centre of the ruin were once at the entrance of the Temple of Apollo, which housed some of the many artworks Rome plundered from Greece.

CAPITOLINO & PALATINO

The best preserved sights of ancient Rome are found here. There are fine views of the city from the Capitoline and Palatine Hills.

Visit the Forum and Colosseum early in the day, before it gets too hot. The Forum is free, but you will need tickets for the Colosseum and Palatine. At the same time, purchase an Electra Vision Guide that illustrates how the area once appeared.

To view the layout of the Forum, climb the Capitoline and walk behind Palazzo Senatorio. The museums on the Capitoline contain many of the sculptures and art treasures that were removed from the Forum's ancient buildings.

The Forum and Palatine are designated archaeological areas so there are no refreshment stands or restaurants. Have a picnic on the Palatine, visit the café at the top of the museum, or find a restaurant on Via Capo d'Africa, east of the Colosseum.

V. D. PLEBISCITO
PIAZZA VENEZIA
Monumento Vittorio Emanuele II
LARGO MAGNANAPOLI
VIA PANISPERNA
Esquilino
V. GIOVANNI LANZA
VIA CAVOUR
Santa Maria in Aracoeli
V. D. FORI IMPERIALI
VIA D. ANNIBALDI
V. ARENULA
Ghetto
Musei Capitolini
LGT. DEI CENCI
V. D. TEATRO DI MARCELLO
Capitolino
Foro Romano (Roman Forum)
VIA SACRA
Colosseo
PIAZZA DEL COLOSSEO
Arco di Constantino
P. D. BOCCA DELLA VERITÀ
Ponte Rotto
Trastevere
Palatino
VIA DEI CERCHI
VIA DI S. GREGORIO
Laterano
Circus Maximus
LGT. D. RIPA GRANDE
LGT. AVENTINO
Celio
Aventino

Capitoline Museums
• classical sculpture
Forum
• centre of ancient Rome
Colosseum
• arena for gladiators
Circus Maximus
• chariot racetrack
Santa Maria in Aracoeli
• a special church for mothers and children

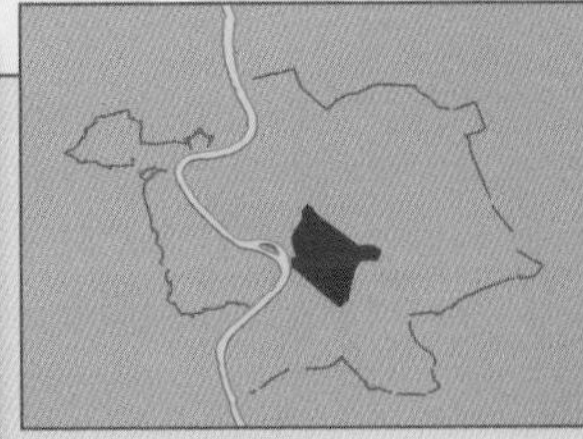

Palatine Hill
Ancient ruins in a park-like setting

restaurants p.237

Bocca della Verità
Children will enjoy putting their hand in the 'mouth of truth'.

Did you know that..?
Julius Caesar combed his hair forward and wore a laurel wreath to cover his baldness.

Foro Romano (Roman Forum)

Via dei Fori Imperiali
06 399 67700
09.00-1hr before sunset
admission free
map 12, I6
GPS (for Capitoline entrance)
41.89206, 12.48310

It is acceptable to join in with guided tour groups; just ask and you'll be made welcome. If you decide to stay until the end it is customary to make a donation.

Entrances:

1. From the Capitoline take the steps behind the Palazzo Senatorio.
2. Descend a flight of steps located between the Temple of Antoninus and Faustina and the Basilica Aemilia.
3. Walk up the Via Sacra through the Arch of Titus.
4. A tree-lined path off Via San Teodoro.

The Roman Empire lasted over a thousand years. Its rise and fall occurred during three distinct periods of government, traces of which are found in the Forum. As with most archaeological remains, the oldest layer is at the bottom.

- The Kings (753 BC - 509 BC)
- The Republic (509 BC - 45 BC)
- The Emperors (31 BC - AD 476)

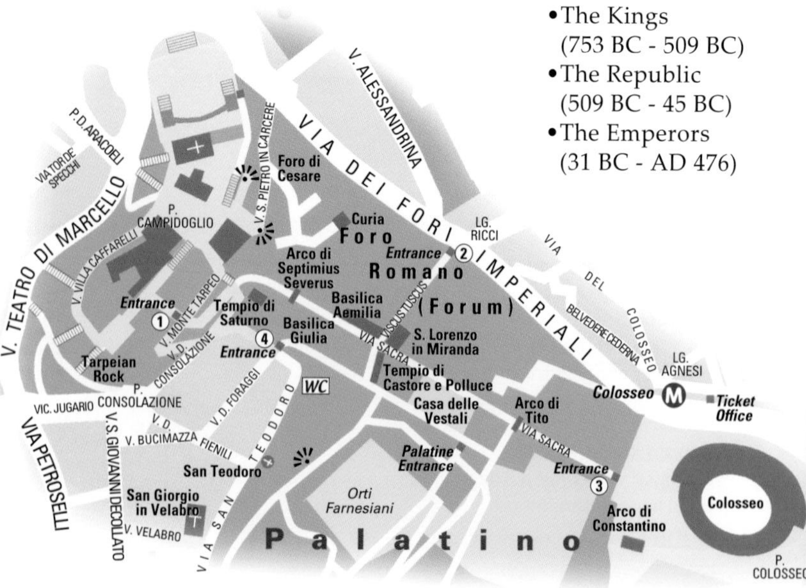

In the 8th century BC, the site was a swamp where villagers living on the Palatine and Capitoline hills would bury their dead. The Etruscan kings were superb engineers; they drained and paved the area to create a marketplace which then became the centre of politics, justice and worship. With the advent of the new Republic, the Forum required bigger and better buildings and temples. And as Rome's population increased, the Foro Romano expanded. In 46 BC Julius Caesar built his new Foro di Cesare at the very edge of the Capitoline, pushing the boundary outwards and setting a building trend that was followed by successive emperors from Augustus to Trajan.

The Foro Romano was the heart of the Empire: a bustling marketplace with wheeler-dealers, money traders and backroom politics. This was where decisions were made, profits distributed, and debts repaid. It was also a place of worship, with temples dedicated to Rome's most prominent gods.

In the Middle Ages the site became known as Campo Vaccino (cow field). Ancient remains were abandoned and forgotten, and the swamp was allowed to reclaim land and buildings. Only the temples and monuments that had been converted into churches remained in use. Pope Paul III (Farnese) and subsequent popes exploited the Forum as a quarry for materials. Between 1540-50 the building projects of the Farnese saw the temples of Saturn, Castor & Pollux, and Julius stripped of their columns, pediments, marbles and flooring. Michelangelo protested but to no avail. There developed a popular saying:

'They destroyed the Rome of the Caesars to build the Rome of the Popes.'

Some excavation took place in the 18th and early 19th centuries, but it was after the reunification of Italy in 1870 that two leading archaeologists, Pietro Rosa and Giuseppe Fiorelli, began the thorough and systematic excavations that are continuing today.

Forum Highlights

Tempio di Saturno

The temple was the focus of the *Saturnalia* celebrations each December. Schools were closed, slaves dined with their masters, presents were exchanged and a fête with a large market was held. In the Republican period, Saturn was the second most important deity after Jupiter. At the entrance to the temple are the remaining Ionic columns that date from the 3rd century BC.

Arco di Septimius Severus

With three passages built entirely out of marble in AD 203, this triumphal arch was made to celebrate the tenth anniversary of the accession of Septimius Severus and the victory over Parthia (modern Iran and Iraq) and Arabia. The inscription at the top of the arch was originally to Septimius and his two sons Caracalla and Geta. After Septimius died, Caracalla murdered his brother and had his name removed. The holes in which the letters of Geta's name were attached are still visible. During the Middle Ages, the central arch – half buried in earth and debris – was used to shelter a barber shop.

Curia

When Caesar built the Foro de Cesare under the Capitoline, he demolished the Basilica Comitia, which had housed the Republican Senate. He built the new Curia for the Imperial Senate in a position much closer to his own forum, perhaps to keep a close watch on their activities. In the 8th century the Curia was transformed into the church of Sant'Adriano. Inside is a marble floor dating to the time of Diocletian. There are two large relief panels depicting the Emperor Trajan: in one, Trajan is portrayed destroying the records of unpaid taxes to free citizens from debt; in the other he sits on a throne receiving a mother and child.

Basilica Giulia

Recent probing has discovered the remains of the house of Scipio Africanus, the general who defeated Hannibal, beneath the centre of the building. During Republican times the house was demolished to make way for the Basilica Sempronia, which was then torn down by Julius Caesar to build the Basilica Giulia. This was the home of the Imperial law courts, a splendid building with steps where the common people of Rome would meet. The graffiti, cut into the steps facing the street, marks where games would be played.

Basilica Aemilia

The Republican consuls Marcus Aemilius Lepidus and Marcus Fulvius Nobilor built the Basilica Aemilia in 179 BC. In Republican Rome a *basilica* was a place where justice was administered and financial transactions took place. It was a meeting hall for politicians and moneylenders, and an indoor market during inclement weather. The pavement is splashed with tiny lumps of coins that melted during a fire.

Viscus Tuscus

This was a shopping street located between the Basilica Giulia and the Temple of Castor and Pollux. Etruscans, from a neighbouring district called *Velabrum,* owned many of the shops.

BASILICA GIULIA

During Hadrian's time, the street was improved and a university was founded near the church of Santa Maria Antiqua.

Cloaca Maxima

Rome's first sewer effectively drained the swamp by diverting the stream that flowed into the valley.

CLOACA MAXIMA
...(TARQUINIO IL SUPERBO) DIEDE INIZIO ANCHE
ALLO SCAVO DI CANALI SOTTERRANEI,
ATTRAVERSO I QUALI TUTTA L'ACQUA CHE
SCOLA DALLE VIE SI VERSA NEL TEVERE,
ED E' QUESTA UN OPERA MIRABILE
CHE SUPERA OGNI DESCRIZIONE...
Dionigi di Alicarnasso,
Le antichita' Romane, III, 67, 5

Castor and Pollux

Three great marble columns standing tall on a plinth are all that remains of what was once the largest temple in the Forum. The temple housed the office of weights and measures, and contained a number of money-lending booths and Senate meeting rooms.

San Lorenzo in Miranda, Temple Antoninus and Faustina

The church of San Lorenzo was built inside the temple superstructure. San Lorenzo is the patron saint of chefs. It is said that when the saint was being roasted on the temple steps he requested that his executioners '*turn me over, I'm done on that side*'. Emperor Pius Antonius built the temple for his deified wife Faustina. Before that, this area formed part of the palace of Numa Pompilius, Rome's second king.

Santi Cosma e Damiano

The original building formed part of the Forum library. The small round vestibule of the church was originally the Temple of Romulus. Consecrated by Pope Felix IV in AD 527, the church contains beautiful 6th century mosaics on the arch and apse. Francesco Allegrini added the frescoes when the church was rebuilt in the 17th century.

Tempio di Vesta

Vesta, the goddess of fire, was one of Rome's oldest and most venerated gods. Her flame symbolised the perpetuity of the state; its extinction would prophesy doom for the city. The fire in the centre of the round temple was tended by six

TEMPIO DI VESTA

virgins, selected between the ages of six and ten, each serving as priestess for a term of 30 years. All the girls came from noble families and were physically perfect. If a priestess lost her virginity she was buried alive, and if the sacred flame went out she was whipped by the high priest.

Casa di Vesta

Vesta's priestesses lived in a villa next to the temple. The women had high status, financial security and the freedom to come and go as they wished. Vestal virgins were so highly regarded that if one happened to cross the path of a condemned prisoner, that prisoner would immediately gain his freedom.

Priestesses were permitted to marry after completing their service but few did so.

Arco di Tito

This monument marks the entrance to the Forum along the Via Sacra from the Colosseum. It is situated near the entrance to the Palatine. Emperor Domitian erected the arch in memory of his brother Titus, and to commemorate Titus' military victories – especially in Jerusalem. In medieval times the arch was incorporated as a gate in the Frangipani fortress walls. It was completely neglected and covered with trees and shrubbery until the archaeologist Valadier restored the monument in the 1820s. He is honoured with an inscription on the side facing the Forum.

CASA DI VESTA

The gods

Romans believed that the processes of the world were divinely activated by different gods, with each god responsible for a particular sphere of activity. Apollo was the god of healing, Mercury for prosperity in business, Mars and Diana for success in battle. There were many gods associated with agriculture: Flora (flowers), Pamona (fruit), Consus (storage), Robigus (blight) and Ceres (growth).

It was not necessary to approach the gods with a pure and humble heart – faith did not involve morality. On the contrary, prayer to the god was a ritual that, if conducted properly, would result in material gain in the area of the god's jurisdiction. There was no dogma in Roman religion, no creed and no essential mystery. A Roman was free to think what he liked about the gods; what mattered was the religious action performed.

Unless it was a demon of the underworld, it was important to invoke the god by name. Romans would then add *'or whatever name you please, be hallowed'* just to ensure that they got the name exactly right. It was also important to direct the prayer to the correct address, in the hope of catching the god at home, or to list a series of alternative addresses. Greater gods had many palatial homes and splendid temples dedicated to their glory, both in Rome and abroad. Apollo spent most of his time in Delphi and on the island of Delos, even though he had a magnificent temple on the Palatine Hill.

The same god might have different functions. Janus both opened and closed doors, so it was important to invoke the correct Janus to keep the horses in the stable.

None of the gods were exclusive; it was possible to worship them all. The only religion with an exclusive God was Judaism and later, Christianity. Romans perpetuated their religious beliefs and customs throughout the Empire, and token gestures to a Roman god were required by law. When Jews and Christians refused they became a thorn in the side of the Roman authorities, who lumped them together as troublemakers.

The Seven Kings

Romulus (p.8) founded the city and established its boundaries.

Numa Pompilius (715-673 BC) developed mercantile trade. Under his rule, craftsmen organised themselves into guilds and a system of barter became codified: one head of cattle was worth ten sheep. This developed into a primitive monetary system based on ingots of raw copper broken up into different sizes and values.

Tullus Hostilius (673-641 BC) increased the city's prestige and wealth by moving all the pagan festivals from Latium to Rome. He established the city as a religious centre with temples and sacred shrines dedicated to the gods.

Ancus Marcius (641-616 BC) built the Pons Aemilius, the first bridge to cross the Tiber, and founded the seaport of Ostia at the mouth of the river. The building of a harbour allowed Rome to develop a navy and establish new trade routes. Goods from the Mediterranean began to flood into Rome, generating massive wealth.

Tarquinius Priscus (616-579 BC) was an Etruscan with knowledge of engineering and architecture. Priscus initiated several building projects including the Circus Maximus. His most ambitious project was a monumental temple to Jupiter, built on the Capitoline, that took 200 years to complete.

Servius Tullius (579-534 BC) enlarged the city and built the Servian wall – five miles in circumference with 19 gates. He further developed the monetary system by putting a stamp into the copper ingot.

Tullius established the first Roman constitution and codified the use of wealth to determine status. This divided Roman society into two groups: the patricians and the plebeians, the rich and the poor. Patricians were responsible for providing men and money to the king in times of war and their representatives advised the king in the newly-created Senate.

Tarquinius Superbus (534-509 BC) was Etruscan and extremely unpopular. He raised taxes to pay for the Temple of Jupiter, the project begun by his grandfather. When patricians were unable to pay the higher rates, Superbus seized their property. Many Roman craftsmen were forced to leave their private businesses to contribute to the building of the temple.

The public mood turned ugly when the King's son Sextus raped Lucretia, the wife of a popular Roman patrician. A revolt led by Lucius Brutus resulted in the death of Sextus and the exile of the King with his four remaining sons.

Rome declared the state a Republic in 509 BC.

Government and Law in the Republic

The Senate established by King Servius now had real power. It created two positions of Consul to rule as alternating Head of State. Elected every two years, Consuls were chosen by and from the Senate. Lucius Brutus and Horatius Pulvillus, leaders of the rebellion, were the Republic's first Consuls.

Membership in the Senate was open only to wealthy patrician men who were required to demonstrate a certain personal net worth. Power in Rome rested with fifty men, who were the heads of noble families. All decisions taken by any of the assemblies had to be approved by the Senate. All magistrates and holders of political, civil or religious offices were members of the Senate and many of the positions were elected. In times of crisis, the Senate could appoint a dictator for a period of six months.

It wasn't long before Rome's plebeians revolted. The economic situation was dire and many people found themselves taken into slavery by patricians for non-payment of debt. A boycott was organised against military service and people exiled themselves in the hills around Rome. Patricians found their houses empty and their servants gone. Farmers stopped bringing goods to the markets. The Senate relented and in 471 BC established an assembly for plebeians, called the *Concilium Plebis*, with elected representatives and a leader. The Plebeian assembly had the power of veto over new laws introduced by the Senate, which meant that existing laws had to be codified. The result was the Twelve Tables, acknowledged by historians as the beginning of European law.

Legal Principles from the Twelve Tables

Death sentences were only to be issued by law courts. A patrician could no longer condemn debtors to death.

The crimes of crop theft and slander resulted in capital punishment (death by clubbing).

The penalty for murder depended on the status of the persons involved and was much less than for crimes of debt or theft. Murder committed in the heat of passion or against an adulterous wife often resulted in no penalty.

A declared maximum rate of interest was established.

Anyone confirmed by the courts to owe a debt had 30 days to pay. After this time he could be sold into slavery by his creditors.

If a thief was a freeman, he was flogged and then handed to his victim for reparations. If the thief was a slave, he was flogged and thrown to his death off the Capitoline Hill, from a place known as the Tarpeian Rock.

No burials or cremations were allowed within the city walls.

The maintenance of roads was the responsibility of the bordering property owners.

It was an offence to cast or have a witch cast spells on another person.

Demonstrations for or against a particular cause were allowed. Those against a particular person were forbidden.

It was permitted to remove a branch from a neighbour's tree overhanging one's property.

The levels of punishment for assault were defined by the status of the perpetrator and victim. A patrician received the lightest sentence, often waived if the victim was a slave.

A father had the right to kill his deformed child (usually by exposure on a hillside).

Marius versus Sulla

Gaius Marius and Lucius Sulla were Consuls and enemies. The root of their conflict was the thorny issue of peasant land reform. Their rivalry split Rome in two, resulting in civil war. Patricians made alliances either for Marius or for Sulla, which continued long after both men had died.

During the time of the Republic, patricians did not serve in the military. Conscripts had to come from the next lower class of landowners. When these men joined the army, their farms were abandoned and then bought at bargain prices by the wealthy patricians. Veterans returned to poverty and so military conscripts were getting harder to find. Consuls Tiberius and Gaius Gracchus introduced the idea of a more equitable distribution of wealth and land between patricians and plebeians. Both were assassinated.

Marius took up the Gracchus legacy and recruited volunteers from the peasant class, offering them land allotments at the end of service. Recruits were fully trained and outfitted with the latest weapons. They became widely respected and feared for their discipline and fortitude in battle. These popular reforms resulted in Marius being elected consul an unprecedented six times. The Senate became polarised into two groups: the *Optimates* led by Sulla, and the *Populares,* followers of Marius. Optimates were the conservative members of the patrician class who wanted all powers of state to reside in the Senate. Populares believed in sharing power. They supported the right to veto Senate laws and decrees which had been granted to the Plebeian tribunes.

While Marius and his successor Cornelius Cinna were in Rome reforming the constitution, Sulla was leading a victorious army through Greece. He conquered Athens in 86 BC and then returned to Rome at the head of his legions. The Populares took to the streets but they were no match for Sulla's trained army. The conflict cost 50,000 Roman lives.

Sulla moved quickly to depose Cornelius Cinna and proclaim himself dictator. Then he hunted down the allies of his enemies, including one Julius Caesar who had recently wed Cinna's daughter Cornelia. In 81 BC, Sulla changed the constitution and disbanded the Plebeian tribunes and assemblies. He declared that consuls could serve only one term, were forbidden from holding military command, and must serve a compulsory year in the provinces after completing of their term as Consul.

Sulla had shown that it was possible to rule Rome by force. In 79 BC he suddenly resigned and devoted his final year to wild parties. The Republic would only survive another 50 years.

Julius Caesar (100-44 BC)

As a member of the patrician class, Julius always expected a political career. He was nineteen when he married Cornelia, and was nominated to the priesthood of Jupiter.

It was 81 BC, Lucius Sulla had been dictator for a year, and now this young upstart, the nephew of Marius, had just married the daughter of his enemy's greatest supporter. Sulla stripped Julius of his priesthood, wife's dowry and his inheritance. He was forced into hiding, sleeping in new quarters every night and bribing householders for protection. Julius finally won Sulla's pardon through the intercession of the vestal virgins and his many relatives and friends. Sulla issued a warning with the pardon: '*Very well then, you win! Take him! But never forget that the man whom you want me to spare will one day prove the ruin of the party which you and I have so long defended. There are many Mariuses in this fellow Caesar.*'

Julius left Rome to give Sulla a cooling-off period. On Sulla's death in 78 BC he returned, and began a career as an orator and lawyer. Determined to further his studies in Rhodes, Julius left on a sea voyage, only to be captured and held hostage by pirates for 40 days. When his captors told him they wanted 20 talents as ransom, he said they should demand at least 50. Julius then regaled them with tales of the torture and death he would inflict on them upon his release. The pirates all laughed but the ransom was raised, his freedom was bought, and a fleet was organised to hunt the pirates down. It was Julius Caesar who had the last laugh.

After Cornelia died in 69 BC, leaving a daughter Julia, Caesar seized the opportunity to once again marry above his station. In a strange irony, he married Pompeia, grand-daughter of Sulla, his old enemy. Pompeia was also the daughter of the powerful general Pompey. When it was rumoured that Pompeia had committed adultery, Caesar quickly divorced her. Adultery was common in Rome, but the nature of the act was so scandalous that the Senate ordered a judicial inquiry. A story had circulated that Pompeia was seduced by Publius Clodius Pulcher at the Feast of the Good Goddess, held at the Caesar residence. All men were excluded from this sacred rite and it was claimed that Publius had dressed as a woman to gain entry. Since Publius and his sister Clotide, who also attended the feast, were both notorious for their sexual appetites, few doubted the veracity of the rumours.

Caesar was appointed to the post of *aedile,* responsible for the public buildings of Rome and for games and festivals. He spent extravagantly to increase his popularity, and initiated subtle changes to laws and government; procedures that would allow Caesar to legally proclaim himself temporary dictator 15 years later. Many senators formed a strong dislike for him as he bribed his way up the political ladder in the most undignified fashion. Caesar was then named *pontifex maximus,* the chief priest. The holder of this office was considered sacrosanct as a person and above criticism.

In 59 BC Caesar formed a pact with two of the most prominent Romans of the day: Marcus Crassus, Rome's wealthiest patrician, and Gnaeus Pompeius Magnus, known as Pompey the Great because of his military victories. To strengthen the alliance, Caesar arranged a marriage between his daughter Julia and Pompey. Crassus and Pompey had been serving as Consuls for ten years. When Caesar was elected Consul, the three ruled together in an alliance known as the First Triumvirate.

Caesar's first act as Consul was to grant lands to returning soldiers. The vote was only achieved because Caesar had restored the Plebeian assemblies and he had silenced the opposition with a detachment of veteran soldiers sent to 'guard' the Senators. The vote carried. Caesar had his reforms but he was very unpopular in the Senate. To the plebeians he was a hero, the one reliable source of help they had for all legal difficulties or debt problems.

'Veni, vidi, vici.'

I came, I saw, I conquered.

In the years 58 to 49 BC Caesar's reputation as a great general was firmly established in the Gallic Wars. During this time he brought all of Gaul under Roman control and in 54 BC he defeated the Britons. In the same year his beloved daughter Julia died. And when Crassus was killed in Parthia the following year, Pompey began to turn against Caesar.

With Caesar still in Gaul, the Senate elected Pompey as sole Consul. The Plebeian assemblies protested, demanding Caesar be summoned back to Rome to stand for election. Pompey and the Senate voted to impeach him for irregularities in the Gaul campaign. Pompey declared that all who were not actively with the government were against it and should be treated as public enemies. Caesar was ordered to disband his army. He countered with a threat to invade if force were used against the Plebeian tribunes who had vetoed the Senate's decree. In 49 BC Caesar crossed the Rubicon and led his army to Rome.

Thus began the civil war. Caesar and Pompey's armies chased each other around the Mediterranean. Pompey was defeated in Thessaly and fled to Alexandria where he was assassinated by King Ptolemy. When Ptolemy handed Caesar the head and signet ring of Pompey, Caesar promptly had Ptolemy executed. He then ensured that his lover Queen Cleopatra was ruler of all Egypt. In 47 BC,

Caesar returned to Rome victorious, riding his triumphal chariot through the Forum and ascending the steps of the Capitol between two lines of 40 elephants acting as torchbearers.

Caesar was first declared dictator for one year and then for a further ten years. He paid every infantryman a war-gratuity of 240 gold pieces and a farm, making him a very popular leader with the plebeians. The Senate was rankled and disapproved of his plans for reform. Caesar's stated philosophy was that all who were not actively against him were for him. Perhaps naïvely, he pardoned many of Pompey's followers and supporters, some of whom would later be his assassins. In 45 BC Caesar was proclaimed dictator for life.

On 15 March 44 BC, Caesar was stabbed 23 times in the portico of the Teatro di Pompeo, the present-day location of Largo Argentina. Few of the assassins outlived Caesar by more than three years. All were condemned, some died in shipwreck, some in battle and some killed themselves with the very daggers used to murder Caesar. It was the end of the Republic.

The Emperors

The assassination of Julius Caesar plunged Rome into civil war once again. Gaius Octavius formed the Second Triumvirate and ruled as Consul with Marcus Antonius (Marc Antony) until 32 BC. In true Caesar style, the alliance was sealed with the marriage of Marcus to Octavia, the sister of Octavius. But Marcus was madly in love with Cleopatra and he soon returned to Egypt. Octavius declared war on Egypt and his victory secured the bounty of Cleopatra's treasury.

Octavius was a patient man. His transformation to official *Imperium Majus* (Emperor) status was gradual and, perhaps mindfull of Caesar's downfall, he was always careful to allow the Senate to believe they were making the decisions. Octavius retained continuous Consulships from 31-23 BC and had the designation *Augustus* conferred upon him in 27 BC. He ended his term of Consul in 23 BC, lacking the strength for official duties. He was elevated to an office above Consul, which was separate from the mundane and practical but with power to summon the Senate; and he was called Emperor Augustus. In 19 BC his authority was broadened to more conveniently govern all the Roman territories and provinces.

Ninety-three Emperors ruled the Roman Empire for just over 500 years. The names of some of Emperors and their family dynasties are listed below. These are remembered either for their great service to Rome or for their notorious behaviour.

Julio-Claudian Dynasty

Augustus *Gaius Octavius* (31 BC-AD 14)
Tiberius *Tiberius Claudius Nero* (14-37)
Caligula *Gaius Julius Caesar Germanicus* (37-41)
Claudius *Tiberius Claudius Nero Germanicus* (41-54)
Nero *Nero Claudius Drusus Germanicus* (54-68)

Augustus reorganised every branch of government to create a Roman Principate in which all but the humblest classes benefited economically. He declared his stepson Tiberius heir and thereby established a system of dynastic transfer of imperial power. Nero later set fire to Rome and blamed the Christians – igniting persecutions that would continue for two centuries.

Flavian Dynasty

Vespasian *Titus Flavius Vespasianus* (69-79)
Titus *Titus Flavius Sabinus Vespasianus* (79-81)
Domitian *Titus Flavius Domitianus* (81-96)

Nero's disastrous reign was followed by the Year of Four Emperors. In 69 AD the Emperors Galba, Otho and Vitellus were murdered. Rome was in chaos when the practically-minded Vespasian assumed the Imperial crown and restored morale. He brought peace and prosperity and commissioned the Colosseum as a gift to the people. When Vespasian died it was rumoured that he had been murdered by his son Titus. The rumour was taken as proof when Vesuvius erupted one month after Titus ascended the Imperial throne. Emperor Domitian, youngest son of Vespasian and loyal brother to Titus, dedicated himself to the deification of his father and brother.

Adoptive and Antonine Emperors

Nerva *Marcus Cocceius* (96-98)
Trajan *Marcus Ulpius Trajanus* (98-117)
Hadrian *Publius Aelius Hadrianus* (117-138)
Antoninus Pius *Titus Aurelius Antoninus* (138-161)
Marcus Aurelius *Marcus Annius Verus* (161-180)
Lucius Verus *Lucius Commodus* (161-169, joint emperor)

Trajan was a great builder and he adopted Hadrian as his successor. Hadrian was the restless architect responsible for the Pantheon and the Villa Adriana at Tivoli. The Augustian golden age was revived under Hadrian and Marcus Aurelius. Rome was prosperous once again. After the death of Aurelius revolts against the Roman yoke broke out across the Empire.

House of Severus

Septimius Severus *Lucius* (193-211)
Caracalla *Julius Bassianus* (211-217)
Geta *Publius Septimus* (211, joint emperor)

Septimius ruled jointly with Pescennius Niger for two years, followed by Clodius Albinus until 197. His eldest son Caracalla was nicknamed after the long Gallic cloak he had made fashionable. Caracalla built the famous baths (p.188).

Tetrarchy

Diocletian (Diocles) *Gaius Aurelius Valerius* (284-305, joint emperor from 286)
Maximian *Marcus Aurelius Valerius* (286-305, 307-8, joint emperor)

Diocletian and his co-emperor Maximian were from Dalmatian peasant stock and rose through the military ranks. Diocletian was hailed emperor after a victory in 284 and he proclaimed

Maximian as joint emperor. In 293 Diocletian established the Tetrarchy, a joint rule of two *Augusti* (emperors) and two *Caesari* (junior emperors). He reduced the size of each province for easier management and divided the large Empire into East and West.

House of Constantine

Constantine I the Great *Flavius Valerius Constantinus* (306-37)
Constantine II *Flavius Claudius* (337-40, joint emperor)
Constantius II *Flavius Julius Constantius* (337-61)

Constantine declared the Edict of Milan in 313, finally allowing Christians freedom of worship. His mother Helena was canonised. Constantine began building Constantinople (Byzantium) as a great capital, resulting in a power shift away from Rome.

Palatino (Palatine)

entrance within the Forum
06 399 67700
09.00-1 hour before sunset
€8 includes Palatine Museum
(also valid for Colosseum)
Palatine Museum: 09.00-2 hours before sunset
map 9, C2
GPS 41.89084, 12.48756
(from inside the Forum)

Protected by the Capitoline and Aventine hills, the Palatine was an ideal place for a nomadic tribe to settle, with gentle slopes and an excellent position next to the Tiber. The hill overlooked a strategic route that connected the Etruscan region in the north with Campagna in the south.

This was the seat of government and the royal residence of the six kings who ruled after Romulus. During the Republic, government moved to the Capitoline and this area became the most elegant residential address in the city. Rome's great and good lived here, including the poet and orator Cicero. During the reign of Augustus the Emperor's residence was established here.

Tiberius expanded the palace and Caligula extended it further, right to the edge of the cliff overlooking the Foro Romano. Emperors Claudius and Nero built the *Domus Transitoria,* which burned down in the fire of AD 64. The next palace to be constructed on the site was the Domus Augustana, built by Domitian in honour of the Emperor Augustus. It remained the Imperial Palace until the fall of the Western Empire.

Completed in AD 92, the palace was divided into two sectors: an official public area and private living quarters. The public reception wing featured an audience hall and basilica, a hippodrome, and baths. The lavish domestic quarters were arranged on the slopes of the hill with courtyards, fountains, porticoes, terraces and a reflecting pool.

When Domitian's palace became too small for Emperor Septimius Severus, he sought to enlarge it. The Emperor found there was no room left on the Palatine, so his solution was to enlarge the hill. He constructed a terraced extension of the plateau on the south face of the Palatine, reaching to the stands of the Circus Maximus. It was supported by a series of brickwork arcades on two levels rising to a height of 30 metres. The ruins of these arcades are a distinctive feature. Septimius also erected the *Septizoniu,* a magnificent fountain richly decorated with columns and statues.

IN THE MUSEO DELLA CIVILTÀ ROMANA (P.279) THERE IS A MODEL OF WHAT THE AREA LOOKED LIKE DURING THE TIME OF IMPERIAL ROME.

Orti Farnesiani (Farnese Gardens)

Established in the 16th century by Pope Paul III's grandson and namesake, Cardinal Alessandro Farnese, the terraced Italianate gardens once included an aviary at its centre. The symbolic setting of the Palatine was the ideal location for Farnese receptions and parties, which were accompanied by the sound and colour of hundreds of birds. In the 18th and 19th centuries it became fashionable for those on the Grand Tour (p.156) to picnic on the Palatine, followed by a stroll through the Farnese gardens.

Colosseo (Colosseum)

Piazza del Colosseo
06 399 67700
€8 (also valid for Palatine)
map 9, D2
GPS 41.88959, 12.49194

09.00-one hour before sunset
last entrance 1 hour
before closing
English guided tours €3.50
09.30, 10.15, 11.15, 12.30
summer only: 15.00, 16.15, 17.00

To fully appreciate what you are seeing, a guided tour is recommended. Tours in English occur frequently and also include the Palatine. There is no need to book in advance as this is more expensive and space is usually available.

IF THERE IS A LONG QUEUE AT THE COLOSSEUM TICKET OFFICE, BUY YOUR TICKET AT THE PALATINE – TICKETS ARE GOOD FOR BOTH SITES.

Emperor Vespasian commissioned an *Amphitheatrum Flavium* in AD 72 on the site of Nero's former palace – the *Domus Aurea* in Parco Oppio. He drained Nero's lake and built a theatre for public games to disassociate himself from the hated tyrant and make himself popular amongst his citizens. But Vespasian didn't live to see his vision completed. It was his son Titus who presided over 100 days of lavish inauguration games in AD 80.

The oval-shaped building is 190.25 metres long, 157.5 metres wide and 50 metres high. The outer façade is comprised of four arcades of arches, one above the other, with the fourth storey filled in and framed. In ascending order the arches are decorated with Doric, Ionic and Corinthian columns. The exterior was once covered in blocks of travertine marble like the five remaining on the east side. A huge retractable awning, the *velarium*, was used to shade spectators from the sun. Numbers are carved over the arches at street level, indicating separate entrances for different seating areas.

With the rise of Christianity and the decline of Roman paganism, the Colosseum fell into ruin. Walls and supporting arches collapsed in the earthquake of 1349 and what remained was stripped for use in rebuilding the city. Pope Sixtus V (Peretti) considered demolishing the Colosseum when he rebuilt Rome for the pilgrims. Instead he decided to include it in the pilgrimage route to St Peter's. In the 18th century, Benedict XIV sanctified the building by dedicating it to the passion of Christ, putting an end to repeated pillaging.

The Roman Games

The Romans did not regard their games as degrading or cruel, and they were not seen as mere entertainment. The games were designed to demonstrate the triumph of Roman imperialism over nature and nations. They were state occasions at which the principles of justice, religion, courage in battle and the ability to die bravely were uppermost. These were the virtues that made Rome great and this is what Emperors wanted their subjects to see.

In the Colosseum, a typical games day would begin in the morning with the entrance of the Emperor, accompanied by the sound of applause from 55,000 spectators. The Master of the Games would signal the start of the proceedings. A religious ceremony would follow, invoking the favour of a particular god. Next it was time for justice to be dispensed: criminals, slaves, prisoners of war, Christians and other offenders were executed with gladiatorial weapons or by wild animals. Slaves removed the bodies and then prepared the arena for a great beast hunt. Lions, tigers and other exotic animals imported from all corners of the Empire would be let loose, to be killed by skilled animal handlers and expert hunters, all dressed in colourful outfits.

During a break for lunch, the wealthy would depart to their town houses. Those remaining would be supplied with food – probably bread – thrown by attendants. Bookies would be kept busy taking bets during the interval. Incense burners were lit all around the amphitheatre, in an attempt to conceal the smell of death – especially nasty on a hot summer's day.

In the afternoon the gladiators entered the arena, acknowledged the Emperor and the contests began. The audience would be watching for a skilful move, a potential fatal thrust or a flash of brilliance. If this was evident, even the loser might be allowed to live. Before the Master of the Games signalled the end of the day's proceedings, there was a draw, with lucky ticket holders receiving prizes. The grand prize might have been an estate in Tuscany.

As time went on, the games became increasingly mindless and violent. Not even the impact of Christianity did much to halt them. Ironically, it was barbarian invaders who succeeded in putting an end to the games.

Gladiators

On the wall of an ancient cemetery in Rome, the following advertisement is written in red paint:

'Weather permitting, 30 pairs of gladiators provided by A. Clodius Flaccus, together with substitutes in case any get killed too quickly, will fight 1st, 2nd and 3rd May at the Circus Maximus. The fights will be followed by a big wild beast hunt. The famous gladiator Paris will fight – Hurrah for Paris! Hurrah for the generous Flaccus who is running for Diumvirate!'

Then there is an additional small ad:

'Marcus wrote this sign by the light of the moon. If you hire Marcus, he will work night and day to do a good job.'

Gladiatorial contests began in 264 BC at a funeral, when the sons of Junius Brutus honoured their late father with a battle featuring three pairs of slaves trained as gladiators. By the time of Augustus Caesar, there were four huge gladiator schools providing a constant supply of young men ready to die for the entertainment of others. The most popular methods of fighting would be either as a *secutor* (with helmet, sword, breastplate and shield) or a *retiarius* (weighted net and three-pronged trident). It would be at the discretion of the *Lanista* (the school manager) to match up suitable opponents for a show.

Death was a certainty for untrained gladiators. They were given scant protection – some even fought with blindfolds to create fun for the audience, who would shout instructions from the terraces. Average fighters knew death was inevitable but there were some advantages: in a school they were part of a big family and their dependents received their earnings.

If a gladiator began to win fights, his social status would soar. Skilled fighters could achieve the status that famous footballers or pop stars have today. Wealthy Roman women would buy their bottled sweat as an aphrodisiac. If they fought exceptionally well, they might be awarded their freedom. Although the 'thumbs down' gesture is a Hollywood invention, hand motions were used to indicate life or death. Well-trained and costly gladiators would not be needlessly sacrificed; their presence might be needed for future events.

Circo Massimo (Circus Maximus)

map 9, B1; GPS 41.8877, 12.4827

Located in the valley between the Palatine and Aventine hills is a large grassy area that once held the largest stadium in the world. It was on this field that Romulus had the Sabine women kidnapped (p.8-9). King Tarquinius Priscus built the first Circus to commemorate the event. Subsequent rulers improved and extended the structure. Today it is a popular picnic spot in the summer, albeit accompanied by the roar of traffic on the Via dei Cerchi. On the side of the Aventine is a viewpoint and photo opportunity looking over the Circus to the Palatine.

The closest restaurants are to be found in the side streets off the Piazza della Bocca della Verità.

The Circus Maximus measured 600 by 200 metres and could seat 300,000 spectators. The Imperial box was on the side that faced the Palatine, where the emperors lived. Other spectators were seated in sections according to their class: patricians at the bottom, plebeians in the middle and slaves further up. Women sat in the wooden seats at the top. These upper rows were not only very hot in the Roman summer, they were also unstable. Records indicate the structure was subject to frequent collapse: 1,112 spectators were killed under Emperor Antoninus Pius; during the reign of Diocletian some 13,000 perished.

Arguably the largest building ever constructed for entertainment purposes, the Circus Maximus was primarily used for chariot racing. The track had two Egyptian obelisks, one at each end of the central barrier that ran down the middle of the arena. Charioteers were required to race around the track seven times to complete the circuit. The final race was held in AD 549 for the benefit of King Totila of the Ostrogoths.

When Rome declined, the races ceased. What could be recycled into new buildings was removed after an earthquake in the 14th century. The two obelisks lay buried in the ground until they were discovered in 1588. One is now in the Piazza del Popolo and the other at San Giovanni in Laterano.

Capitoline Hill

The Capitoline has a long history as a centre of Roman government and worship. Archaeologists have discovered traces of Bronze Age settlements dating back to 1200 BC when the hill consisted of two wooded heights known as the *Capitolium* and the *Arx*.

The Capitolium was the location of the Temple of Jupiter. Begun under the Etruscan King Tarquinius, it was consecrated by the Republic in 509 BC. The temple became a symbol of Roman civilisation and the place where all triumphal processions culminated. Victorious generals, Julius Caesar included, marched through the Forum along the Via Sacra to the Capitolium where they performed ritual sacrifices to the gods. The *Tempio di Juno Moneta*, the public mint, was on the Arx.

From street level it is impossible to miss the enormous white *Monumento a Vittorio Emmanuele II*, which houses the *Museo di Risorgimento*. Beside the monument are two long flights of steps leading up the Capitoline: one goes to the church of *Santa Maria in Aracoeli* and the other, known as the *Cordonata*, leads to the *Campidoglio*, the piazza at the centre of the *Musei Capitolini* (Capitoline Museums). On either side of the piazza are the two buildings of the Capitoline Museums: the *Palazzo dei Conservatori* and the *Palazzo Nuovo*. The distinctive yellow ochre façade of the central building belongs to *Palazzo Senatorio*, now the offices of the Mayor of Rome.

In the centre of the piazza is a copy of a 2nd century bronze statue of *Emperor Marcus Aurelius*. The original is in the courtyard of Palazzo Nuovo. The museums occupy the site of the old Temple of Jupiter and the church stands on the site of the former mint.

Campidoglio

map 12, H5; GPS 41.89346, 12.48258

In 1538, Michelangelo was commissioned by Pope Paul III (Farnese) to rebuild the area for the processions that were planned for Charles V's triumphant re-entry to Rome. As Holy Roman Emperor, Charles showed his power by sacking Rome in 1527. The Pope was keen to make a good impression.

The Temple of Jupiter once sat imperiously above the city and faced the Forum. Michelangelo redesigned the Capitoline to face northwards, looking out over the new city and the roads leading to the Vatican. His grand staircase features colossal statues of Castor and Pollux at the entrance to the Campidoglio.

The bronze Marcus Aurelius was placed high on a domed oval pavement in the centre of a twelve-pointed stellate pattern, radiating out from a sunburst. The mounded pavement evokes the earthly sphere; the star shape alludes to the heavens and the signs of the zodiac; the sunburst is the symbol of Apollo, who was used in the Renaissance as a metaphor for Christ. Michelangelo's design symbolises the temporal and spiritual universality of the Pope.

CAMPIDOGLIO

Musei Capitolini (Capitoline Museums)

Piazza del Campidoglio
06 3996 7800
www.museicapitolini.org
map 9, B1
GPS 41.89346, 12.48258

09.00-20.00 Tues-Sun
admission €6.20

The Capitoline Museums are spread across two buildings: the Palazzo Nuovo and the Palazzo dei Conservatori. There is a ticket office on the ground floor of each building and tickets are valid for both buildings. *Caffè dei Musei Capitolini* provides excellent views from the rooftop of Palazzo dei Conservatori. A ticket to the museums is not required to access the restaurant. There is an entrance along the narrow staircase to the right of the main entrance.

THE EXTERIOR RESTAURANT HAS TABLE SERVICE, SO DON'T PURCHASE ANYTHING IN THE CAFETERIA IF YOU WANT TO SIT OUTSIDE.

Sixtus IV (Francesco della Rovere) began the museum's collection in 1471 with a donation of the Lateran bronzes. These were sculptures that were found in the Forum and the Temple of Jupiter and then housed at San Giovanni in Laterano. In 1566 Pius V (Ghislieri) added to the Capitoline's statuary collection to *'purge the Vatican of pagan idols'*. The collections expanded with continuing papal donations. Napoleon once made off with much of the statuary. But the sculptor Antonio Canova, then a director of the museum, had them recovered. Today the collection is enhanced by archaeological finds in excavations at Largo Argentina and Trajan's Market.

Be sure to see four noteworthy bronzes from the original Lateran collection: *Constantine, Capitoline She-Wolf, Spinarius* (Boy Removing a Thorn), and *Camillus*. They are displayed on the first floor of the Palazzo dei Conservatori. On the second floor is the Capitoline Picture Gallery with paintings by Titian and Caravaggio. The Palazzo Nuovo is primarily a sculpture gallery. The Hall of Emperors contains busts of many illustrious emperors and their wives. It is interesting to note the evolution of Roman hair and beard fashions through the centuries. The Palazzo dei Conservatori and the Palazzo Nuovo are connected by an underground passage that was excavated in the 1930s to reveal the existence of an ancient road between the Arx and the Capitolium.

Palazzo dei Conservatori

In the **Courtyard** on the ground floor are fragments of the giant statue of *Constantine,* dating from 313-24, that once stood in the Basilica Maxentius in the Forum. It was built using the acrolithic technique where only the exposed parts of the body – head, hands and feet – were carved in marble. Stucco or concrete made up the other parts; robes and clothing were made of gilded bronze.

On the **staircase** leading to the first floor are five relief panels: three depicting the triumphant commander Marcus Aurelius and two of Hadrian, the great statesman and scholar. The collections on the first floor are located in the former meeting rooms of the magistrates, the *Conservatori,* established in 1363 as an autonomous body to administer and control public taxation and customs duties.

In the **Hall of the Horatii and Curiatii** at the top of the stairs is the bronze *Constantine.* The large head and hand dominate the gallery. The head is remarkable for the character expressed in the face: focused strength in the eyes, cruelty in the set of the mouth. The gilded bronze statue of *Hercules* was found in the round Temple of Hercules near the Piazza della Bocca della Verità. The 16th century frescoes are by Cesari d'Arpino. They depict the myths of ancient Rome that were fashionable during the Renaissance period. Romulus and Remus are depicted at the moment they were discovered by the peasant couple. Of the statues of the popes that once filled this room only two remain: a Bernini sculpture of his patron Pope Urban VIII (Barberini) and a bronze of Innocent X (Pamphilj) by Alessandro Algardi.

The **Hall of Triumphs** features *Spinarius,* which dates from the 1st century BC around the time of Sulla and the sack of Athens. Inspired by Greek sculpture, the pose is unusual in that it is so natural: a boy removing a thorn from his foot, his face full of intense concentration. Nearby is the *Capitoline Brutus,* whose penetrating eyes are made of ivory and glass. *Camillus* is another statue also dating from the 1st century BC. Because of the drapery and fine features, the subject was considered to be a woman, but is now thought to be a man belonging to a religious sect. The eyes are made with silver inlay.

SPINARIUS

In the centre of the **Hall of the She-Wolf** is the *Capitoline She-Wolf,* suckling the twins Romulus and Remus. The wolf is Etruscan and dates from the 5th century BC. The baby boys were added in 1509 by a Florentine sculptor. Also in this gallery is a marble *Medusa* by Bernini and a sensitive portrait of Michelangelo by an unknown artist.

The **Capitoline Picture Gallery** displays Italian painting from the Medieval period to the late Renaissance. The collection is organised by location and time. There are rooms dedicated to painting from Ferrara, Venice, Bologna and, of course, Rome. **Hall II,** the Ferrara Gallery, has a beautiful *Annunciation* by Garofalo and in **Hall III,** the Venice Gallery, there is an early Titian, *Baptism of Christ,* and a Paolo Veronese, *Rape of Europa*. **Hall V** displays paintings from Emilia Romagna and Rome, including a gentle portrait of *Diana the Huntress* by Cesari d'Arpino. **Hall VI** contains a delicate portrait *Girl with a Crown* by Guido Reni. In the **Hall of Saint Petronilla** are two paintings by Caravaggio: *The Fortune Teller* and *St John the Baptist*. There is also a Peter Paul Rubens, *Romulus and Remus.* The collection of Francesco Cini in the **Cini Gallery** contains two portraits by Giovanni Bellini, one by Van Dyck, and a self-portrait by Velasquez.

Palazzo Nuovo

In the **Lobby** on the ground floor is a sculpture of the goddess *Minerva* that stands almost ten feet tall. Nearby stands a sculpture of *Ceres*, goddess of agriculture. The model for the head was the Empress Faustina, wife of Emperor Antoninus Pius. The body was copied from a Greek sculpture of Aphrodite.

The **Courtyard** contains a fountain with *Marforio*, one of the 'talking statues' (p.72). In the niches on both sides of the fountain are two sculptures, known as *Satyrs of the Valley*, depicting the Greek god Pan. These originate in ancient Greece and were once used as part of an architectural support structure in the Theatre of Pompey. The restored original bronze *Marcus Aurelius* is the most impressive sculpture in the courtyard. It was once mistakenly thought to be a rendering of the Emperor Constantine holding out his arm in Christian blessing. This spared the statue from being melted down during the Middle Ages.

On the first floor **Gallery** is a sculpture of the baby *Hercules* strangling a snake. This was actually a portrait of Annius Verus, the son of Marcus Aurelius. Other family portraits of Roman emperors can be found in the **Hall of Emperors**, which also exhibits the bust of *Agrippina*, mother of Nero. In the **Hall of Philosophers** are works portraying the poets and orators of ancient Greece that once decorated the houses of Roman patricians. Mosaics were another popular item in the homes of wealthy Romans. Two beautiful pieces dating from the time of Hadrian are found in the **Hall of Doves**: one depicts four doves drinking from a bronze bowl and the other shows theatrical masks of *Comedy* and *Tragedy*.

Further pieces from the Capitoline collection (previously undisplayed) are housed in the **Centrale Montemartini** south of the city centre. The black iron machinery of this former power station provides a striking contrast to the white marble statuary.

Via Ostiense 184
06 574 8030, €4.20
09.30-18.30 Tues-Sun

Santa Maria in Aracoeli

Scala dell'Arce Capitolina 12
06 679 8155
9.00-12.30, 15.00-18.00 daily
map 12, H5
GPS 41.89383, 12.48270

This church is considered one of the most important in Rome. As well as being renowned for music, it has special appeal for mothers and children.

There are 124 steps on the long climb to the church, whose name translates as 'St Mary of the Altar in the Sky'. The staircase was built in 1348 as a gesture of thanks to the Madonna for ending the latest outbreak of plague. The exterior appears stark and forbidding, but the interior of the church is light and airy. A coffered golden ceiling commemorates the victory at Lepanto in 1571. In the chapel to the right of the altar are frescoes dedicated to the life of *San Bernardino da Siena* by Pinturicchio.

Be sure to find the little **Chapel of the Holy Infant**, to the left of the main altar. The altarpiece, the *Santo Bambino,* is a replica of the original, carved in Jerusalem in the late 15th century by a Franciscan friar. Legend has it that the friar could not finish his work and an angel completed the piece. It was then lost at sea as the friar returned to Rome, only to arrive safely in Livorno, still in its case, in the wake of the friar's ship.

Today mothers and children from around the world visit the chapel to obtain blessings, and pregnant women have their unborn children blessed. Beside the *Bambino* there is a touching collection of letters written by children.

Santa Maria in Aracoeli presents superb concerts; some have featured the London Philharmonic Orchestra. Christmas Eve is especially magical, when the church is glowing with light from candles in the chandeliers.

EXIT FROM THE RIGHT OF THE ALTAR TO FIND STEPS LEADING DOWN TO THE CAMPIDOGLIO.

Monumento a Vittorio Emanuele II (Il Vittoriano)

Piazza Venezia
09.30-18.00 daily
admission free
map 12, H4
GPS 41.8953, 12.4818

Museo del Risorgimento
Via di San Pietro in Carcere
06 678 0664
09.00-18.30 Tues-Sun
closed Monday, admission free
www.risorgimento.it

Built between 1885 and 1911 to celebrate the unification of Italy, the monument completely changed the character of a neighbourhood that was once home to Michelangelo. The building owes its stark white colour to a government minister who insisted that, instead of using the traditional brownish-grey travertine, it should be built with marble from his native Brescia. Known locally as the '*wedding cake*' and the '*typewriter*', most Romans complain that the edifice is an eyesore. They also quip that the monument is the best place to stand because then you aren't forced to look at it. Superb views are to be had from the top, which is reached from the inside. Climb part way up and look for an entrance to the building.

The monument houses the *Tomb of the Unknown Soldier* and the **Museo del Risorgimento**. The museum is dedicated to Italian soldiers, both in their struggle for nationhood and in memory of two world wars. Cavour, Garibaldi, Mazzini and King Vittorio Emanuele II are honoured here. Entrance is from the side of the monument, off Via dei Fori Imperiali.

Piazza della Bocca della Verità

map 9, A2
GPS 41.8894, 12.4813

The piazza is nestled between the Capitoline, Palatine and Aventine hills and is easy to miss because of its low elevation. Once settled by Greek dock workers, this was the harbour and warehousing district for the markets in the Foro Romano. Cattle were traded in the shadow of the **Arch of Janus**. The ruins of warehouses built by Agrippa are still visible along Via San Teodoro at the base of the Palatine.

There is an interesting mix of pagan temples and early Christian churches. The temples to Fortuna and Vesta, known as the **Forum Boarium**, are located in a grassy area of the piazza. The temple of Vesta was originally dedicated to Hercules, the Greek hero. A giant gilded statue of Hercules, now found at the Capitoline Museums, was taken from here. The temple was renamed because its round shape echoed the Tempio di Vesta in the Forum.

Near the temples is **Santa Maria in Cosmedin**, a church built in the 6th century on the site of the old farmer's market. Under the church portico there is an old drain cover mounted on the wall. It is known as *Bocca della Verità* (mouth of truth). Visitors are challenged to place their hand in the open mouth to

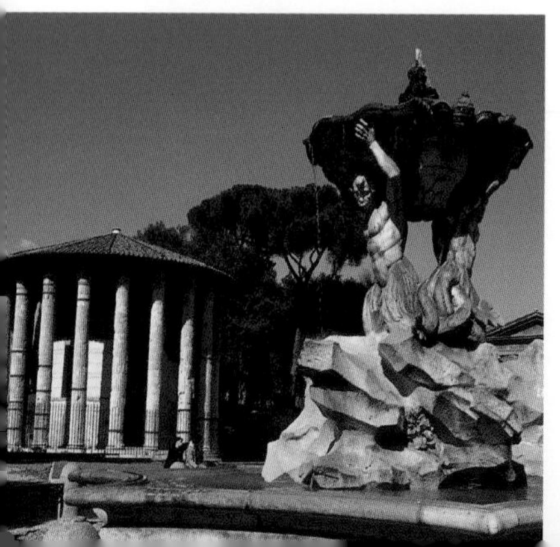

TEMPIO DI VESTA

determine their veracity. Legend says that the formidable jaws will close on the hands of those who tell lies.

Across the piazza, hidden behind the Arch of Janus, is **San Giorgio in Velabro,** one of the oldest churches in Rome. It is said to most closely resemble the original St Peter's, which was built in the 4th century. Attached to the exterior is the *Arch of Silversmiths,* built in AD 204 by Septimius Severus. Materials to build the church were salvaged from surrounding temples. As a result, the 16 columns inside are all different. Decorating the apse are mosaics by Pietro Cavallini dating from 1300. Each year over 200 brides choose to be married here.

Turn left along Via San Teodoro for the newly restored Greek Orthodox church of **San Teodoro.** The small, round building is located in the centre of what once was Rome's central storehouse area for grain and corn. In the 4th century, these buildings were converted into shelters for the poor.

THE NEARBY RESTAURANT, *SAN TEODORO* (P.237), IS A GOOD PLACE TO STOP FOR LUNCH.

SAN GIORGIO IN VELABRO

VATICANO

PIAZZA SAN PIETRO

The smallest country in the world, the Vatican is a pilgrimage site for the world's Catholics. Its galleries house some of mankind's greatest art treasures.

There's a lot to see – don't try and visit everything in one day. A suggested itinerary would be St Peter's on one day and the Vatican Museums on another. If time is short, go to the galleries first; they always close before St Peter's. Summer visitors may find afternoons a quieter time to see the museums. In winter they close after lunch. With a view of the gardens, the cafeteria in the museums is a good place to eat.

Proper attire is required throughout the Vatican. Knees, shoulders and midriffs should be covered for visits to St Peter's and the museums.

Adventurous travellers can make the climb up to the dome of St Peter's, for the best viewpoint in Rome.

The huge armoury once required to protect the popes is on display in Castel Sant'Angelo. A secure passage – used in times of danger – connects the castle to the Vatican palace.

SWISS GUARDS IN UNIFORMS DESIGNED BY MICHELANGELO

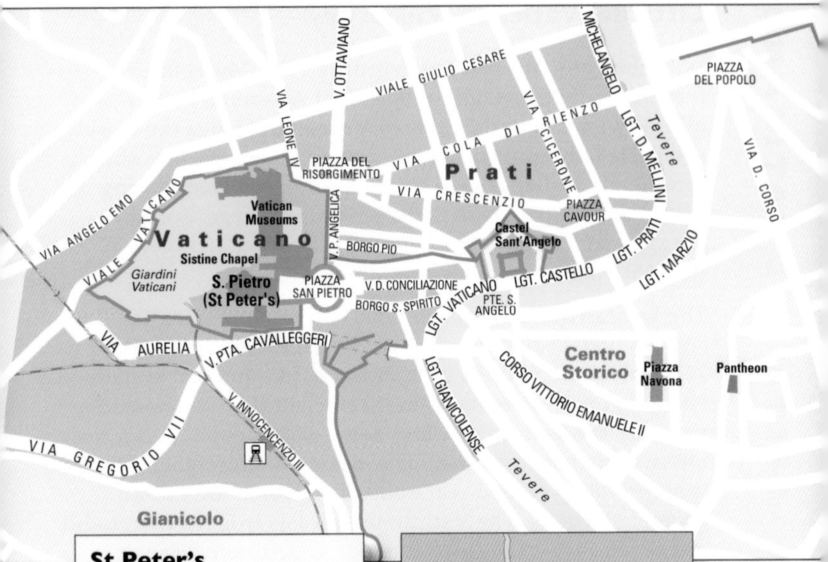

St Peter's
centre of the Catholic faith
- Michelangelo's *Pietà*
- Piazza San Pietro

Vatican Museums
- Raphael Rooms
- Pinacoteca

Sistine Chapel
- Michelangelo's ceiling
- wall frescoes by famous Renaissance artists

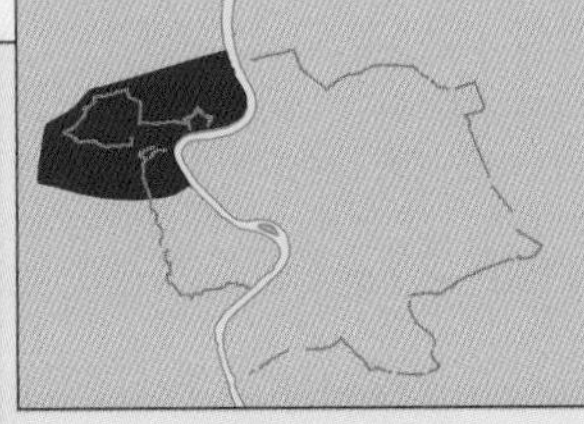

Vatican Gardens
Book a guided tour of these historical gardens.

restaurants p.238
shopping p.258

Ponte Sant'Angelo
Bernini's angel sculptures.

Via Cola di Rienzo & Via Ottaviano
A quieter area for mainstream shopping, with a large indoor market at Piazza dell'Unità.

Did you know that..?
Just after he was named Pope, Cardinal Ratzinger's 1999 VW Golf sold for €45,000 on eBay.

Città del Vaticano (Vatican City)

With the Lateran Treaty of February 1929, Mussolini formally established an independent sovereign nation, officially known as the State of Vatican City. It is the world's smallest state, comprising 108.7 acres in a trapezium shape, completely walled except for the great open space facing Piazza San Pietro. Latin is the official language. Today the state sovereign is Benedict XVI (Joseph Ratzinger) the 265th pope.

The Vatican accommodates 1,000 citizens including the Pope and his household, 46 curial cardinals, 89 Swiss Guards and 201 diplomats. With its own shops, banks, judicial system and post office (one that is more efficient than the Roman version), the Vatican employs some 4,000 people. It is a truly international state; nobody is considered a foreigner. There is no privately owned real estate, no income tax and no general elections. The Vatican broadcasts from its own radio station and publishes a newspaper: *Osservatore Romano*.

The purpose of the Vatican state is to provide complete political independence to the Pope. As head of the Catholic Church, he is subject to no government or political power. Neither are the state-run Vatican banks. A case in point is when John Paul II secretly donated large sums to the Polish Solidarity movement to aid the cause of freedom: he was not required to seek permission or advice from outside the Vatican.

This is the territorial home of the Holy See. A 'see' is a diocese, with the name derived from the Latin *sedes*, meaning 'seat'. Headed by the Pope, the Holy See is a sovereign and distinct entity, separate from the territory of the Vatican state. It is the Holy See, with its 1.1 billion Catholic adherents, that has diplomatic relations with 123 countries, not the Vatican state. Hence, Mussolini signed the Lateran Treaty with the Holy See, which also has sovereignty over a dozen buildings outside the walls of the Vatican.

Basilica di San Pietro (St Peter's)

The Apostle Peter is considered the father of the church. He is buried where the Basilica now stands, linking papal authority with the most important church in the Catholic world. The church is built on land that was once a pagan burial ground known as the Vatican cemetery. The Apostle's body was brought here after his crucifixion at Nero's Circus in AD 67. He was given a simple burial; his bones put to rest in a grave dug into the hillside and covered with tiles. The gravesite was well known amongst Christians, who came to pray and keep vigil against grave robbers. Sometime around AD 160, a red-coloured wall was erected as a barrier and a shrine was built above the grave to protect the sacred ground from encroaching pagan mausoleums. Remains of the shrine, the reddish wall and the Apostle's bones were found in the *Scavi*.

Scavi

Excavations beneath the Basilica in the 1940s revealed a larger than expected necropolis. This included an underground street used by Christians forced into hiding by Nero's persecutions. There are remains of houses and shops, along with a mosaic of Christ dating from the third century depicting him as a beardless charioteer. A limited number of visitors are permitted to visit the Scavi (p.127).

Constantine's church

Emperor Constantine donated the land to build the first church on this site, which was consecrated in 326 by Pope Sylvester I. The ground sloped steeply away from St Peter's grave on two sides. To create a firm foundation, huge concrete walls were constructed along the boundary of the church. The area within the walls, which encompassed many pagan tombs, was filled in with compacted clay and sand until the ground was level with the tomb. More than a million cubic feet of earth was used. The walls were made of brick and a timber roof was covered with bronze and lead tiles. The church was spacious, with five aisles divided lengthwise by four colonnades of 22 marble columns.

Emperor Constantine was honoured with a triumphal arch placed between the congregation and the altar. St Peter's tomb was covered by a large canopy, from which hung a golden crown-shaped lamp embellished with 50 dolphins.

Pilgrims flocked to St Peter's in the thousands, each one bringing offerings. Royal benefactors enriched the interior and soon the church housed the most precious artefacts in Christendom. Barbarian raiders and vandals sacked Rome many times in the Middle Ages. Each time the crumbling church was robbed and damaged and then restored. By 1454 the decision had been taken to demolish the old building.

The Renaissance church

During an inspection of the Basilica in 1505, Pope Julius II (Giuliano della Rovere) discovered Michelangelo's *Pietà* tucked away in the Chapel of St Petronilla. The Pope was so impressed he immediately summoned the artist to Rome and commissioned Michelangelo to carve him a magnificent tomb. When it became apparent that Michelangelo's massive design would not fit into the existing St Peter's, Julius organised a competition of architects to build a new church, one that would '*embody the greatness of present and future, and surpass all other churches in the universe.*' Donato Bramante won the contest. He designed a church based on a Greek cross plan with a great central dome inspired by the Pantheon. If Bramante's plan had been executed without compromise, St Peter's size would be increased by 11,350 square yards.

Construction commenced in April 1506, with over 2,500 labourers employed on the project. Costs soared and soon Julius II faced a financial crisis. His schemes to raise money included the selling of 'indulgences' (a practice which fuelled the growing Reformation movement), levying taxes on Rome's prostitutes, and selling some of his own personal art collection. Julius died in 1513, Bramante in 1514.

Leo X (Medici) succeeded Julius. He appointed Bramante's nephew Raphael, who had decorated the papal apartments, as chief architect. But Raphael's inexperience and his agreeable personality meant the builders took advantage; workmen were allowed to leave gaps in the foundations so that they could store their lunches and tools in convenient locations. Years later these gaps began to fracture and crumble under the weight of the church. Raphael's death in 1520, followed by the sack of Rome in 1527, meant building slowed to a halt.

In 1546, Paul III (Farnese) put Michelangelo in charge of the project. He returned to Bramante's original plan, which he made smaller and more compact – completely redesigning the dome. The design followed the same multiple-shell system used by another Tuscan architect, Filippo Brunelleschi, for the *Duomo* in Florence. Michelangelo accepted no payment for his work on St Peter's, dedicating his labours to God, St Peter and the Madonna. When he died in 1564, the building was not finished.

Giacomo della Porta and Domenico Fontana executed Michelangelo's design for the dome in 1589. Della Porta modified the contour to be 20 feet higher than Michelangelo had planned. The dome's huge drum is 137 feet (41.8 metres) in diameter, compared to the Pantheon's 142 feet (43.3 metres). There are 16 windows, each more than 20 feet high. Between the windows are double sets of Corinthian columns, 50 feet tall, designed to act as a transition from the base of the drum to the curve of the dome. Three chains were set into the dome to prevent it from spreading; two were embedded into the solid brick where the curve begins, and another midway to the summit. The completed dome is topped by a 16 foot bronze cross, attaining an overall height of 452 feet.

In 1606, Paul V (Borghese) secured the services of Carlo Maderno as chief architect. Maderno extended the nave, changing the structure back to a Latin-cross plan. He completed the colossal façade, which is 375 feet wide and 167 feet tall, with statues of Christ and the Apostles on top of the balustrade. The Corinthian columns and pilasters on the façade are more than 90 feet tall. The frieze is adorned with the Borghese name engraved in bold Roman letters. Urban VIII (Barberini) consecrated the new church in 1626.

Piazza San Pietro
(St Peter's Square)

When the church façade was completed, its grandeur completely dwarfed the piazza in front. Medieval houses surrounding the original piazza were demolished and Bernini was commissioned to define and beautify the space. He made the piazza almost twice as long as it is wide: 1,110 by 650 feet. Colonnades with four rows of columns, made from Tuscan travertine, outline the piazza in a keyhole shape. There are 284 columns in all. The overall height of the colonnaded structure is 64 feet, allowing a view of the windows of the papal apartment in the Vatican palace from which the Pope gives his blessing.

On the balustrade above the columns stand 96 travertine statues of saints and martyrs, each 12 feet tall. Clement XI commissioned 78 more statues after Bernini's death, bringing the total to 174.

In the centre of the piazza is an Egyptian obelisk, originally brought from Heliopolis during Caligula's time. The cross on the top is said to contain a relic of the Holy Cross.

COLONNADE

Visiting St Peter's

Information office on the left (south) side of the piazza.
Toilets are outside the church on the left and right sides, and in the bag check area on the lower right side of the façade.

St Peter's
Piazza San Pietro
open daily, admission free
www.stpetersbasilica.org
Apr-Sep 07.00-19.00
Oct-Mar 07.00-18.00
map 2, C3
GPS 41.9023, 12.4575
You are likely to be offered a free guided tour of the church while you are in St Peter's Square. These tours are interesting and informative. If you stay until the end, you may be expected to make a donation. Audio tours available in the bag check area.

Cupola (Dome)
Apr-Sep 08.00-18.00
Oct-Mar 08.00-17.00
€4 without lift, or €5 with lift to first level. There are 323 steps to climb after you get out of the lift.
There is usually a queue of at least 30 mins for the dome. Exit from the lift and climb up the dome or down to roof level where you can walk around the gallery and look down into the Basilica. There is a large outside area with a gift shop, coffee bar, water fountains, restrooms and a post box. If you want to view the roof statues in more detail, the roof level is ideal.
Grottoes same opening times as the church, free admission.
Located below the church and accessed from inside via stairs by the St Longinus or St Andrew statues, near the papal altar. Many popes and a few royals are buried here. The **tomb of John Paul II** is housed in a private niche. A white marble slab bears his name in Latin, carved in gold letters.
Scavi Book a 90 minute tour well in advance. Email the Excavations Office with names and number of visitors, contact info in Rome, language, and time period desired (scavi@fsp.va). Groups are limited to 15 (no children under 11). You may also apply in person at the Office of the Scavi, outside the church on the left, through the Arch of the Bells. Just walk up to the Swiss Guards and say 'Scavi'.
Treasury Apr-Sep 09.00-18.00
Oct-Mar 09.00-17.00, €5
Enter from the left transept inside the church. View precious objects saved from the old basilica.
Vatican Gardens 2 hour tours
10.00 Mon, Tues, Thurs-Sat
(book and collect tickets in advance)
arrive 15 mins beforehand, €9
Book at the Information Office
06 698 84466, fax 06 698 85100
Encompassing 40 acres behind St. Peter's, the gardens are a masterpiece of Renaissance landscape architecture. Look behind the scenes at daily life in the Vatican. See the railway bringing goods for the Vatican's own supermarket, and the tower where Radio Vatican is based.

Inside St Peter's

Clearly designed to inspire awe in even the most jaded of visitors, the vast interior can hold 90,000 people. There are 44 altars, 27 chapels, 11 domes, 800 chandeliers, 778 columns, 395 statues and 135 mosaics. St Peter's central nave is the longest in the world at 186 metres (611 feet). Set in the floor are 28 marks, comparing the length with other naves found in the world's largest churches. St Paul's in London is second longest at 158 metres; St Patrick's Cathedral in New York is in 28th position at 101 metres.

Above the walls there are Latin inscriptions, written in letters six feet tall, black on gold, quoting passages from the Bible. The inscription on the drum of the central dome translates as: '*... you are Peter, and on this rock I will build my Church... I will give you the keys of the kingdom of heaven...*' Matt 16:18-19

Baldacchino

Common in Italian churches, a *baldacchino* is an elaborate fixed canopy over a main altar. In 1624, Urban VIII (Barberini) commissioned Bernini to build the baldacchino over the tomb of St Peter, located beneath the altar. This was the beginning of a lifelong work for Bernini, who was primarily responsible for the decoration of the church interior. The baldacchino rises to a height of 100 feet. Its construction required some 93 tonnes of bronze, some of which was taken from the roof and portico of the Pantheon. The four spiral columns are modelled on the original baldacchino from the Constantine church. Pairs of angels above the valance hold the symbols of St Peter and St Paul: a tiara and keys for Peter, a sword and book for Paul. On the very top is a golden orb and cross.

Cattedra San Pietro (St Peter's chair)

Looking through the baldacchino you will see golden light shining from an oval window. The dove in the centre is a metaphor for the Holy Spirit. The 12 rays symbolise the apostles. Carved clouds surround the glass, along with a multitude of golden angels. The chair, a gift to the church in the 9th century, is placed in the centre, below the window.

The statues at the base, each over 16 feet tall, are of Saints Ambrose, Augustine, Athanasius and Chrysostom.

On the left of the Cattedra is the *Tomb of Paul III,* designed by Michelangelo. The figure of Justice (holding a torch) was said to be an image of the Pontiff's sister-in-law and was first depicted fully nude. It caused such a scandal that Bernini was later commissioned to drape it in a tunic of bronze, which was painted to match the marble.
The *Tomb of Urban VIII,* made by Bernini, is to the right.

St Peter

In front and to the right of the main altar, facing the nave, is a life-sized bronze statue of *St Peter*. He is seated, his hand held out in blessing. His extended right foot has been worn away by centuries of veneration by pilgrims.

Near the altar

Four large statues, symbolising crucial moments of Christ's passion, are set in niches that face the main altar. To the right of St Peter and holding a lance is *St Longinus* – he was the soldier who pierced Christ's side with his lance but then later converted. Holding the cross, *St Helena* was Emperor Constantine's mother. She made a pilgrimage to Jerusalem and returned to Rome with pieces of the true cross and nails. *St Veronica,* represented by the statue holding the veil, wiped Christ's brow on the road to Calvary. Leaning against a cross is *St Andrew,* who was Peter's brother and was himself crucified in Greece. *St Longinus* was made by Bernini, the other statues came from his workshop.

Monuments

Just off the left transept is Bernini's *Monument and Tomb of Alexander VII,* created when the artist was aged 80 and facing his own end. Bernini depicts a skeleton holding an hourglass, symbolising the brevity of life on earth. The figure on the right is meant to be Religion. Under her foot is a map of England, referring to the Pope's unsuccessful attempt to end conflict with the Anglican Church.

Along the right aisle is Antonio Canova's *Monument to the*

three Stuarts who abdicated claims to England's throne in favour of the Catholic Church.

Mosaics

In the 17th century, it was discovered that damp was destroying priceless frescoes and oil paintings above the altars. A decision was taken to replace the original works with mosaic copies. Artisans of the papal mosaic factory made the reproductions and they took 100 years to complete. Most impressive is the copy of Raphael's *Transfiguration,* near the bronze *St Peter,* off the left side of the nave. The original painting is on view in the Pinacoteca, the Vatican picture gallery.

Pietà (pictured right)

Near the entrance, in the first chapel on the right aisle, is Michelangelo's *Pietà,* protected by glass since an attack in 1972. Made in 1499 when he was aged just 25, this is the masterpiece of Michelangelo's youth. Pursuing what he called 'the heart's image', Michelangelo disregarded conventional reality in the *Pietà*. The Virgin, traditionally represented as a woman disfigured by grief, is here much younger than her son; she is depicted as the 'personification of perpetual purity'. And while the Christ is life-sized, the Virgin is larger than life. Were she to stand she would be seven feet tall, yet her head is the same size as the Christ's. One of the wonders of the *Pietà* is that proportions like these don't disturb the viewer.

Michelangelo overheard a pilgrim credit the work to Christoforo Solari, a Lombard. In a fit of rage, he returned that night with hammer and chisel to carve '*Michelangelo Buonarroti, Florentine, made this*' on the sash across Mary's breast. It is his only signed work.

NOREM PRINCIPIS·APOST PAVLVS·V·BVRGHES

OMANVS·PONT·MAX·AN·MDCXII·PONT·VI

The early popes

In the beginning, the community of Christians in Rome shared authority among a group of elders. There was no pope, there were no bishops. As the faith spread, so did a number of false prophets and teachers all claiming to understand 'true Christianity'. And so it became important to establish that the tenets of the faith had been reliably passed down by an unbroken succession of bishops, the first of them chosen and consecrated by the Apostles themselves.

The pope is considered by Catholics to be the living heir of Peter but the Apostle himself is not reckoned as a pope. Two years after Peter was martyred in AD 67, Linus was elected Bishop of Rome. In AD 180 Irenaeus of Lyons recorded the first six popes as Linus, Anacletus, Clement I, Evaristus, Alexander I, and Sixtus I (116-125). The unbroken line of popes was established to ensure that there was accurate teaching obtained from the Apostles, providing a pedigree for authentic Christian truth and a political focus for unity.

The Edict of Milan, proclaimed in 313 by Emperor Constantine, secured Christians' freedom to practice their religion. The edict gave Christianity legal recognition throughout the Roman Empire. It was a bonanza for the struggling church. In his writings, Pope Sylvester (314-335) lovingly details Constantine's benefactions which included the Vatican.

Constantine established the priesthood as a viable career by declaring that clerics should be paid. This legitimacy propelled the bishops of Rome into the heart of the Roman establishment. Already powerful and influential men, they were now on par with senators; they took on political roles and became judges and governors. The practice of the Christian religion could now be codified. Councils were held to determine qualifications for holy orders and a liturgical calendar was established. Local bishops in far-flung territories sought guidance from Roman bishops, much as governors had previously received direction from the Emperor.

INAUGERATION OF BENEDICT XVI: *PREVIOUS PAGE*

Pope Joan

According to legend, Joan was unanimously elected in 853 to succeed Leo IV under the name of Pope John VIII and ruled over the Catholic world for two years, five months and four days.

Pope Joan was believed to have been born in Germany to English missionaries. She was exceptionally clever and became proficient in the liberal arts at an early age. With her parents she visited the monastery at Fulda, celebrated as a centre of scholarship. As a woman, she was not allowed to continue her studies and so she began to dress as boy. Joan took a lover at Fulda and went with him to Athens, still in men's clothes, where she established her reputation for superior knowledge in the sciences. From Athens Joan went to Rome and became a celebrated lecturer. Her abilities were recognised by Rome's cardinals and she was elected Pope.

Unfortunately she became pregnant. Historians aren't certain whether the father was her lover from Athens or a secretary-deacon within her household. Joan hid her pregnancy well as most clerics tended to be portly. But one hot July day, during a papal procession from St Peter's to San Giovanni in Laterano, she gave birth to a son in a narrow street between the Colosseum and San Clemente.

Accounts vary as to what happened next. Some say Joan was set upon and killed by the outraged populace, and was buried where she fell. Others claim she was thrown into prison and died, or that she entered a convent and her son became the Bishop of Ostia. Joan was succeeded by Benedict III, who was declared Pope on 29 September 855.

The legend goes on to say that there was a monument to Pope Joan in the Cathedral of Siena. In 1601 Clement VIII (Aldobrandini) ordered the statue renamed. Historical records extended the life and rule of the preceding Pope Leo IV until 17 July 855. Years later another Pope took the name John VIII, ruling from 872-882.

Renaissance popes

In 1378 the papal court moved to Avignon. It was a financial disaster for Rome, which had come to rely on the economic activity generated by the church. The city had a well-developed agricultural sector but unlike Florence, Venice or Milan, it had no banking, manufacturing or trade. With the papacy located in Avignon the population of Rome halved to 17,000. The city became smaller than Siena.

When Pope Martin V (Colonna) negotiated the papal return to Rome in 1420, he found a dilapidated city. Residents were living in filth, streets were covered in excrement and the ancient aqueducts had collapsed. Martin brought civic government under papal authority and hired two managers to rebuild the infrastructure, giving priority to the circulation of pilgrims. Broad avenues were built to direct the flow of pilgrim traffic from the city's gates towards St Peter's. The expanding papal court resulted in a building boom. By 1600 Rome's population had increased to 100,000. Only London and Paris had greater populations.

The Catholic year offered the populace a continuous series of processions and parades. For a new pope the most dangerous of these was the *possesso*, the ritual post-coronation procession from St Peter's to San Giovanni in Laterano. This event provided an opportunity for discontented noblemen to try to knock the newly crowned pope off his horse, or attempt an assassination. Sometimes they were successful. At the death of a pope, power over the administration of the city reverted to Roman nobles and officials until the next pope was elected.

In the 250 years between 1417-1667 the pope was the most powerful person in Christendom. A delicate balance of power existed between the papacy, the kings of Europe and the Holy Roman Emperor, with the pope maintaining absolute control over Rome and the Papal States. Popes invariably came from the most wealthy and influential families of the day; some supplied the papal court with several cardinals and more than one pope. Four popes were from the Medici family, the Borgia and the della Rovere each produced two.

'God has given us the Papacy. Let us enjoy it.' Leo X

Martin V (1417-31)
Odo Colonna

Eugenius IV (1431-47)
Gabriel Condulmaro

Nicholas V (1447-55)
Tommaso Parentucelli

Calixtus III (1455-58)
Alfonso Borgia

Pius II (1458-64)
Aeneas Silvio Piccolomini

Paul II (1464-71)
Pietro Barbo

Sixtus IV (1471-84)
Francesco della Rovere

Innocent VIII (1484-92)
Giovanni Battista Cibo

Alexander VI (1492-1503)
Roderigo de Borgia

Pius III (1503)
Francesco Todeschini

Julius II (1503-13)
Giuliano della Rovere

Leo X (1513-21)
Giovanni de'Medici

Hadrian VI (1522-23)
Adrian Dedel

Clement VII (1523-34)
Giulio de'Medici

Paul III (1534-49)
Alessandro Farnese

Julius III (1550-55)
Giovanni del Monte

Marcellus II (1555)
Marcello Cervini

Paul IV (1555-59)
Giovanni Pietro Caraffa

Pius IV (1560-65)
Giovanni Angelo de'Medici

St. Pius V (1566-72)
Michele Ghislieri

Gregory XIII (1572-85)
Ugo Boncampagni

Sixtus V (1585-90)
Felice Peretti

Urban VII (1590)
Giambiattista Castagna

Gregory XIV (1590-91)
Nicolò Sfondrati

Innocent IX (1591)
Giovanni Antonio Fachinetti

Clement VIII (1592-1605)
Ippolito Aldobrandini

Leo XI (1605)
Alessandro de'Medici

Paul V (1605-21)
Camillo Borghese

Gregory XV (1621-23)
Alessandro Ludovisi

Urban VIII (1623-44)
Maffeo Barberini

Innocent X (1644-55)
Giambattista Pamphilj

Alexander VII (1655-67)
Fabio Chigi

Popes versus Emperors

After the fall of the western Roman Empire, when waves of barbarians came through Rome looting and pillaging, the Pope had little defence. Rome was in decline and needed help. In 754 Pope Stephen II called on the French king Charlemagne to oust the Lombards from Roman territory. He was successful and as a reward, Pope Leo III crowned Charlemagne the first Holy Roman Emperor in 800. Emperor and Pope neatly divided authority into the temporal and spiritual realms. It must have seemed like a perfect compromise. The Pope still had complete spiritual authority, including the divine power to crown kings, and he had military protection. The Emperor had political power over all of Europe.

The Holy Roman Emperor was often a German or French king and there were many instances when the pope did not support the coronation. When Pope Gregory VII (Hildebrand) refused to crown Henry IV as Holy Roman Emperor, Henry's army sacked Rome in 1084.

In 1519 Leo X (Giovanni de'Medici) opposed the selection of Charles V as Holy Roman Emperor. But Charles was crowned the next year at Aachen and in 1527 took revenge by sacking and burning Rome. Nearly 12,000 people were slain by the Emperor's Spanish and German troops. From May to October, the Vatican became their headquarters as a third of Rome's dwellings were burned to the ground. The troops stabled their horses in the Sistine Chapel and thoroughly plundered St Peter's. Three years later, Leo's cousin Clement VII confirmed Charles V as Holy Roman Emperor. Paul III (Farnese) rebuilt the Capitoline in preparation for the triumphant re-entry parade of Emperor Charles V in 1538.

Napoleon later sought a papal blessing in his bid to be crowned Emperor. He kidnapped two popes before achieving his goal. When Pius VI (Giovanni Braschi) refused to bless Napoleon, he was bundled into a carriage on 15 February 1798 and driven north to Valence where he died. Napoleon was ready to appoint his own pope, but Cardinal Carmerlengo insisted on holding a conclave at San Giorgio Maggiore in Venice. The cardinals deliberated for three months before electing Pius VII (Barnaba Chiaramonte). Pius proved reluctant to crown Napoleon and was held prisoner in the Quirinale Palace for six months, with eight French cannons trained on his window. Napoleon then had him bundled into a carriage and driven north to Savona, before demanding that the Pope sign away his sovereignty over the Papal States. These were governed as a monarchy by the Pope as both temporal and spiritual ruler. As well as land in and around Rome, the States comprised a large part of Italy, including present-day Emilia Romagna and the Marches. The great cities of Ravenna, Bologna, Palma, Ferrara, Urbino, and the seaport at Ancona were included in the Papal States. Napoleon wanted all of it.

Tired of waiting, he sent French troops into Rome and annexed the Papal States. French republican law and government were imposed and all the ruling cardinals were removed to Paris. Church property was confiscated. Cardinals and bishops were now appointed and paid by the state. After negotiating for four years, Pius VII finally crowned Napoleon Emperor at Notre Dame in 1804.

Citizens were not overjoyed when, after the fall of Napoleon in 1815, the Papal States were returned to the control of the papacy. People had become used to a more efficient system of government and were not keen to return to the old ways. In the fight for Italian unification the Papal States became a battleground for freedom during the Risorgimento in the middle of the 19th century.

As the Church was losing temporal authority in Italy and France, it gained greater spiritual authority. The Vatican Council of 1870 called by Pius IX (Giovanni Mastai-Ferretti) introduced the doctrine of papal infallibility, thereby guaranteeing the spiritual authority of the Pope. The formal transfer of papal temporal authority to the Italian state didn't occur until the Lateran Treaty of 1929.

John Paul II (1978-2005)

Karol Jozef Wojtyla was born on 18 May 1920 in Wadowice, an industrial town outside Krakow in the foothills of the Tatras mountains. He decided to become a priest in 1942, the year that Nazis imprisoned all parish priests and the year his father died. Karol studied in secret and two years later was forced underground; he spent some time hiding out in the residence of the Archbishop of Krakow. In 1946 Karol was ordained; in 1963 he was made Archbishop of Krakow. Appointed Cardinal in 1967, he was elected Pope on 16 October 1978.

Perhaps John Paul's greatest legacy will be his contribution to the restoration of freedom and nationhood for Eastern bloc countries. While visiting Poland in 1979, John Paul drew huge crowds and preached a message of courage and freedom, which the faithful took as encouragement to stand up to Soviet oppression. He openly supported the Solidarity strikes of 1980, secretly channelled funds to the movement, and personally wrote to President Brezhnev demanding freedom for Poles. Locals in Poland's Tatras mountains claim that John Paul held many secret meetings there, planning a co-ordinated strategy for freedom with dissident leaders.

The Soviet response was to order John Paul's assassination. In 1981 he was shot in St Peter's square by a Turkish assassin, hired by the Bulgarian arm of the Russian KGB. Undaunted, John Paul kept up the pressure on the Soviets. In 1989 the iron curtain was finally torn down. John Paul visited his would-be assassin in prison and forgave him.

John Paul achieved many firsts in his long reign. He was the first Polish pope, the first to attend an Anglican service at Canterbury, the first to pray in a synagogue and a mosque, and he was the most travelled pope in history. His reign was characterised by a conservative orthodoxy that saw falling numbers of active Catholics in Europe but rising numbers in Latin America and Africa.

In a return to early Christian tradition, Karol Josef Wojtyla died penniless, without worldly goods. More than 3 million people came to view his body and pay their last respects. His funeral was attended by every world leader and was seen by a billion people on television.

Benedict XVI (2005-)

Cardinal Ratzinger gave the homily to his lifelong friend John Paul saying, *'We can be sure that our beloved Pope is standing today at the window of the Father's house, that he sees us and blesses us.'* Both men shared deeply conservative beliefs; few expect Benedict to liberalise church theology. However, like John Paul, Benedict is more accessible to the public than earlier popes.

Joseph Ratzinger was born in 1927 and raised in Catholic Bavaria. His father was a police officer who opposed the Nazi regime. To keep the family safe, he moved them several times. Membership in the Hitler Youth was compulsory, so Joseph was drafted into an anti-aircraft unit that built engines. In 1944 he deserted and was sent to a POW camp. He claims never to have fired a gun.

When explaining his choice of papal name, Benedict referred to his predecessor Benedict XV, who sought to avert World War I and then tried to limit the slaughter: *'In his footsteps I place my ministry, in the service of reconciliation and harmony.'*

Papal Audiences

Benedict is continuing the tradition of papal audiences initiated by John Paul. Weekly meditations on the psalms and canticles of the Bible are usually held on Wednesday mornings in Piazza San Pietro.

Attendance is free but you must obtain a ticket in advance. Several methods are explained in Travel Basics (p.284). Winter audiences may be held in St Peter's or in the Sala Nervi. Summer audiences are held at 10am on Wednesdays at the Pope's summer residence in Castel Gandolfo.

Musei Vaticani (Vatican Museums)

entrance on Viale Vaticano
(10 min walk from St Peter's)
06 698 83333
€12 cash only
credit cards accepted in gift shops
last entrance is 1½ hrs before closing
Mar-Oct 08.45-16.45 Mon-Fri,
08.45-13.45 Sat
Nov-Feb 08.45-13.45 Mon-Sat
open last Sunday of each month all year 08.45-13.45 (free admission)
closed for religious and public holidays, see website for details
www.vatican.va
Special permit needed for Raphael Loggia, Vatican Library, Lapidary Gallery & Vatican Archives.
map 3, C1
GPS 41.9071, 12.4535
There are some well-placed toilets off the Raphael Rooms.

The galleries are well signposted with information provided in many languages. Hire your audio guide at the top of the escalator. Turn right to visit the Pinacoteca and other museums or left into the main galleries, heading towards the Raphael Rooms and the Sistine Chapel. For the main galleries you can choose from four colour-coded routes, 1½-5 hrs in length, each one ending at the Sistine Chapel. If time is short, you can whizz straight through to the Chapel and then double back to the Quattro Cancelli to join one of the marked routes. For a first visit, we recommend you see the Raphael Rooms, Sistine Chapel and the Pinacoteca.

BRING A HAND MIRROR TO VIEW THE CEILINGS.

One of the first sights on the visit is the 4 metre tall bronze pinecone in the **Cortile della Pigna.** The Roman bronze *pigna* (pinecone) sits in the centre of the north staircase, flanked by two peacocks removed from Hadrian's mausoleum. On your way to the Raphael Rooms, you walk through the **Galleria di Carte Geografiche** (map gallery). There are 40 maps, painted between 1580-83 by Antonio and Ignazio Danti, showing the lands belonging to the Catholic church. Rome is placed at the epicentre of a flat world, illustrating the scientific beliefs of the Renaissance papacy.

Stanze di Raffaello (Raphael Rooms)

These were the new apartments of Julius II who refused to inhabit the rooms of his predecessor, Alexander VI (Rodrigo Borgia). Raphael was commissioned to decorate the walls in 1508, the same time Michelangelo was painting the Sistine

Chapel ceiling. Though separated by just one flight of steps, both artists were extremely possessive of their art and each forbade the other to view work in progress. There are four rooms known as the Raphael Rooms, but only the final two were painted by the artist. The first two were painted by Raphael's followers, Giulio Romano and Francesco Penni.

Sala di Constantino, the largest hall in the rooms of the Vatican Palace, was used for official ceremonies. Frescoes depicting the story of the Emperor Constantine were painted in 1519-25, after the death of Raphael. They represent the triumph of Christianity over paganism and the supremacy of the papacy. Shortly after the frescoes were completed, Rome was sacked by the troops of Charles V and the signatures of invading soldiers are still visible today.

The fresco cycle in the next room was painted under the direction of Raphael between 1514 and 1517. The paintings glorify Leo X by placing his visage into episodes from the lives of his predecessors, Leo III and Leo IV. *Fire in the Borgo* depicts the fire of 847 in the Borgo district near the Vatican. Leo X (in place of Leo IV) is shown giving the solemn blessing that was said to have miraculously extinguished the flames.

The **Stanza di Eliodoro** (Room of Heliodorus) was entirely painted by Raphael in 1512-14. It was commissioned by Julius II but completed under Leo X. The change meant that in *The Meeting of Leo the Great and Attila,* the figure of Leo X can be seen twice: first as cardinal and then as pope. In the lunette above the window, Raphael's mastery of light is beautifully displayed in *The Liberation of St Peter*. Peter is shown at the moment of being miraculously freed from prison by an angel, while guards lie sleeping.

Stanze della Segnatura was the library of Julius II and it was here that he signed his official documents. Painted between 1508 and 1511, these are Raphael's most famous frescoes and his first work in the Vatican. The allegorical paintings are: *Disputation of the Sacrament* (Faith), *School of Athens* (Reason) and *Parnassus* (Beauty). In the roundels are Justice, Poetry and Theology.

SCHOOL OF ATHENS: DETAIL

In *School of Athens*, the central figures are Plato (his hand raised towards the sky) and Aristotle on the right. Many of the ancient philosophers depicted are in reality portraits of contemporary characters: Bramante is seen on the bottom right with Euclid, who has a compass in his hand. Raphael can be found on the lower right, wearing a black beret. Michelangelo is situated lower left, leaning on a pedestal and posing as Heraclitus. Raphael added this tribute to Michelangelo after seeing the completed Sistine ceiling.

On the opposite wall in *Disputation of the Sacrament*, the world is horizontally divided into heaven and earth. A clean-shaven Christ is enthroned in heaven with a bearded God above. John the Baptist and the Virgin Mary are seated alongside Christ on his throne, and to either side of them are Old Testament prophets with the Apostles. Around the altar are prominent Renaissance figures. Among them are several popes and a figure in a brown cloak: Dante Alighieri (author of the Divine Comedy). Above the window, *Mount Parnassus* depicts Apollo with his lyre surrounded by the Nine Muses. The *Cardinal and Theological Virtues* above the opposite window personifies the virtues in the figures of women and cupids.

The **Cappella Niccolina** is a small chapel, often overlooked by visitors who flock directly to the Sistine Chapel. This leaves it relatively empty and a pleasure to visit. Built for Nicholas V, the chapel contains frescoes by Beato Angelico and an altarpiece by Giorgio Vasari, *Stoning of St Stephen*.

MICHELANGELO: DETAIL FROM THE SISTINE CHAPEL

Capella Sistina (The Sistine Chapel)

In 1508, Pope Julius II commissioned Michelangelo to fresco the chapel's vaulted ceiling. The artist tried to refuse, insisting he was a sculptor and not a painter. Michelangelo also had the commission to carve the monumental tomb for Julius and he wanted to keep working on it. At that time Michelangelo knew little about fresco technique, which had to be carried out quickly without interruptions and changes. Raphael learned that Michelangelo refused the commission and, seizing an opportunity to engineer the great sculptor's humiliation, he and his uncle Bramante manipulated Julius into insisting that Michelangelo paint the Sistine ceiling. Julius' tomb was put on hold.

The ceiling vault covers 800 square metres and it took four years to paint. Michelangelo hated every moment: lying on a scaffold 65 feet high, arms exhausted from holding the brush straight up, face covered with drops of paint, with the nagging voice of Pope Julius spurring him on. Old as he was, Julius did not hesitate to venture up the scaffolding to inspect Michelangelo's progress. Things came to a head in 1510 when the Pope struck the artist. Michelangelo packed his bags; Julius offered money and apologies. Michelangelo fled to Florence and Julius sent a special emissary bearing gifts. Eventually, Michelangelo returned and finished the ceiling. With great acclaim, Julius II inaugurated the chapel on 1 November 1512. Everyone hailed Michelangelo as a genius, including Raphael and Bramante.

The ceiling depicts the creation story, which is told in nine rectangles along the middle of the vault. In the centre is God Creating Adam, the expulsion of Adam and Eve from the garden, the separation of light from darkness and scenes of Noah. Christ's ancestors, as listed in the gospel of Matthew, are portrayed in the triangles above the windows. Between the triangles are paintings of seven prophets from the Bible and five pagan sibyls. The figures are seated on massive thrones and each is caught mid-gesture: writing, reading a book, or unrolling a parchment.

Last Judgement

Michelangelo painted the *Last Judgement* (on the end wall) after the sack of Rome as a warning to the unfaithful. When unveiled in 1541, it shocked many with its expressions of anger and tormented writhing bodies. That the bodies were naked only added to the controversy; clothes were added to some at a later date. Michelangelo's self portrait can be seen in the flayed piece of dead skin hanging in the middle of the piece.

The Walls

The large paintings on the side walls illustrate stories from the Bible, with scenes from the Old Testament on the left (as you face the *Last Judgement*) and the New Testament on the right. *The Journey of Moses into Egypt* is by Pinturicchio and Perugino. *Events in the life of Moses* and *Punishment of Korah* are by Sandro Botticelli. Michelangelo's master, Domenico Ghirlandaio, painted *Crossing of the Red Sea* and *Vocation of Peter and Andrew*. Cosimo Rosselli is credited with *Sermon on the Mount* and Roselli painted *Moses on Mount Sinai* with

Piero di Cosimo. The most beautiful painting of the series is *Christ Giving the Keys to St Peter* by Perugino, Raphael's teacher and former master.

WHEN EXITING THE SISTINE CHAPEL, LOOK FOR SIGNS DIRECTING YOU BACK TOWARDS OTHER VATICAN GALLERIES SITUATED NEAR THE ENTRANCE TO THE MUSEUMS.

Pinacoteca

The Vatican Picture Galleries are located on the west side of the main entrance to the Vatican Museums. The galleries contain a stunning collection of paintings from some of Italy's best artists and should be third on your must-see list after the Sistine Chapel and the Raphael Rooms. The original paintings that were removed from altarpieces in St Peter's and replaced by mosaics are housed here. There are works by Raphael, Giovanni Bellini, Leonardo da Vinci, Titian and Caravaggio.

Room 3 contains two exquisite paintings by the patron saint of artists, Beato Angelico: *Madonna and Child with Saints Dominic and Catherine* and *Stories of St Nicholas*. Botticelli's master, Fra Fillippo Lippi, painted *Coronation of the Virgin* and *Angels and Saints*. **Room 4** has paintings of the most extraordinary musical angels by Melozzo da Forlì. They are all beautiful. The angels are perfect company for Marco Palmezzano's simple and luminous portrayal of *Christ carrying the Cross*.

Room 5 houses a *Pietà* by German painter Lucas Cranach the Elder. The Venetian painter Bellini's influence can be seen in Bartolomeo Montagna's *Madonna with Child. The Miracles of St Vincent Ferrer* is by Ercole de'Roberti, founder of the Ferrara school of painters. In **Room 6** visit the Madonna triptych by Bartolomeo di Tommaso: *Birth, Coronation, Annunciation*. **Room 7** has several paintings by the Umbrian artists Perugino and Pinturicchio.

Room 8 is dedicated to Raphael. There are five great paintings and nine tapestries made from Raphael's drawings. The paintings show the growth in his talent and mastery. The early *Coronation of the Virgin* (1502-3) is the

MARCO PALMEZZANO: *CHRIST CARRYING THE CROSS*

closest in style to his master Perugino. *Transfiguration* (1516-20) is Raphael's last painting and perhaps his most spiritual depiction of divine beauty.

Room 9 contains an unfinished canvas depicting *St Jerome* by Leonardo da Vinci. Giovanni Bellini's *Burial of Christ* is a particularly emotional depiction of Mary Magdalene, Joseph and St Nicodemus. **Room 10** has two paintings by Paolo Veronese, *Allegory of the Arts* and *Vision of St Helen,* and two mature works by Titian, *Madonna with Child and Saints* and a portrait of *Doge Niccolò Marcello.*

Room 12 has Caravaggio's beautifully tragic *Deposition from the Cross,* originally commissioned for the Chiesa Nuova in Rome. Guido Reni's *Crucifixion of St Peter* is obviously a copy of Caravaggio's painting of the same subject in Santa Maria del Popolo. Peter is shown upside down at the gruesome moment of the nail entering his foot.

Room 17 contains Bernini's preparatory models for *St Peter's Chair* in the Basilica. **Room 18** displays a collection of Russian icons from 15th and 16th centuries, including episodes from the life of St Nicholas.

Museo Pio-Clementino

The most important Greek and Roman works in the Vatican collections are displayed here, in a musem established by Clement XIV and Pius VI in the late 18th century. The museum was made to house sculptures that were found in excavations ongoing in Rome during the Renaissance and Baroque periods. One of the first works to greet the eye is the *Apoxyomenos* sculpture, depicting a classical athlete removing sweat from his body after a competition. The **Cortile Ottagonale** exhibits the sculpture collection of Julius II. Michelangelo admired the *Laocoőn Group,* a sculpture found on the Esquiline Hill, and asked Julius II to bring it to the Vatican. Julius was particularly fond of the statue *Apollo del Belvedere*. Near the courtyard is the **Sala degli Animali**, with a veritable zoo of stone and marble beasts on display.

Other galleries off the Cortile Octagonale lead to the **Sala delle Muse** and **Sala Rotonda**, with a bronze sculpture of *Hercules* standing 3.8 metres tall and dating from the 2nd century AD.

Museo Chiaramonti

Between 1807 and 1810, Pius VII (Chiaramonti) had Antonio Canova assemble this collection of fragments of busts, *bas reliefs* and small statues. At the time, Canova was busy negotiating the return of art that had been looted by Napoleon. At the end of the gallery is the **Braccio Nuovo** built in 1817-20. It contains Roman mosaics and a sculpture of *Augusto di Prima Porta* from the 1st century BC with Augustus depicted at the height of his reign. Also of note is the huge *Nilo*, a personification of the River Nile with sixteen little cupids clambering all over him.

Etruscan Museum
Founded in 1837 by Gregory XVI to house objects discovered in excavations in southern Etruria (Vulci, Cerveteri, Tarquinia, Perugia and Orvieto), this collection holds Etruscan artifacts dating from the 9th to the 1st century BC. On the second floor is the **Sala della Biga** which includes Francesco Antonio Franzoni's *Chariot Sculpture* of 1788, made from fragments of other sculptures. Exit through the **Galleria dei Candelabri** which contains copies of candelebra from various epochs and different styles. Next is the **Galleria degli Arazzi** which is hung with tapestries.

Ethnological Museum
This collection of religious artifacts from all continents of the world includes Taoist, Buddhist and Hindu objects. There are also plaster portraits of native Americans by German sculptor Ferdinand Pettrich and a collection of ceremonial objects from New Guinea.

Gregory XVI founded the **Museum of Profane Arts** in 1844 to house ancient Roman works that were pagan in subject matter. These include marble reliefs with scenes from everyday life and sculptures inspired by mythology. Pius IX extended the collection further with the **Museo Cristiano** (Museum of Christian Sculpture).

The **Gregorian Egyptian Museums** contain one the world's finest collections of Egyptian art. Works are arranged chronologically in nine rooms, beginning with funerary pieces dating from 2600 BC. The most outstanding sculptures in the collection were removed from necropoli at Giza and Thebes. These include a large Ramses II seated on a throne. **Room 3** contains pieces removed from Villa Adriana (p.215). **Room 5** displays busts and funerary statues from Egypt's long reign of Pharoahs. Iron Age ceramics, Assyrian reliefs and bronze figurines are found in **Rooms 6-9**.

TRIDENTE & BORGHESE

SPANISH STEPS

Top designer boutiques and lively restaurants define Tridente. Villa Borghese is known as 'the park of museums'.

Start at the Spanish Steps and climb up to Trinità dei Monti for a view down Via Condotti, Rome's famous shopping boulevard. While you are up here, stop in at *Ciampini* for ice cream.

Piazza San Lorenzo in Lucina is Tridente's most pleasant piazza. It's free of traffic and there are two good restaurants. Via di Ripetta is a quieter way to reach Piazza del Popolo, a dramatic and historical entrance to Rome. From there it is a climb up to the formal Pincio Gardens, a good place to watch the sunset. Villa Borghese has an Etruscan museum in Villa Giulia; a modern art gallery at the Galleria Nazionale d'Arte Moderna; and Galleria Borghese, full of Renaissance and Baroque masterpieces. The park, with a boating lake and zoo, has something for everyone.

Near Via del Tritone is the Borromini-designed church of San Andrea delle Fratte which contains two of Bernini's original angels from Ponte Sant'Angelo.

GALLERIA COLONNA

Spanish Steps • Rome's most famous staircase

Villa Borghese • A large park with a zoo and three museums

Galleria Borghese • Raphael, Caravaggio, Titian and Bernini

Santa Maria del Popolo • one of Rome's finest art churches

Explora
A children's museum just outside Villa Borghese.

Piazza San Lorenzo in Lucina A quiet piazza with a pleasant church.

Mercato delle Stampe
An outdoor market selling old prints, maps, coins and books. Held in Piazza Fontanella Borghese.

restaurants p.239
shopping p.260

Did you know that..?
An apartment in Keats' house is available for holiday rentals from the Landmark Trust.

The Spanish Steps

map 5,C2; GPS 41.9062, 12.4815

This is a popular meeting place in the heart of Rome's most fashionable shopping district. Both the steps and the piazza take their name from the *Palazzo di Spagna,* the Spanish embassy to the Holy See. Francesco de Santis built the steps in 1726 to connect the piazza with the Trinità dei Monti church and the Pincio Gardens. At the beginning of May the steps are adorned with pots of beautiful azaleas. At the bottom is the *Fontana di Barcaccia* ('fountain of the worthless boat') – a marble fountain made in the shape of a leaking boat. The design is an ingenious solution to the problem of low water pressure. Pietro Bernini, father of Gian Lorenzo Bernini, conceived the idea when a boat was stranded here after the Tiber flooded.

This area has been a magnet for the English since the days of the Grand Tour when both Keats and Shelley lived here. There are two quintessentially English establishments on the Piazza di Spagna: Babington's Tea Rooms (opened by two English ladies in 1896) and the Keats-Shelley Memorial House. The Hotel d'Inghilterra, with its English-style bar, is found on nearby Via Bocca di Leone.

The Grand Tour

The influence of Italian culture, with its philosophy, art, music and literature, came to dominate Europe during the 16th century. It became fashionable amongst the English aristocracy to fill their classically designed houses with Italian objects, especially sculpture. In 1780, 40,000 Britons were being carried in litters across the Alps to Florence, taking a journey that was known as the Grand Tour. There was a prescribed itinerary: travellers visited Tuscany first, followed by Rome, Naples and finally Venice. The Napoleonic Wars interrupted the Tour in the late 1790s. After 1815 it resumed and subsequently influenced a generation of Romantic artists. Seeing the Colosseum was said to render many travellers speechless; the ruins were often viewed by moonlight to lessen the overwhelming assault on the senses. It also became fashionable to have a portrait painted while in Rome – with the Colosseum as background – not only as a souvenir, but as proof that the subject had really been there. The Tourist was thus seen to be a man of taste, versed in the classics and antiquity.

Keats-Shelley Memorial House
Piazza di Spagna 26
06 678 4235
09.00-13.00, 15.00-18.00 Mon-Fri
11.00-14.00, 15.00-18.00 Sat
admission €3
www.keats-shelley-house.org
map 5, C2

Dedicated to the British Romantic poets, the museum has a collection of paintings, objects and manuscripts celebrating the lives of Keats, Shelley and Byron as well as first editions and letters by Wordsworth and Robert Browning.

Romanticism flowered between the French Revolution in 1789 and the coronation of Queen Victoria in 1837. Where the Age of Enlightenment honoured science and reason, Romanticism was more concerned with expression, imagination and a response to nature. The Romantic movement produced many writers (Goethe, Hugo), painters (Constable, Delacroix) and composers (Beethoven, Schubert). There were six outstanding English poets: William Blake, William Wordsworth, and Samuel Taylor Coleridge, followed by Lord Byron, Percy Bysshe Shelley and John Keats.

Keats arrived in Rome with the painter Joseph Severn in November 1820. They took cheap rented rooms at 26 Piazza di Spagna, overlooking the Spanish Steps. Too ill from consumption to write, Keats had travelled to Italy hoping the Italian climate would affect a cure. It was not to be. He died in February 1821 aged just 25.

Percy and Mary Shelley arrived from Naples on 7 March 1819. Their short time in Rome was marked by the death of their son William on 7 June. Three days later they departed for Tuscany where Shelley's life ended three years later. He drowned off the coast of Livorno in 1822. Shelley, his son William and Keats are buried in the Protestant cemetery in Testaccio. Their graves are maintained by the Keats-Shelley Memorial Society, which is based in the house in Piazza di Spagna.

Piazza del Popolo

map1,D5; GPS 41.91042, 12.47614

During the Renaissance, the *Porta del Popolo* was the most important gate in Rome. Since most pilgrims came from lands to the north, this was their first point of entry. Modelled on a Roman triumphal arch, the gate led the traveller into an impressive piazza with a large Egyptian obelisk – the second most important in Rome – at the centre. The obelisk was a trophy of Augustus' victory over Antony and Cleopatra. Once located in the centre of Circus Maximus, it was installed in the piazza in 1588, and topped with the mountains and star symbol of Pope Sixtus V (Peretti).

The south side of Piazza del Popolo leads to three streets: the Via di Ripetta, the Via del Corso and the Via Babuino. Designed by the architect Antonio da Sangallo the younger (1485-1546), the geometrically precise configuration of the streets constitutes a trivium or trident *(tridente)*. Pope Alexander VII (Chigi) commissioned the twin churches of Santa Maria di Montesanto and Santa Maria dei Miracoli – both designed by Carlo Rainaldi – to accentuate the triangle shape. Seen from the gate, the piazza and the churches make a powerful impact on the visitor.

Bernini completed Santa Maria dei Miracoli and installed his trademark angels at the top. He also embellished the inner façade of the gate. When Giuseppe Valadier enlarged the

piazza in 1816, he constructed the terraces leading up to the Pincio gardens and the Villa Borghese. In the early 20th century, the piazza was used for Communist demonstrations. Afterwards people would gather at one of two bars on the south side. *Rosati's* was favoured by the left wing, *Canova* by the right. Today both establishments serve a less politically-defined clientele.

Santa Maria del Popolo

Piazza del Popolo 12
06 361 0836

07.00-12.00, 16.00-19.00 Mon-Sat
07.30-13.30, 16.30-19.30 Sun

Just inside the gate is Santa Maria del Popolo, the della Rovere family church. In the early Renaissance, this was the first church that a pilgrim from the north would encounter in Rome. It was commissioned by Sixtus IV (della Rovere) in 1472 and the family emblem, oak branches laden with acorns, is conspicuous in the decoration of the interior. In the apse are frescoes by Pinturicchio: *Coronation of the Virgin, Evangelists, Sibyls,* and *Four Fathers of the Church.*

Raphael designed the **Chigi chapel** as a family mausoleum for his patron, the banker Agostino Chigi. Lorenzo Lotti supervised the work and carved *Jonah Emerging from the Whale* from a design by Raphael. The mosaics in the dome, depicting the planets surmounted by angels, are by the Venetian artist Luigi de Pace. One hundred and forty years later, Fabio Chigi (Alexander VII) commissioned Bernini's two sculptures: *Habakkuk and the Angel* and *Daniel in the Lion's Den.*

In the **Cerasi chapel** are paintings by two very different artists: Annibale Carracci and Caravaggio. Painting with elegant grandeur in the Roman High Renaissance style, Carracci made the altarpiece *Assumption of the Virgin*. Working in oil on cypress panels, Caravaggio painted *Crucifixion of St Peter* and *Conversion of St Paul* in a style that was stark and aggressive by comparison. When Caravaggio learned that Caracci's altarpiece would hang between his two paintings, he showed his opinion of his fellow artist by pointing the large rear-end of Paul's horse towards Carracci's altarpiece.

SANTA MARIA DI MONTESANTO, *LEFT;* SANTA MARIA DEI MIRACOLI, *RIGHT*

Tridente is the best district in Rome for shopping. In a city where all layers of history co-exist happily, the ultra-modern and chic will be found sitting right beside the traditional and long-established. As well as being the home of designer labels, Tridente also has a number of historic shops that date from the 19th century.

Association of Historic Shops in Rome
(Associazione Negozi Storici di Roma)
Via Cassiodoro 14
06 679 2717
www.negozistorici.it
The purpose of the association is to promote shops and eating places that have existed for more than 100 years. With ownership often residing in the same family, these establishments are considered to be Roman institutions. Many of them still have their original shop fittings. They usually provide excellent customer service. We list those found in Tridente, but for a complete list of members visit their website.

Historical shops in Tridente

Antica Farmacia Reale
Via del Gambero 11-13
06 679 2220
Chemists since 1687

Biagini
Via del Gambero 5-6
06 679 2717
Leather goods since 1885

Catello d'Auria
Via Due Macelli 55
06 679 3364
Gloves and socks since 1894

Farmacia Chieffo-Santi
Via Capo Le Case 47
06 679 0894
Chemists since 1870

Tabaccheria Campaiola
Via Sistina 108
06 474 0687
Tobacconists since 1850

Venier-Colombo
Via Frattina 79
06 679 2979
Lace and embroideries since 1870

Franchi
Via della Croce 14
06 679 3514
Silversmiths since 1886

Merola
Via del Corso 143
06 679 194[illegible]
Leather gloves since 1885

Schostal
Via del Corso 158
06 679 1240
Linen and lingerie since 1870

Radiconcini
Via del Corso 139
06 679 1807
Hatters since 1914

Massoni
Largo Goldoni 48
06 679 0182
Jewellers since 1790

Annibale
Via di Ripetta 236
06 361 2269
Butchers since 1870

Carucci
Via di Ripetta 68
06 322 7209
Leather and shoes since 1902

Farmacia Ripetta
Via di Ripetta 23
06 361 2137
Chemists since 1860

If you're looking for the big names, then head for the Spanish Steps. Most designer shops are concentrated in a grid of streets at the bottom.

Via Condotti
Armani, Gucci, Prada, Dolce & Gabbana, Bulgari, Hermés, Cartier, Ferragamo, Max Mara, Alberta Feretti and Battistoni

Via Borgognona
Fendi, Zegna, Versace Uomo, Valentino Uomo, Moschino, Ferrè, Laura Biagiotti and Gai Mattiolo

Via Bocca di Leone
Yves Saint Laurent, Versace and Valentino

Via Frattina
Tiffany, Versace and Byblos

Piazza di Spagna
Missoni, Sergio Rossi

Villa Borghese

map 1-2

open from dawn to dusk all year

Given to the people of Rome in 1903, this large and beautiful park is the place to go for children's activities, culture, sport, or just a gentle stroll. Refreshments can be found next to the Galleria d'Arte Moderna, in the museums, or at the entrance to Bioparco.

Galleria d'Arte Moderna (p.275)

Villa Giulia (p.276)

Galleria Borghese (below)

Bioparco (zoo)
06 360 8211, www.bioparco.it
09.30-18.00 last admission 17.00
€8.50 adults, €6.50 children

This zoo is more sensitive to conservation issues than it has been in the past. Around 200 animal species can be viewed in environments sympathetic to their natural habitats.

Giardini Segreti (Secret Gardens)
06 820 7734
free guided tours in Italian
10am Sat and Sun, no pre-booking
Meet near the Borghese Gallery at the corner of Viale dei Daini.

These restored walled gardens were originally planted in the 1500s.

Tempio di Esculapio is a neoclassical temple surrounded by a small lake, found at the end of Viale del Lago. Rowing boats can be hired here.

Piazza di Siena is used for horse-jumping and other events. It also has a long running track.

Anchored balloon
Galoppatoio, 06 321 11511
09.30-sunset, every 15-20 mins
€14 adults, €6 children

Ascending from its fixed base to a height of 150 metres, there are spectacular views of the city.

Giardini del Pincio

A lovely place for an evening walk with views of Piazza del Popolo and the city. You can hire cycles outside Casina Valadier, a beautiful restaurant and café, recently restored and re-opened.

Just outside the park on the west side is **Explora**, the city's first hands-on museum for children (p.275).

Galleria Borghese

Piazzale Scipione Borghese
06 328 10
www.galleriaborghese.it
€8.50, advance booking essential, collect tickets 30 mins before timeslot
map 2, H4; GPS 41.9146, 12.4926

08.30-19.00 Tues-Sun

THERE IS A STRICTLY TIMED ADMISSION POLICY. VISITS ARE LIMITED TO TWO HOURS WITH HALF AN HOUR ALLOWED FOR THE FIRST FLOOR.

Once the residence of the Borghese family, the villa that houses the gallery was specially commissioned by Cardinal Scipione Borghese to display his precious collection of ancient art and sculpture. One of the great Roman dynasties, the Borghese name is inscribed in the pediment above the entrance to St Peter's. Pope Paul V (Camillo Borghese) and his nephew Scipione were patrons of Caravaggio and Bernini. The gallery displays some of their best works, as well as masterpieces by Raphael and Titian.

The **ground floor** is organised following the 18th century model. Sculptures displayed in the centre of the room relate in subject matter to the paintings and frescoes on the walls and ceilings. **Room 1** contains Antonio Canova's provocative marble portrait of the nude Paulina Bonaparte Borghese (sister of Napoleon) as *Venere Vincitrice*. Because women of high status were always portrayed properly clothed, the piece created a huge scandal when it was unveiled.

Rooms 2, 3, 4 contain early sculptures by Bernini who used his own face for that of *David*. In *Apollo and Daphne*, the nymph Daphne, chased by the sun god Apollo, transforms into a laurel tree to escape from her aggressor. Cardinal Borghese justified the pagan theme of the work by having an inscription placed on the base: '*he who chases fleeting pleasures will find leaves and sour grapes in his hand.*' In *Pluto and Persephone*, Pluto, the god of the underworld, kidnaps Persephone. Bernini perfectly captures the skin and musculature of three ages of man in *Aeneas and Anchises* in **Room 6**. The young Aeneas flees from Troy bearing his father Anchises on his shoulders, while his son Ascanius carries the sacred fire of the hearth. Also in this room is *Truth unveiled by Time*. Made during Bernini's exile from the papal court, this is perhaps his most personal piece.

Room 8 displays six Caravaggio paintings: *Boy with a Basket of Fruit* and *Ailing Bacchus* are early works from 1593-4; *Saint Jerome in his Study* depicts the aged man writing the Bible. Soon after he painted *Madonna dei Palafrenieri* (also known as *Madonna and Child with St Anne*), Caravaggio was on the run for murder. The Palafrenieri family rejected the piece and any association with the artist. Scipione quickly stepped in to acquire the painting. *David with the Head of Goliath*, thought to be Caravaggio's last work, was painted for Paul V to secure a papal pardon. The face on Goliath's disembodied head is Caravaggio's own.

On the **first floor**, **Room 9** displays paintings by Raphael: *Lady with a Unicorn, Portrait of a Man* and *Deposition from the Cross.* Also in this room is Pinturicchio's *Crucifixion with St Jerome and St Christopher* and *Adoration of the Christ Child* by Fra Bartolomeo.

In **Room 12** *Leda and the Swan* depicts the god Zeus transformed into a swan in order to seduce Leda. Leonardo da Vinci is said to have left the painting unfinished at his death. His pupil Salai completed the work.

Room 14 exhibits a series of self-portraits by Bernini, made when he was 15, 25, and 40 years old. **Room 15** contains a sweet painting of *Tobias and the Angel* by Savoldo. Jacopo Bassano's *Last Supper* depicts the Apostles as a group of barefoot fishermen. In **Room 18** is Rubens extraordinary

depiction of the *Pietà*. All the colours of the spectrum are reflected in the skin of the dead Christ. **Room 19** displays Barocci's grand *Flight of Aeneas from Troy* (1598), which inspired Bernini's *Aeneas and Anchises.*

Room 20 contains several works by Venetian masters: *The Impassioned Singer* by Giorgione; *Portrait of a Woman* by Carpaccio; Giovanni Bellini's *Madonna and Child* (1510), painted when the artist was aged 84; Veronese's *St Anthony Preaching to the Fish* and *St John the Baptist Preaching.* There are also four paintings by Titian: *Venus Blindfolding Cupid, St Dominic, The Scourging of Christ* and the most famous, *Sacred and Profane Love.* Titian was 25 when he was commissioned to paint this work to celebrate the marriage of Niccolò Aurelio and Laura Bagarotto in 1514. The nude represents a heavenly, celestial Venus (divine love) whilst the earthly Venus is clothed (profane love). In 1899, the Rothschilds offered to buy this one painting for a price higher than the estimated value of the lands and gallery together, but the Borghese refused to sell.

TITIAN: *SACRED AND PROFANE LOVE*

POSITIS SIGNIS ET

QUIRINALE & ESQUILINO

TREVI FOUNTAIN

Quirinale has been home to popes, kings and presidents. Esquilino is a bustling mixture of modern and ancient Rome.

One of the area's star attractions is the Trevi Fountain but there's much more to see. Walk up to Piazza del Quirinale for a splendid view. The palace guards are an elite branch of Carabinieri known as *Reggimento Corazzieri.* There is a daily changing of the guard at 4pm.

Compare two Baroque churches built by arch-rivals Bernini (*Sant'Andrea al Quirinale)* and Borromini (*San Carlo alle Quattro Fontane).* At the corner of Via del Quirinale and Via delle Quattro Fontane are four fountains. Look around and you can see three obelisks in the distance.

From here you can either go to Palazzo Barberini to see Renaissance art treasures or to *Santa Maria degli Angeli,* Michelangelo's church built inside the Baths of Diocletian. More of ancient Rome is on view at Palazzo Massimo, Domus Aurea and Trajan's Market.

If it's all too much, take a break in the gardens at Villa Aldobrandini but don't miss the magnificent church of Santa Maria Maggiore.

The perfect day in Esquilino would finish with dinner at *Agata e Romeo* (p.244).

GUARDS FROM THE *REGGIMENTO CORAZZIERI*

Tridente
PIAZZA BARBERINI
V. BARBERINI
Palazzo Barberini
Santa Maria degli Angeli
Terme di Diocleziano
PIAZZA D'INDEPENDENZA
V. D. TRITONE
Quirinale
San Carlo alle Quattro Fontane
Palazzo Massimo
Termini
VIA DEL CORSO
Fontana di Trevi
Pal. del Quirinale
V. D. QUIRINALE
VIA NAZIONALE
TORINO
VIA
VIA MARSALA
Sant' Andrea al Quirinale
CAVOUR
Santa Maria Maggiore
VIA GIOVANNI GIOLITTI
Trajan's Column
Villa Aldobrandini
VIA PANISPERNA
V. CARLO ALBERTO
PIAZZA VENEZIA
Esquilino
Trajan's Market
V. GIOVANNI LANZA
VIA CAVOUR
San Pietro in Vincoli
PIAZZA VITTORIO EMANUELE II
V. D. FORI IMPERIALI
Capitolino
VIA MERULANA
Foro Romano (Roman Forum)
Domus Aurea
VIALE MANZONI
Colosseo
VIA LABICANA
Palatino

Trevi Fountain
• Rome's most famous fountain

Palazzo Barberini
• Raphael with Titian and Caravaggio

Santa Maria Maggiore
• one of the four main basilicas

San Pietro in Vincoli
• Michelangelo's *Moses*

Baths of Diocletian & Santa Maria degli Angeli • ancient Rome meets the Renaissance

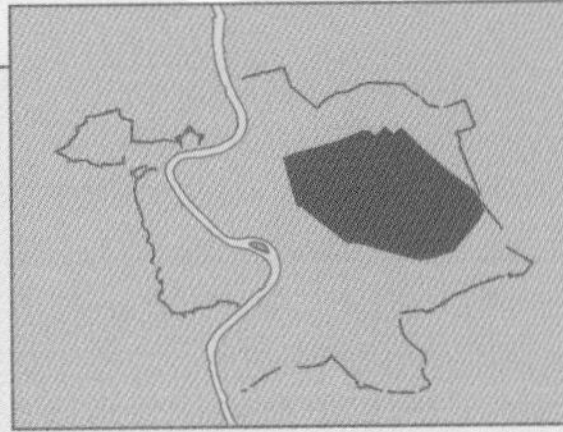

Villa Aldobrandini
An oasis near a busy intersection.

restaurants p.245
shopping p.262

Palazzo Massimo
Early Roman mosaics and frescoes.

Did you know that..?
Charlton Heston was cast as Moses because of his resemblance to Michelangelo's statue in San Pietro in Vincoli.

Fontana di Trevi (Trevi fountain)

Piazza di Trevi; map 5, C3; GPS 41.90083, 12.48334

Lights illuminate the fountain beautifully at night, evoking images from Fellini's film *La Dolce Vita* (1960). In the 15th century, Pope Nicholas V (Parentucelli) first commissioned a fountain on this site, to celebrate the repair and reopening of the Acqua Vergine aqueduct. It was one of the first construction projects undertaken after the papacy returned to Rome. Since that time the aqueduct has remained in nearly constant use, providing water for fountains in Centro Storico.

Originally constructed in 19 BC by Marcus Agrippa, Augustus' son-in-law, the Acqua Vergine was designed to bring water to his baths near the Pantheon. It is said that a young woman showed the original feeding spring to Roman soldiers. The aqueduct is named after her. If you look in the upper panels above the large figure on the right, you can see a depiction of the event.

The current fountain dates from 1732, when Nicola Salvi began the project for Pope Clement XII (Corsini). Salvi's ambitious design resembles an open-air theatre. The central arch surrounds a large statue of *Neptune*, god of the sea. Neptune stands on a seashell carriage pulled by two horses, which are led by Tritons. Dating from 1762, these sculptures are the work of Pietro Bracci. Filippo della Valle carved the two large figures on either side of the central arch, which symbolise the life-giving properties of water: *Abundance* (left) and *Health* (right). There is a story that Nicola Salvi was suffering constant criticism from a barber who had a shop in the square. To silence him, Salvi created a large basin (known familiarly as *Ace of Cups*) situated on the right-hand balustrade. This addition would forever block the barber's view of the fountain.

Quirinale

According to legend, the hilltop was home to a small village of Sabines whose god was named *Quirinus*. In the 3rd century AD, Emperor Constantine's baths were located here. Equestrian statues of Castor and Pollux once stood in the baths; they are now the centrepieces in Piazza del Quirinale. The Roman obelisk between the two statues is a companion to the one on top of the Esquiline. Across the piazza is Scuderie Papali, an art exhibition space.

Castor and Pollux are also known as the *Dioscuri* (from the Greek *dios kouroi*) meaning 'sons of Zeus'. The father of the pantheon of Greek gods once disguised himself as a swan to seduce Leda, a beautiful mortal. Leda produced twin boys, one mortal and one immortal: Castor and Polydeuces (Pollux). The mortal Castor was a great horseman, whereas Pollux was a boxer and a god. The twins accompanied Jason on his quest for the Golden Fleece.

Palazzo del Quirinale (Quirinale Palace)

06 469 91
admission €5
map 5, D4; GPS 41.8993, 12.4863

08.30 -12.30 Sun only
changing of the guard 16.00 daily
closed July and Aug

Many of the great Renaissance and Baroque architects and artists worked on the palace, which became the summer papal residence for Clement VIII(Aldobrandini) in 1592. Napoleon also lived here while he occupied Rome in 1809-14. The papacy regained possession and kept it until 1870 when King Vittorio Emanuele II made it his royal residence in Rome. In retaliation, Pope Pio IX shut himself up in the Vatican and excommunicated members of the Italian government and the monarchy. The papacy refused to recognize the legitimacy of the recently formed Italian state. For nearly 60 years the situation remained unresolved until Pius XI signed the Lateran treaty in 1929. King Umberto II went into voluntary exile at the end of World War II and the Quirinale Palace then became the residence of the President of Italy. When Benedict XVI made a visit on 24 June 2005, it was a hugely symbolic event. At the time of writing, the palace is the residence of President Carlo Ciampi. Saying that the place 'needed life', the president opened the door to visitors on Sunday mornings. You can wander freely through large reception rooms, decorated with 17th century frescoes depicting the glories of various popes, before reaching salons filled with 19th century triumphal paintings of Savoy monarchs.

Palazzo Barberini (Galleria Nazionale d'Arte Antica)

Via delle Quattro Fontane 13
06 32810
admission €6
map 5-6, E3; GPS 42.90289, 12.48918

08.30-19.30 Tues-Sun
last admission 30 minutes before closing
www.galleriaborghese.it

The palazzo was designed by Carlo Maderno for Maffeo Barberini, who became Pope Urban VIII. After Maderno's death in 1629, both Bernini and Borromini worked on the building. The gallery offers another opportunity to visit works by Raphael, Caravaggio and Bernini, along with Titian, Tintoretto, Hans Holbein, El Greco and Canaletto. After a recent refurbishment (due for completion by the end of 2005), the paintings will return to their original rooms. Regardless of when you are visiting, the collection is always hung in chronological order.

Raphael's celebrated *La Fornarina* (1518-19) is a portrait of one of his lovers. She has been identified as Margherita Luti, daughter of a Sienese baker who had a shop in Via del Governo Vecchio, near Piazza Navona. Raphael's possession of her is made clear by the signature *Raphael Urbinas* on the bracelet adorning her upper arm. It was rumoured that her passionate desires were the cause of the artist's death. This portrait has inspired other artists such as Goya and Ingres.

Henry VIII by Hans Holbein (1540) was painted on the day of the King's wedding to Anne of Cleves. Attributed to Guido Reni, the portrait of *Beatrice Cenci* dates from the 17th century. After suffering years of rape and abuse at the hands of her father Francesco, Beatrice collaborated with her stepmother in in his murder. They were both convicted of conspiring to kill him and executed in 1577 on the bridge of Ponte Sant'Angelo. Legend has it that she is one of the ghosts that inhabit Rome, her spirit appearing on the bridge. Beatrice's story is the subject of Shelley's play *The Cenci*. Reni's rival Caravaggio has two paintings in the gallery: *Judith Beheading Holofernes* (c.1599) dramatically depicts a bloody execution; *Narcissus* is a mythical young man enchanted by his own reflection.

The three bees from the Barberini coat of arms are in evidence throughout the palazzo. An example is found in a ceiling fresco in the **Gran Salone** – *Triumph of Divine Providence* by Pietro di Cortona. Look for the Barberini bees flying heavenward, a metaphor of the family's industriousness and social status.

Those with an interest in 18th century decoration and art should find their way to the **second floor**, to see paintings by Canaletto, Guardi and Fragonard.

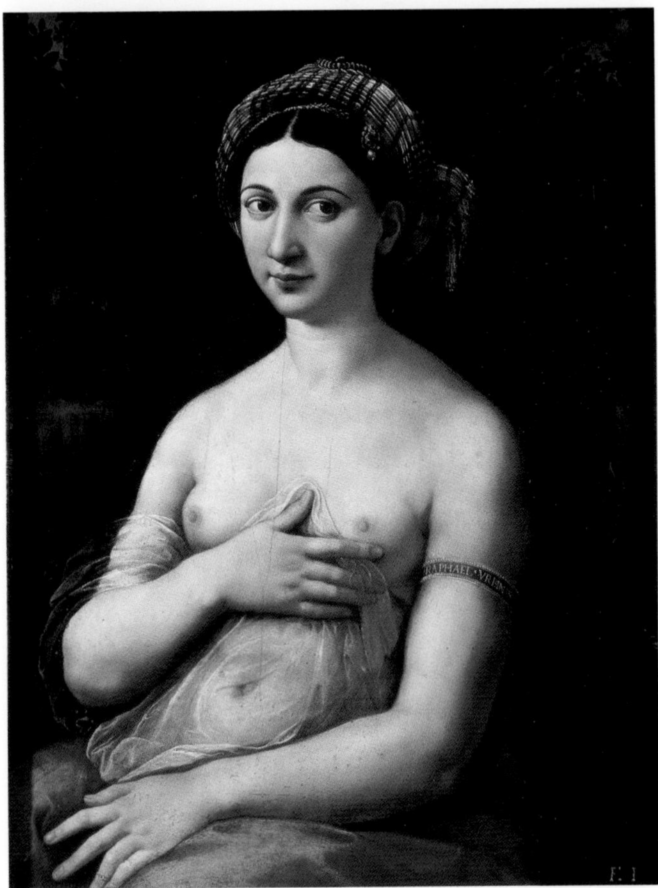

RAPHAEL: *LA FORNARINA*

MICHELANGELO, *TOMB OF JULIUS II* (DETAIL: MOSES)

San Pietro in Vincoli

Piazza di San Pietro in Vincoli 4A
06 488 2865

07.00-12.30, 15.30-19.00 daily
map 6, F6; GPS 41.89379, 12.49249

There has been a church on this site since the 5th century. A bronze and crystal casket below the high altar contains the two chains, the *vincoli*, that shackled St Peter in prison. These chains were later used to exorcise devils in the Middle Ages.

To the right of the altar is Michelangelo's *Tomb of Julius II*, first commissioned in 1505. The three figures just above ground level are: *Rachel* (left) *Moses* (centre) and *Leah* (right). The only sculpture by Michelangelo is *Moses*, with a face modelled on that of Julius II who died in 1513 with the tomb unfinished. Raffaelo da Montelupo carved the top three figures. The piece was completed and placed in the church in 1545.

Michelangelo in Rome

Michelangelo Buonarroti (1475-1564) came from Tuscany. He was born in Arezzo and raised by a family of stonemasons because his natural mother was too ill to care for him. At 13 he was sent to Florence to apprentice with the fresco painter Domenico Ghirlandaio. Michelangelo then studied sculpture under Donatello's master, Bertoldo di Giovanni. While in Florence, he was invited into the Medici household by Lorenzo de'Medici. Lorenzo's son was the future Pope Leo X and his nephew became Clement VII.

At this time there was a booming trade in fraudulent antiquities. To fund his trip to Rome, Michelangelo carved a cupid and aged it. He sold it to a cardinal, who discovered later that it was a forgery. Despite the fraud, the cardinal was so impressed by the artist that he commissioned an original. Michelangelo's first stay in Rome was a success: he carved the *Pietà* for St Peter's, finishing the sculpture at the age of 25.

His next commission was the tomb of Julius II, a project Michelangelo first conceived as a monument to himself and his art. This was to be a new Colossus of Rhodes, with *Moses* as just one of more than 40 intended sculptures. He spent months in Tuscany, searching the Carrara quarries for perfect blocks of marble, only to arrive with them in Rome and find his project cancelled. In frustration, Michelangelo returned to Florence. Julius summoned him back to Rome to paint the ceiling of the Sistine Chapel. Michelangelo consented on the condition that he would also carve the tomb. Julius agreed to a monument half the size of the artist's original vision.

Michelangelo loved sculpting and hated painting. In many of his letters, he complained that *'painting is not my profession.'* Resenting the time spent working on the Sistine ceiling, Michelangelo would often sneak away to carve in secret, and this resulted in Julius continually spying on him. The sculptor's failure to complete the tomb became an obsession, one he called the *'tragedy of the tomb.'* For this Michelangelo blamed Raphael, who had recommended him to paint the Sistine ceiling. Michelangelo disliked Raphael for being handsome and having the social graces he lacked. Dislike turned to hatred as Raphael was favoured by the Medici popes, men Michelangelo once knew almost as brothers. Michelangelo was furious when Raphael inherited Bramante's position as architect of St Peter's and continued to blame Raphael long after the painter's death in 1520. Michelangelo wrote, *'All the discord that was born between Pope Julius and me was from the envy of Bramante and of Raphael; and this was the reason for the Pope not continuing his tomb during his lifetime, in order to ruin me. And Raphael had good reason for this, because everything he had in art, he had from me.'*

Once again, Michelangelo retreated to his beloved Florence. He stayed there until 1534, when Paul III (Farnese) succeeded the Medici popes. Michelangelo was summoned to Rome to paint the *Last Judgement* in the Sistine Chapel. Paul III was also keen to use Michelangelo's skill as an architect on many different projects – including the *Campidoglio* (1538) and the dome of St Peter's, begun in 1546. When the Farnese papacy ended in 1549, Michelangelo returned to Florence where he planned to open a school to teach sculpture (a task accomplished in 1563 when he started the Accademia). Michelangelo continued as papal architect through succeeding popes, dividing his time between Rome

SANTA MARIA DEGLI ANGELI

and Florence. In 1561, Pius IV (Giovanni Angelo de'Medici) commissioned Michelangelo to design Santa Maria degli Angeli at the Baths of Diocletian. It was to be Michelangelo's last architectural work.

Santa Maria degli Angeli

Piazza della Repubblica — 07.00-18.00 daily
06 488 0812 — map 6, G3; GPS 41.9029, 12.4958

Pius IV commissioned this church because the Baths of Diocletian had been taken over by gangs of thieves. By converting the vast *Tepidarium* at the heart of the baths, he hoped to rid the area of undesirables. Michelangelo's plan made no changes to the structure of the huge Tepidarium; he merely raised the floor and installed altars. Building commenced in 1565, one year after Michelangelo's death. The work was supervised by Giacomo del Duca, who remained completely faithful to the original design, including the particular marble columns that Michelangelo had demanded for the cloister.

Terme di Diocleziano (Baths of Diocletian)

Viale Enrico de Nicola 78 — 09.00-19.00 Tue-Sun
06 399 67700, €5.00 — map 6, H2; GPS 41.9022, 12.4985

The baths were situated here, on the plateau of the Quirinale and Viminale hills, because it was the most densely populated area of Rome. Begun in AD 298 under Emperor Diocletian, they were the biggest in Rome, accommodating up to 3,000 bathers. The baths fell into disrepair after the year 536, when invading barbarians destroyed the aqueduct that supplied the water.

Santa Maria Maggiore

Piazza di Santa Maria Maggiore 07.00-19.00 daily
map 6, H5; GPS 41.89744, 12.49935

Sitting atop the Esquiline Hill, this is one of the four main pilgrimage churches of Rome. Dedicated to Mary, mother of Jesus, it is the most important Marian church in the Catholic world. The building seen today dates from 432, one year after the Council of Ephesus affirmed the dual nature of Jesus as truly God and truly man. Thereafter, Mary was confirmed as the Mother of God.

The column in Piazza di Santa Maria Maggiore was taken from the Basilica of Constantine in the Forum. It is topped with a bronze *Virgin and Child* that dates from 1615. Bernini completed the rear façade, with its ancient obelisk matching the one on the Quirinale.

Vision of the Madonna On a hot August night in 352, the Virgin Mary appeared to Pope Liberius in a dream. She bade him build a great church in her honour on the site of a miraculous snowfall. The next morning it snowed on the Esquiline and the Pope commissioned a church. The story is depicted in a bronze bas-relief high above the altar. Every year on 5 August, white flower petals are released to fall like snow in the church. After the service these are collected by the faithful as tokens of special grace.

The true story is more prosaic: the church was built on the site of a pagan temple dedicated to Juno Lucina, goddess of childbirth. Under the **main altar** is a precious wooden relic of the Sacred Crib allegedly brought to Rome in the 4th century by St Jerome. Mary's life story is told in 5th century mosaics above the altar in the triumphal arch: *Annunciation, Adoration of the Magi* and *Flight into Egypt*. Mosaics depicting scenes from the Old Testament – emphasizing the link between Christ's birth and the Messianic prophecies – are high up around the nave.

The inlaid marble floor of the **nave** is an original 12th century work by the Cosmati family. Alexander VI (Borgia)

commissioned the coffered ceiling, made with the first gold brought to Spain from the New World by Columbus. The gold was a gift from Ferdinand and Isabella.

To the left of the main altar is the **Pauline chapel**, which houses the tomb of Pope Paul V (Borghese). The altarpiece contains an icon of Mary attributed to St Luke the Evangelist. Legend says that Luke (who is called Mary's biographer) also painted her portrait. A number of icons are attributed to him in Bologna, Venice, Poland and Mexico. Proof that all of them were painted around the 13th century has done nothing to discredit the legend. One story claims that when a fire raged in the Borgo district around the Vatican, this particular icon was marched through the streets, causing the flames to die out. Buried in the crypt under the altar are Gian Lorenzo Bernini, his father Pietro, and the extended family. Paulina Bonaparte Borghese is also buried here.

To the right of the main altar is the **Sistine chapel** dedicated to Pope Sixtus V (Peretti), who built Rome's pilgrim routes in a star-shaped plan around Santa Maria Maggiore. Sixtus installed his own tomb here, along with a tomb for St Pius V (Ghislieri).

GLORIA

LATERANO & CELIO

SAN CLEMENTE

Religion has been the business of Laterano for two thousand years. Celio has more green space than any of the seven ancient hills.

As designated parklands, Terme di Caracalla and Via Appia Antica are pleasant for a Sunday stroll. Walk up the medieval street of Clivo Scuaro to find the well-tended gardens of Villa Celimontana. Halfway up the road, beneath the church of Santi Giovanni e Paolo, is the tiny entrance to the Museum of Roman Houses. Excavations have uncovered more than twenty rooms dating from the 3rd-12th centuries, many with frescoes.

In Laterano, San Clemente provides an excellent opportunity to explore three layers of Roman history that span more than a thousand years. To appreciate the power of the growing church, walk down to San Giovanni in Laterano, the Cathedral of Rome, with its beautiful cloisters.

Musicians will enjoy a visit to the Museum of Musical Instruments in the Piazza di Santa Croce in Gerusalemme. The network of small roads between the Colosseum and San Clemente offers many lively restaurants and bars. Via Capo d'Africa has something in every price range.

Just outside the walls and down the Via Appia Antica are the ancient catacombs where many of the first popes are buried.

CLIVO SCUARO

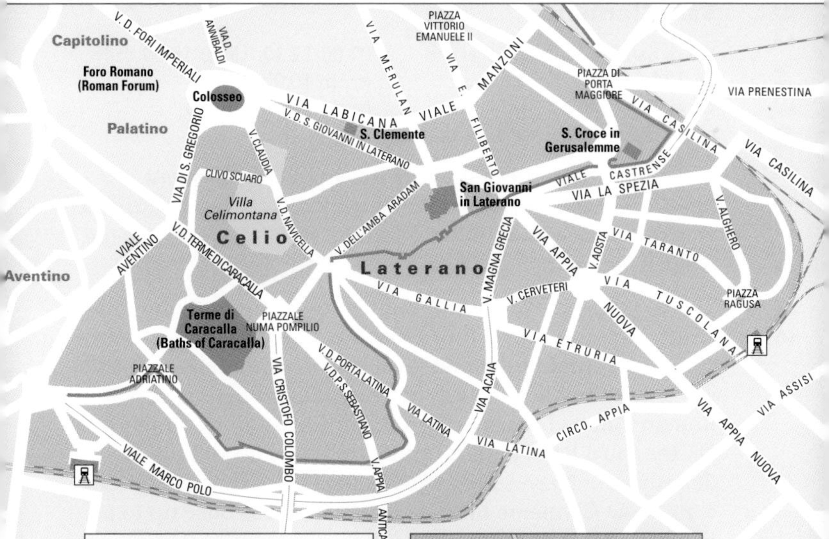

LATERANO & CELIO

San Clemente
• descend through time
San Giovanni in Laterano
• peaceful cloisters
Terme di Caracalla
• Roman baths
Via Appia Antica
• ancient Imperial highway
Catacombs
• early Christian burial grounds

Gardens
Villa Celimontana
07.00-dusk daily.

restaurants p.246

Music
• Summer jazz festival at Villa Celimontana
• Annual opera season at Terme di Caracalla
• Museum of Musical Instruments

Did you know that..?
The only way to be disqualified in a Roman wrestling match was to poke someone's eye out.

San Clemente

Via di San Giovanni in Laterano
06 704 51018
€3 excavations
map 10, F3; GPS 41.8894, 12.4981

09.00-12.30, 15.00-18.00 daily
(from 10.00 Sun)
last admission 17.30

The church is dedicated to the third pope, St Clement (88-97). Clement was a contemporary of Peter and Paul and was referred to as a 'fellow labourer' in Paul's letters of the New Testament.

The building is a multi-layered trip back through time. At street level is a 12th century basilica. The original Christian church is found in the first level below ground. Deeper still is a temple to Mithras (an ancient god) and the remains of a Roman villa, which became a secret Christian meeting place. On the third level underground are remnants of houses destroyed in Nero's fire (AD 64). Beneath all this is running water. San Clemente lies in a valley that was once up to 60 feet lower than it is today.

San Clemente has been under the care of Irish Dominicans since 1677, when the Order was given refuge here after the English outlawed the Irish Catholic church and expelled the entire clergy. The medieval basilica has an original Cosmati marble floor and mosaics of brilliant gold depicting Jesus as the Holy Lamb. The coffered gold ceiling and the large paintings were added in the 18th century. Father Mullooly discovered the layers beneath the church in 1857. He was acting on intuition, with little more than a pick and shovel.

On the level just below ground, the 4th century church has a nave and side aisles defined by thick walls and square pilasters that support the basilica above. Remnants of frescoes depict the legend of St Clement, who was banished to the Crimea in AD 98 by the Emperor Trajan and forced to work in the mines. Clement's passionate evangelising of soldiers and prisoners was so disruptive the Romans tied him to an anchor and threw him into the Black Sea. According to legend, he was taken by angels and placed in an underwater tomb, one that was revealed to believers once a year at the ebbing of the tide.

The second level down is the lowest one open to the public. Originally from Persia and India, the cult of Mithras was becoming widespread in the Roman Empire by the 1st century AD. The dark room is the *mithraeum* – a meeting place where the faithful received instruction and initiation before being permitted to proceed to the *triclinium*. This was a place of worship with two rows of stone benches facing a central altar that featured a carved image of Mithras killing a sacrificial bull.

On the same level is the villa of a Roman Consul, Titus Flavius Clemens (cousin to Emperor Domitian), who was martyred in AD 95 for '*godlessness and following Jewish practices.*' The space is divided into two areas split by a narrow passageway. One side has small apartments and the other a large open space that was used for Christian meetings. According to tradition, St Clement was once a slave in Consul Clemens' household.

The third level can be seen through an iron grille at the end of a corridor. Part of a brick wall and pavement are visible. The sound of rushing water is coming from a tunnel five metres below, which was made to carry water to the Cloaca Maxima in the Forum. It is not known whether the source is an underground spring or a submerged ancient aqueduct.

4TH CENTURY FRESCOES

San Giovanni in Laterano

Piazza di San Giovanni in Laterano 4
06 6988 6452
admission charge for cloisters
map 10, H4; GPS 41.8867, 12.5042

Cloister: 07.00-19.00 daily
Museum: 09.00-13.00 Sat and first Sun of month
Baptistry: 07.30-12.30, 16.00-19.00 daily

This is the cathedral of Rome, one of the four major basilicas and one of the seven pilgrimage churches. On the façade stand 15 statues, with Jesus placed in the highest position. The others include John the Baptist, the Apostle John and theologians who studied and wrote about Christ. Each figure is seven metres tall. The façade faces east, towards the Piazza Porta San Giovanni. Enter the church from this side to get the full effect of Borromini's nave and altar. If you enter from the Piazza di San Giovanni, you will emerge behind the altar near the apse, and miss the splendour completely.

The Lateran Palace is the long ochre building attached to the church. This was the official papal residence for the first thousand years of Catholic history. When the papacy returned from Avignon in the 14th century, the court moved to the Vatican. San Giovanni fell into disrepair and was demolished by Sixtus V (Peretti), who commissioned Domenico Fontana to build the present-day church. Innocent X (Pamphilj) gave Borromini just six years to complete the interior in time for the Jubilee of 1650. In earlier days, Boniface VIII (Caetani) proclaimed the first Jubilee in 1300 from the Loggia of San Giovanni. A fresco by Giotto commemorating the event can be seen on a pillar to the right of the main doors. On an adjacent pillar is a monument to Pope Sylvester II, said to emit sounds of creaking bones before the death of a pope.

The interior, with a large nave and two side aisles, is based on a typical Roman basilica plan. The decoration and architecture is essentially as Borromini conceived it. He restored the Cosmati floor and placed grand niches along the side aisles, occupied with statues of the Apostles. The altar is designed by Giacomo della Porta. The *confessio*, beneath the altar, houses relics of the ancient wooden altar at which St Peter and succeeding popes celebrated mass in San Giovanni from the 1st to the 4th centuries. Above the altar, in the midsection of the towering Gothic baldacchino, are relics of the heads of Saints Peter and Paul. The baldacchino is decorated with fresco panels linking the history of Constantine with the history of the basilica.

Only the Pope is permitted to celebrate mass at the main altar because this is the church where he fulfils his obligations as Bishop of Rome. On Maundy Thursday, there is a special service when he symbolically washes the feet of priests chosen from around the world. Then, from the Benediction Loggia facing Piazza di San Giovanni, the pope gives his blessing.

Until 1870 all popes were crowned in San Giovanni. The cathedral is also the head office for all the churches of Rome. Many important events have been held here, including the signing of the Lateran Pact of 1929, which established the Vatican as a sovereign state.

Be sure to visit the quiet **cloister**, built by the Vassallettos between 1215-32. Fragments found in excavations under the basilica are exhibited, one of which is thought to be a portrait of St Helena, mother of Constantine.

The nearby **baptistery** is the oldest in the Western world. The **obelisk** in the piazza is Egyptian. The largest and most ancient of all the obelisks in Rome, it is placed in exactly the right spot to be seen from Santa Maria Maggiore.

Terme di Caracalla (Baths of Caracalla)

Viale delle Terme di Caracalla 52
06 399 67700
€5 (museum cards apply)
map 9, D6; GPS 41.8802, 12.4904

09.00-1hr before sunset Tue-Sun
09.00-14.00 Mon, ticket office closes 2 hrs before sunset

Built by an infamous emperor and given to the people of Rome as a means to gain their favour, these public baths were completed in AD 217. The complex was square with sides of over 1,000 feet (305 metres). Colonnaded buildings contained bathing areas, gymnastic facilities, restaurants, libraries and lecture rooms. These were surrounded by pleasant gardens, kept green and watered by cisterns holding 80,000 litres of water. Used by 1,600 people at a time, they functioned for more than 300 years.

From AD 211, Caracalla and his brother Geta ruled jointly for one year. Caracalla murdered Geta at an official meeting and followed through by killing all those he considered enemies. Then he tactfully took himself off on military campaigns, leaving the unhappy citizens with the promise of the best baths ever to be built in Rome.

Public bathing was an important form of ritualistic social activity. Having paid a small entrance fee, a typical visit to the baths would begin with exercise. After scraping the skin, the *tepidarium* (a warm room for bringing on sweat) awaited, followed by a hot bath in the *caldarium*. The *frigidarium* was a large room for meeting friends before taking a plunge in the *natatio*, the open-air swimming pool. All of these activities were sexually segregated, with women bathing early in the day. Men would usually arrive after 2pm. There was plenty to do besides bathing: stroll in the gardens, visit the library, or watch jugglers and acrobats perform. An army of slaves was on hand to ensure that everything worked.

Early baths were primitive affairs heated by large bronze braziers. In the 1st century BC, Romans invented central heating, and this allowed individual rooms to be temperature controlled. The technology that was used to create vaulted concrete roofs ultimately developed into the great dome of the Pantheon.

Via Appia Antica
(Appian Way)

overview map G6

Today Via Appia Antica begins at Porta San Sebastiano, the best-preserved gate of the Aurelian Wall. Dating from the 3rd century, the wall once stretched for about 12 miles (19 km) around the city. Designated a park (with the road closed to traffic on Sundays), the area now offers recreational activities.

Beneath the fields on either side of the road are the *catacombs,* the secret underground graveyards of the early Christians, who were brought here because they could not get a proper burial elsewhere. So many saints were entombed underground that the catacombs became shrines and places of pilgrimage.

Appius Claudius Caecus built the first section of the road in 312 BC to link Rome with Capua. It was later extended to Benevento, Taranto and then Brindisi in 190 BC. The road once began at Porta Capena in the old Servian wall. This was the route taken by the funeral processions of Caesar and Augustus. It was on this road that St Paul entered Rome in chains in AD 56.

Sights

Take a tourist bus from Termini (p.283). For cycle hire see p.288.
www.parcoappiaantica.org

Museo delle Mura
(Museum of the Walls)
Via di Porta San Sebastiano 18
06 704 75284, €2.60
09.00-19.00 Tue-Sat, 09.00-17.00 Sun
overview map G6
Walk on the Aurelian Wall. Learn about its history.

Catacombs (on Via Appia Antica)
08.30-12.00, 14.30-17.30 daily, €5

- Basilica San Sebastiano (136)
06 785 0350
closed Sundays and 10 Nov-10 Dec
One of the seven pilgrimage churches.

- San Callisto (110)
06 513 01580
closed Wednesdays and February
Early popes are buried here.

- Tomb of Cecilia Metella (161)
06 399 67700
09.00-1 hr before sunset Tue-Sun
Tomb built for a Roman noblewoman.

- Circus of Maxentius (153)
06 780 1324
09.00-1 hr before sunset Tue-Sun
Mausoleum of Romulus.

- Domitilla (off Via Appia Antica)
Via delle Sette Chiese 283
06 513 3956
closed Tuesday and January
Frescoes of Christ as the Good Shepherd.

AVENTINO & TESTACCIO

SAN ANSELMO

Aventino is a quiet and exclusive residential area. Testaccio, a working class district, comes alive at night.

Start from Piazzale Ugo La Malfa to reach the top of the Aventine Hill. Via di Santa Sabina and the *Giardini degli Aranci (*Garden of Oranges) have views across Trastevere to St Peter's. Stroll along Via Sabina to the Piazza Cavalieri di Malta. Enclosed by four walls, the piazza has a large bronze door on the west side with a 'keyhole' view of St Peter's. Look through the keyhole to see the Basilica framed by a long green arbour. There are no restaurants or bars on the Aventine.

The name Testaccio comes from *testae,* meaning 'pots'. Broken *amphorae,* previously dumped in the Tiber, were stacked in a pile which eventually became a large hill called Monte Testaccio. The area around the food market has clubs and discos.

There are two cemeteries in Testaccio: the Protestant Cemetery and the British War Cemetery. Nearby is the Pyramid of Caius Cestius, the tomb of a wealthy Roman caught up in the Egyptian craze at the time of Augustus.

VIEW FROM THE AVENTINE

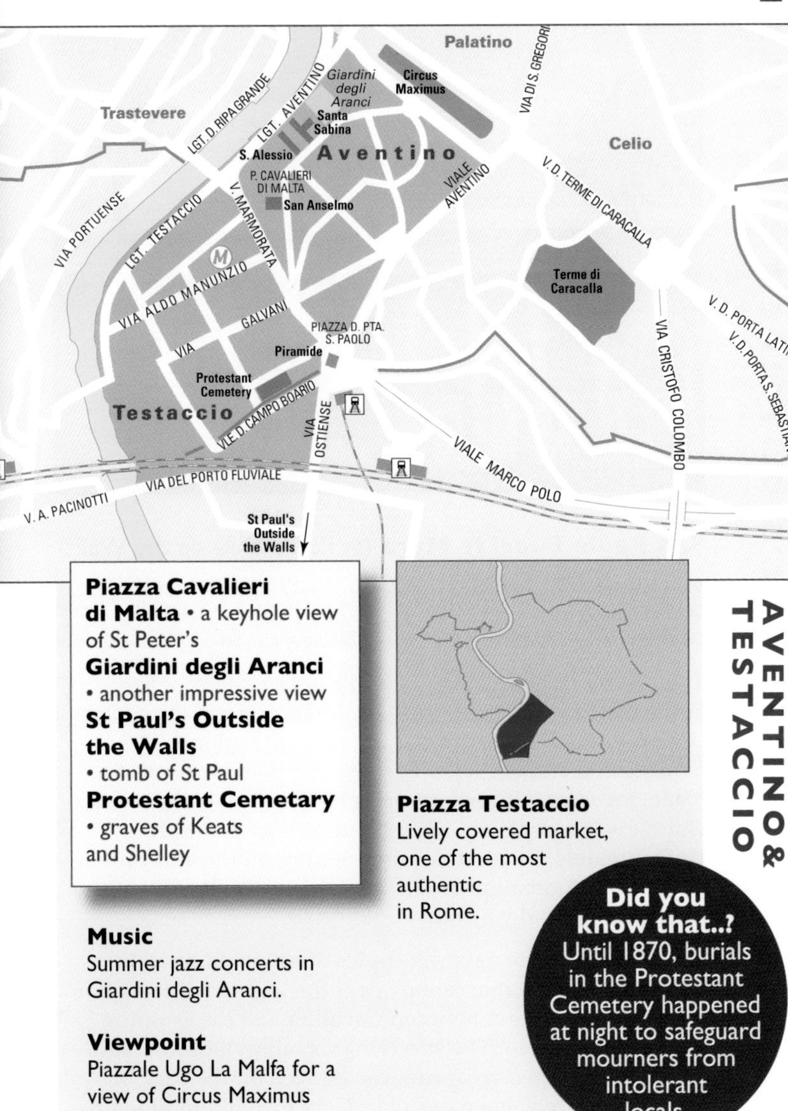

AVENTINO & TESTACCIO

Piazza Cavalieri di Malta • a keyhole view of St Peter's
Giardini degli Aranci • another impressive view
St Paul's Outside the Walls • tomb of St Paul
Protestant Cemetary • graves of Keats and Shelley

Piazza Testaccio
Lively covered market, one of the most authentic in Rome.

Music
Summer jazz concerts in Giardini degli Aranci.

Viewpoint
Piazzale Ugo La Malfa for a view of Circus Maximus and the Palatine.

restaurants p.248

Did you know that..?
Until 1870, burials in the Protestant Cemetery happened at night to safeguard mourners from intolerant locals.

San Paolo Fuori le Mura (St Paul's Outside the Walls)

Via Ostiense 186 (bus 23)
06 541 0341
off map; GPS 41.8558, 12.4772

07.00-19.00 daily (summer)
07.00-18.30 daily (winter)
Cloister closed 13.00-15.00 daily

The second largest church in Rome after St Peter's, San Paolo contains the tomb of St Paul. The original 4th century church burned to the ground in 1823. Miraculously the baldacchino and the relics beneath the altar survived the blaze, together with two mosaics by Pietro Cavallini. The church was completely rebuilt and consecrated in 1854. Unfortunately, the vast new interior has all the atmosphere of a marble football pitch. However, four small side chapels offer comfort and warmth.

The frescoes in the nave are copies of original Cavallini paintings. The marble canopy over the high altar dates from 1285, a collaboration between Cavallini and the sculptor Arnolfo di Cambio. The surviving Cavallini mosaics, with distinctive winged creatures, can be seen on the back of triumphant arch above the altar. Gold medallions along the sides of the nave contain portraits of the popes.

Pietro Vassalletto decorated the charming cloister, and also completed the one at San Giovanni in Laterano. St Paul's is the only great pilgrimage basilica not to have an obelisk – instead it has a bell tower. The striking gold mosaics on the exterior façade depict Christ in the centre, with Paul at his left and Peter on his right.

St Paul (10 BC-AD 67)

Named Saul at his birth in Tarsus (in modern day Turkey), St Paul was both a Jew and a Roman citizen. He was educated in Jerusalem and was a Pharisee, a member of an ancient Jewish sect that believed in strict observance of Mosaic law. Saul actively persecuted Christians and was present at the stoning of St Stephen. In the book of Acts, the story is told of how Saul was struck blind on the road to Damascus. A heavenly voice asked him: *'Saul, Saul why do you persecute me?'* After reaching Damascus, a man named Ananias restored his sight and baptised him. Saul changed his name to Paul to represent becoming a new man in Christ. He went to Jerusalem and met with the other Apostles.

Paul embarked on an evangelical mission, undertaking three journeys in the years 47-49 and 57-58. He travelled 7,800 km on foot and 9,000 by sea. Tireless and stubborn, Paul was reputedly a short bald man, bandy-legged with a large flat nose. Paul wrote letters to the churches he helped found: thirteen epistles in the New Testament are directly attributed to him. Four of them were written from prisons in Ephesus and Rome. Paul was the first man to write about Christ in his epistle to the Thessalonians, which pre-dates the earliest Gospel of Mark by 15 years.

Finally, Paul's preaching enraged authorities in Jerusalem and he was arrested. As a Roman citizen he was sent to Rome for trial. Here he was placed under house arrest for two years while he continued to preach. Eventually Paul was tried and convicted. Because he was Roman, he was beheaded rather than crucified. His body was laid to rest outside the city walls, in the place where the church now stands.

TRASTEVERE & GIANICOLO

PIAZZA DI SANTA MARIA IN TRASTEVERE

Locals who live in Trastevere consider themselves to be the true Romans. The view from Monte Gianicolo is the best in Rome.

Trastevere means 'across the Tevere'. The area was originally inhabited by Jews, slaves and foreigners who couldn't live elsewhere. Today it has a lively neighbourhood feel, with lots of colourful shops and restaurants. Access to the centre is easy and, if you are staying here, Trastevere is a good refuge at the end of the day. The heart of the district is Piazza di Santa Maria in Trastevere, one of the best people-watching locations in Rome. Locals will appreciate the correct pronounciation: *Trahs*-**tev**-*eh-ray*

Monte Gianicolo stands between Trastevere and the Vatican. The climb to the top is worth it but take a taxi or the 115 bus if the weather is hot. Locals say that Villa Doria Pamphilj provides essential oxygen for Rome. The garden is kept green all year round.

CAMPO DE' FIORI
Centro Storico
Pal. Corsini
Villa Farnesina
V. ARENULA
LGT. R. SANZIO
Gianicolo
VIA NUOVA D. FORNACI
Monumento Garibaldi
GARIBALDI
S. Maria in Trastevere
VIA AURELIA ANTICA
VIA GARIBALDI
S. Pietro in Montorio
VIA
Fontana dell' Acqua Paola
S. Cecilia
Villa Doria Pamphilj
V. D. S. PANCRAZIO
Trastevere
S. Francesco a Ripa
LGT. D. RIPA GRANDE
VIA G. CARINI
VIALE DI TRASTEVERE
VIA FONTEIANA
V. MARMORATA
Aventino
VIA G. BARILLI
VIA PORTUENSE
Tevere
Testaccio

Santa Maria in Trastevere
• Cavallini mosaics

Santa Cecilia in Trastevere
• Cavallini frescoes

Villa Farnesina
• Chigi's pleasure palace

Villa Doria Pamphilj
• Rome's greenest garden

Gianicolo
• fresh air and good views

Porta Portese
Huge Sunday morning flea market.

Piazza di Santa Maria in Trastevere
A vibrant meeting place.

Piazza San Cosimato
Daily market with local atmosphere.

restaurants p.249
shopping p.263

Did you know that..?
The local Trastevere dialect includes more than 2,000 words to describe human genitalia.

Santa Maria in Trastevere

Piazza Santa Maria in Trastevere
06 581 4802
07.00-21.00 daily
map 8, F2
GPS 41.88938, 12.47031

First dedicated by Pope St Calixtus sometime around AD 220, Santa Maria in Trastevere is the oldest established church in Rome. Legend has it that mineral oil suddenly spouted from the ground here in the year 38 BC, a phenomenon that was later interpreted as a portent of the coming of Christ.

By the 1st century AD a house church was located on this site, a place where Christians met in secret. These first Roman Christians were mainly Jewish slaves and immigrant converts from the Empire, who settled in Trastevere near the ports on the Tiber. Imperial guards would sometimes pay a visit to the area when Christians were needed for the arenas.

In 1140 Pope Innocent II, a Trastevere native from the powerful Papareschi family, commissioned the building we see today. Pietro Cavallini is responsible for the stunning mosaics in the apse. At the top is Christ enthroned with Mary. This was the first time Mary had been depicted as a queen, instead of her usual role as Madonna with Child. On Mary's right are St Calixtus (martyred in 222), St Lawrence and Innocent II (holding the model for the church). On Christ's left are St Peter and three popes. Under Christ's throne is a charming row of sheep on either side of Christ the Holy Lamb. Beneath the sheep are scenes depicting incidents in Mary's life. Take plenty of change for the illuminato.

IF YOU ENCOUNTER A WEDDING, BAPTISM OR FUNERAL, IT IS POLITE TO LEAVE AND RETURN ANOTHER TIME.

Santa Cecilia in Trastevere

Piazza di Santa Cecilia
06 589 9289
09.30-12.30, 16.00-18.30 daily
€2 for excavations
map 8, H3; GPS 41.8874, 12.4768

Cavallini fresco:
10.00-12.00 Tues and Thurs,
11.30-12.30 Sun
€2.60

St Cecilia is the patron saint of music. The story is that she was a Christian, the musical daughter of the patrician Cecili, promised in marriage to Valerian. The couple set about doing good works until Valerian and his brother were arrested and martyred in AD 230. Cecilia was condemned to suffocation by steam in her own baths. After a day and night, she emerged – still singing. Roman soldiers made three attempts to decapitate her, but Cecilia managed to linger on for several days. Legend says that when her grave was opened in 1599, the body was found to be perfectly intact. The artist Stefano Maderno was present and he immediately carved the likeness of her remains. The statue is under the altar of the church.

It is worth making the effort to visit the Cavallini fresco of *The Last Judgement* (a portion of which is the cover image for this book). Located upstairs in the attached cloister, you enter through a large wooden door in the left wall of the church. Be patient, you may have to knock several times. Eventually an aged nun will open the door and direct you upstairs. She may also sell you one of her handmade cards.

The excavations beneath the church reveal foundations of several Roman houses, storerooms and a tannery.

Villa Farnesina

Via della Lungara 230
admission €5
map 8, F1; GPS 41.8933, 12.4669

9.00-13.00 Mon-Sat
last entry 12.40

This plot of land has long been associated with pleasures of the flesh. In 44 BC, Julius Caesar secretly entertained his lover Cleopatra inside a palace located here, and it was from here that she fled with her illegitimate son after Caesar's assassination.

Agostino Chigi, playboy and Sienese banker to the popes, commissioned Balthazar Peruzzi to build him a palace on the river. Chigi was famed for his lavish parties – at an inauguration banquet for Leo X, guests flung their gold dinner plates into the Tiber. No fool, Chigi had his servants lay nets in the river so they could later retrieve the plates. In 1512, Chigi commissioned Raphael to paint frescoes for the **Loggia di Galatea.** The artist was given a suite of rooms in the palace, where he installed his mistress. The *Triumph of Galatea* depicts a statuesque blonde sea-maiden, wrapped in a red cloak, riding the waves on a seashell pulled by two dolphins. It is a beautiful painting, the colours glowing with light – a work that undoubtedly influenced Titian's *Bacchus & Ariadne,* painted for the Duke of Ferrara in 1520. Not all artists were impressed; Michelangelo passed by the villa one day and painted a head on the wall as a mark of his disapproval of Raphael's work.

The **Loggia di Psyche** was the original entrance to the villa. Painted by Raphael, Giulio Romano, and their students, the fresco portrays a bountiful garden with a scantily clad Psyche, Cupid and other naked bodies engaged in erotic scenes. Above the raised hand of Mercury is a tree bearing a very phallic looking fruit.

In the **Stanza del Fregio**, scenes from Ovid's *Metamorphoses* are attributed to Sebastian del Piombo. The constellations on the ceiling, illustrating the position of the stars at Chigi's birth, are the work of Peruzzi.

On the first floor is the grand **Salone delle Prospettive**, painted by Peruzzi for Chigi's nuptial banquet in August 1519, when he married his mistress. The room at the end of the Salon, **Sala delle Nozze di Alexander e Roxanne** was Chigi's bedroom, painted by G.A. Bazzi, an artist known as 'Il Sodoma' because of his sexual preferences. From preparatory drawings by Raphael, the frescoes depict the nuptials of the beautiful Persian princess Roxanne and Alexander the Great.

DETAIL FROM THE BAZZI FRESCOES

Chigi died in 1520 and his heirs squandered his fortune. The villa was later sold to the Farnese who continued to use it for parties. To maintain secrecy, they commissioned Michelangelo to design a private bridge over the Tiber to connect the villa to Palazzo Farnese. It was never built.

Raphael (1483-1520)

Born in Urbino in the Papal States, Raffaello Sanzio was the son of Giovanni Santi, court painter to the Duke of Urbino. The young Raphael was treated like a prince and, unlike Michelangelo, knew the manners and etiquette of life at court. He learned to paint by copying his father, who also provided Raphael with his earliest patrons. At the age of 17 Raphael completed his first commission – the *San Nicolò Tolentino* altarpiece for the church of Sant'Agostino in Città di Castello, Umbria.

Raphael was like a sponge, absorbing the best from each artist into his own developing style. He apprenticed with Pietro Perugino and went on to Florence in 1504, with letters of introduction to the civic authorities. At the time, Leonardo da Vinci and Michelangelo were engaged in painting battle scenes on opposite walls of the Palazzo Vecchio. Their rivalry and exchange of insults came to be known as the *Battle of the Battles*. Raphael was a frequent visitor, observing both artists closely. He also studied and made drawings of the work of Masaccio, Giotto and Donatello.

Raphael in Rome

Galleria Borghese
Deposition of Christ 1507
Lady with a Unicorn 1506
Portrait of a Man 1502
Sant'Agostino
The Prophet Isaiah 1512
Palazzo Barberini
La Fornarina 1519
Musei Vaticani
Stanze della Segnatura 1508-11
Stanza di Eliodoro 1511-14
Stanza di Borgo 1514-17
Vatican Loggia 1517-19
Pinacoteca Vaticana
Resurrection 1499
Coronation of the Virgin 1503
Theological Virtues 1507
Madonna di Foligno 1512
Transfiguration 1520
Villa Farnesina
Triumph of Galatea 1512
Loggia of Psyche 1518
Santa Maria della Pace
Sibyls and Angels 1514
Galleria Doria Pamphilj
Portrait of Andrea Navagero and Agostino Beazzano 1516

Raphael the architect

Santa Maria del Popolo
Chigi Chapel 1513-1516
Sant'Eligio degli Orefici
1509-1516
Villa Madama
(completed posthumously)

Pope Julius II employed Bramante, Raphael's uncle (or cousin) as architect. On Bramante's recommendation, Raphael was appointed artist to the papal court in 1508 and given the task of painting the Pope's private apartments in the Vatican. When Julius died, Raphael was favoured by Leo X.

Agostino Chigi became an ardent patron and friend of Raphael. They both loved women and parties. Raphael once wrote that, *'to paint a beautiful woman I have to see many beautiful ones to choose the best.'* He died on his 37th birthday. Chigi died four days later. Raphael is buried in the Pantheon.

Palazzo Corsini (Galleria Nazionale d'Arte Antica)

Via della Lungara 10
06 688 02323, bookings 06 32810
admission €4
www.galleriaborghese.it
map 8, E1; GPS 41.8933, 12.4669

09.30-13.30 Tue-Sun

The Palazzo was home to Queen Christina after she abdicated the Protestant Swedish throne to convert to Catholicism. She died here in 1689 and the palazzo was purchased by Cardinal Neri Maria Corsini, an art patron and the nephew of Clement XII (Corsini). The Cardinal's outstanding collection was donated to the Italian state in 1883, to form the Galleria Nazionale d'Arte Antica. This is housed in two buildings, with the larger part located at the Palazzo Barberini. The gallery contains beautiful *tromp l'oeil* frescoes as well as masterpieces by Rubens, Van Dyck, Murillo, Beato Angelico and Caravaggio.

Orto Botanico (Botanical Gardens)

Largo Cristina di Svezia 24,
off Via Corsini
06 499 17107, €2
map 8, E1; GPS 41.8924, 12.4661

09.00-18.30 Tue-Sat
(Oct-Mar to17.00)
closed public hols & Aug

Located just behind Palazzo Corsini, these botanical gardens have splendid collections of orchids and bromeliads, along with 7,000 other plant species. The garden is an oasis of peace and calm.

Monte Gianicolo (Janiculum Hill)

This is the tallest of Rome's hills, with a park offering many viewpoints and photo opportunities. To reach San Pietro in Montorio and the first viewpoint, start in Trastevere. Find Vicolo del Cedro (map 8, F2) and climb a set of steps to Via Garibaldi. Cross the street and look for steps on your right. This is a *passaggio pubblico* leading up the hill. Alternatively, catch bus 115 from Via Mameli (map 8, F3).

San Pietro in Montorio

Piazza San Pietro in Montorio 2
06 581 3940
09.00-12.00, 16.00-18.00 daily
map 8, E2; GPS 41.8881, 12.4665

Montorio is a reference to the fact that this was once thought to have been the location of St Peter's crucifixion before it was proven to have taken place at the Vatican. Inside, to the left of the entrance, is Bernini's *Tomb of Maria Raggi*.

Tempietto

Hidden away in a courtyard next door to the church is Bramante's round temple, inspired by the Tempio di Vesta in the Forum.

Fontana dell'Acqua Paola

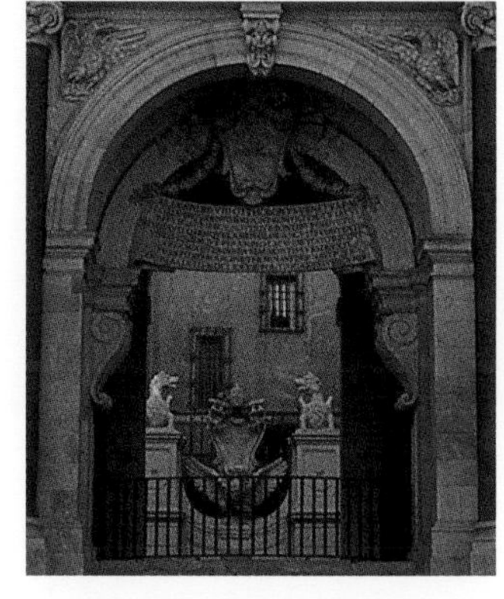

Begun in 1612 to mark the restoration of an aqueduct originally built by Emperor Trajan in AD 109, this fountain was renamed Paola after Pope Paul V (Borghese). Though the fountain is ornate, the tepid water supplied by the aqueduct is rated by Romans as only fit for bathing and washing vegetables.

Garibaldi

In 1849 Gianicolo was the scene of battles between Italian Republicans – led by Giuseppe Garibaldi – and the French. Garibaldi and his forces held out for weeks before surrendering. The general's tomb is located near the fountain. At the summit there are two Garibaldi monuments: one to Giuseppe and one to his wife Anita, located 100 yards away on Viale Aldo Fabrizi. On the base of Giuseppe's monument is the inscription: *Roma o Morte* (Rome or Death). There are good views over Rome and a café just off the piazza.

EXCURSIONS

CASTEL GANDOLFO

Getting there

Ostia: Metro to Piramide, then change for a train to Ostia Antica (30 min).

Colli Albani: To see all of the area, a car is recommended. There are trains from Termini to Castel Gandolfo and Frascati (30 min). COTRAL buses leave from Anagnina Metro station to all towns.

Tivoli: Metro Line B to Tiburtina (one stop past Bologna), then change for trains to Tivoli (40-60 min). From Tivoli, No. 4 bus leaves from Piazza Garibaldi for Villa Adriana. COTRAL bus leaves from Ponte Mammolo and Tiburtina, with stops at Villa Adriana.

Viterbo: Change at Metro Flaminia for trains from Roma Nord Viterbo, or depart from Termini and Ostiense (90 min).

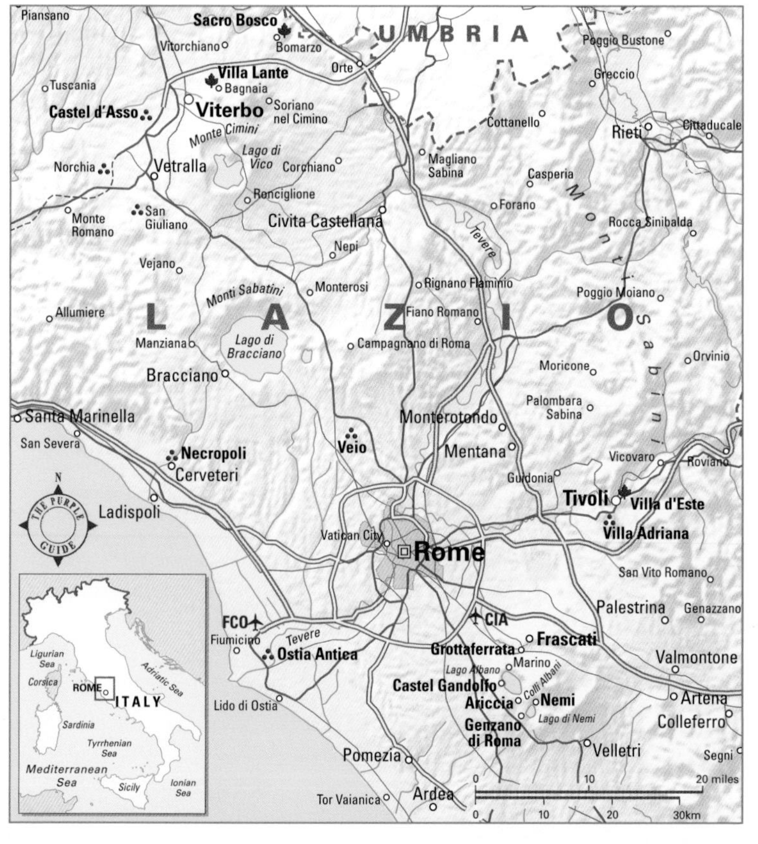

Ostia Antica

Viale dei Romagnoli 717,
Ostia Antica
06 563 58099, €4.50
www.itnw.roma.it/ostia/scavi

Apr-Oct 09.00-19.30 Tues-Sun
Nov-Mar 16.00
ticket office shuts 90 min before closing time

This ancient seaport, founded in 340 BC, was once the gateway to Rome. The ruins are impressive. You can see the remains of a forum, temples, baths and warehouses, a theatre and a well-preserved *thermopoleum* (drinking house). At its height, 80,000 people lived here. There's a lot to see, so it's best to make a day of it. A bar is on site, and food can be bought in the town. We highly recommend a visit to a restaurant in nearby Fiumicino.

Restaurant

Leonardo
(in the Courtyard Marriot)
Via Portuense 2468, Fiumicino
06 999 351
www.leonardorestaurant.it
€€€

It was a complete surprise to discover such a fine restaurant in a chain hotel. There are two menus: creative and traditional. In either case, the food will be superb, with service that is friendly and unpretentious. Have a cocktail in *The Glass*, the adjoining wine/sushi bar, where the manager has invented some astonishing drinks.

Colli Albani

South-east of Rome are two volcanic lakes set in the Alban Hills: Lago Albano and Lago di Nemi. Several attractive fortified towns are dotted around the area. From a distance they appear to be castles, hence the Italian nickname for the region: *Castelli Romani.* Romans have come here since ancient times because it is higher up, out of the heat, and less than one hour from the city.

Castel Gandolfo The first Roman settlers came from Alba Longa, founded in 1100 BC on a ridge of Monte Albano near present-day Castel Gandolfo. Above the shores of Lago Albano, the town is now the summer residence of the pope, with papal audiences held Wednesdays at 10am. The piazza has a fountain and a lovely church, both designed by Bernini. You can walk the 10km trail that circles the lake.

Grottaferrata

The 11th century Abbey of Grottaferrata has a beautiful and unusual Greco-Byzantine church, where Catholic services are held in Greek. The Abbey has a workshop for restoring old books and a museum to visit. There is a fine restaurant nearby.

Lago di Nemi

Emperors once held mock naval battles here. Today there is a small museum with two Roman ships. Situated high above the lake is the pretty town of **Nemi**, known for its tiny wild strawberries. Nearby **Genzano** has a medieval centre and the 17th century Palazzo Sforza Cesarini. **Ariccia** has a palace and church by Bernini.

Restaurant

Taverna dello Spuntino
Via Cicerone 22, Grottaferatta
06 943 15985
www.tavernadellospuntino.com
€€€

The Fortini family serve classic *cucina romana* in comfortable surroundings. The food is excellent, they do everything well and, if you ask, a member of staff will give you a tour of their extensive wine cellar.

Festivals

Nemi: *Sagra delle Fragole*, the strawberry festival (first Sunday in June).

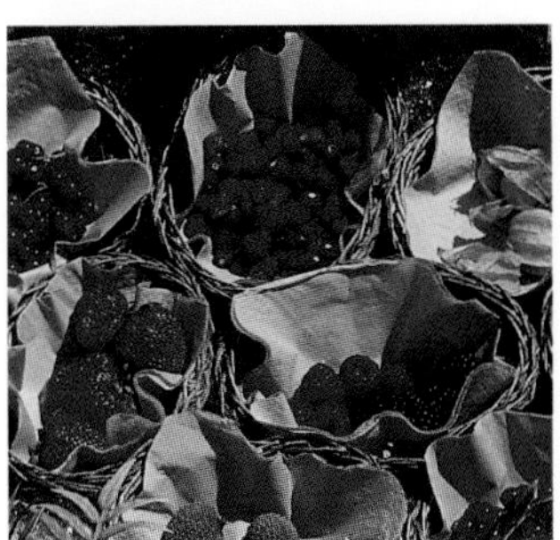

Genzano: *Infiorata*, when the streets are carpeted with paintings made of flowers (June, first Sunday after Corpus Domini). **Marino**: *Sangra del Vino*, a boisterous festival when the fountains flow with sweet white wine (first Sunday of October). **Ariccia**: the locals serve *porchetta* (slow-roasted piglet) with homemade bread, olives and cheese (September).

Villa d'Este

Piazza Trento 1
077 431 2070, €6.50

May-Sept: 09.00-18.15,
21.00-24.00 Tues-Sun
Oct-Apr: 08.30-16.00 Tues-Sun

The terraced gardens of Villa d'Este have more fountains than flowers – there are over five hundred of them. This is a lovely and cool place to spend an afternoon. Stroll along the *Avenue of the Hundred Fountains* and spend a restful moment at the *Oval Fountain*. Bernini contributed the *Fountain of the Goblet*. Children will enjoy watching the owls and birds sing at the *Fountain of the Owl,* and listening to the water organ play a tune at the *Fountain of the Water Organ*.

Originally a Benedictine convent, the villa was developed into a private residence by Cardinal Ippolito d'Este, son of Lucrezia Borgia and Alfonse d'Este, Duke of Ferrara. Lucrezia lived out her life in Ferrara and never visited Tivoli. Franz Liszt lived here briefly while he composed *Fountains of Villa d'Este.*

Restaurant

Sibilla
Via della Sibilla 50, Tivoli
lunch and dinner
0774 335 281
closed Mon
€€€
Located at the edge of a ravine, with a view of an ancient temple. Dine *al fresco* or choose the elegant dining room. Stick to the antipasti and primi and save room for dessert.

Villa Adriana

Via di Villa Adriana
Via Tiburtina 0774 382 733
09.00-1 hr before sunset daily
€6.50, last admission 90 min before closing

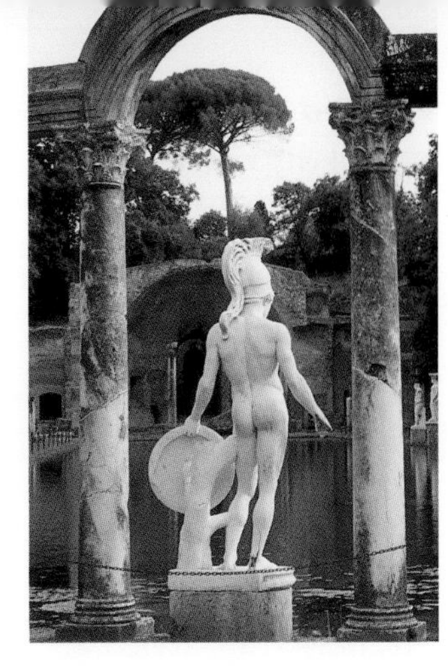

This was the private summer retreat of Emperor Hadrian who acquired the property in his wife's dowry. The architect Appolodorus began building in AD 118. The grounds cover an area of 120 hectares and the complex was more of a small city than a country villa. There were baths, theatres, kitchens, storehouses, barracks for the Imperial Guard, houses for members of court, and grand reception rooms and ballrooms. Today the grounds are a vast open-air museum. To fully appreciate the villa's former glory, be sure to study the scale model located in the building beside the car park. There is a small museum with busts of Emperors and their wives – it's interesting to follow the changing hairstyles.

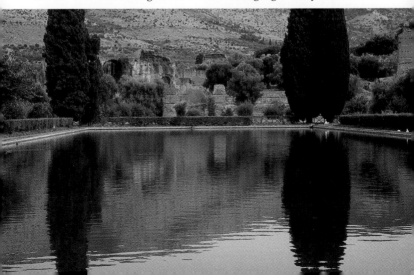

Viterbo

A small city with an interesting history, Viterbo has recently attracted artisans who have left Rome in search of lower prices. This is a good place to shop for ceramics, glass, jewellery and other handicrafts. There is a very attractive medieval quarter – the best-preserved in Lazio – and a lively *passeggiata* in the early evening, when it seems that all the citizens are out to see and be seen.

The papal seat moved to Viterbo in the 13th century when Rome became too dangerous. After the death of Clement IV in 1268, it took three years to elect a new pope. Locals finally locked the Cardinals in the first *conclave* (meaning 'with key') and made them live on bread and water until they elected Gregory X in 1271.

Shops & Restaurants

Artistica
Via S Pellegrino 8
0761 321971
Etruscan ceramics.

Gregorio Gala
Via Cavour 2
Beautiful hand-blown glass.

American Bar
Via della Sapienza 1
0761 220 953, closed Mon
Stylish bar, complimentary nibbles during aperitivo.

Taverna Etrusca
Via Annio 8-10
0761 226 694, closed Sunday
Interesting antipasti choices include buffalo meat. Try the pumpkin and bacon pizza.

Antico Caffè di Neri
Via Saffi 6
Historic cafè.

Villa Lante

0761 288088, located in Bagnaia, 5 kms east of Viterbo
09.00-17.30 in summer, 16.30 in winter, closed Monday

This is one of the most important Renaissance gardens in Italy, with fountains by Carlo Moderno. Cardinal Gambara (whose family symbol is a crayfish) commissioned the garden in 1560. There are two parts: woodlands and formal, symbolising the transition from chaos to order.

Sacro Bosco, Parco dei Mostri (Park of the Monsters)

0761 924 029, located near Bomarzo
08.30-dusk, admission free

An eccentric park with large stone sculptures (monsters) of giant gods and beasts set in the hillsides and grown over with moss. The figures were placed here by Vicino Orsini in 1542.

Necropoli

The area around Viterbo is known for Etruscan burial sites, the nearest of which is at Castel d'Asso, just down the road from the hot springs of Terme dei Papi.

Other sites are found at Norchia and San Giuliano.

PIAZZA
DI S. MARIA
snack gelateria
PARCHEGGIO
CANI
DOG
PARKING

FOOD & DRINK

CAFFÈ DI MARZIO, TRASTEVERE

Rome has always been a marketplace, with goods and people arriving from all parts of the world. Over time, several different culinary traditions have found their way into the Roman diet. Some are Italian and others, such as Jewish and Japanese, come from further afield.

Traditional *cucina romana* originated in the kitchens of the poor. Workers at the main slaughterhouse in Testaccio were paid in offal and unwanted animal parts like heads, tails and hooves. With little else to eat, they created dishes like *trippa alla romana,* tripe flavoured with spearmint and strong *pecorino* cheese. Recipes were handed down through the generations, each established the absolutely correct method for the preparation of a dish. Changes or variations were considered to be a form of heresy.

Romans who favour tradition are deeply suspicious of experimentation and the accompanying high prices found in restaurants that serve *cucina creativa* (creative cooking). There is a saying, *'più se spenne, peggio se magna'* (the more you spend the worse you eat). However, this second type of Roman cuisine is finding favour, particularly with younger people, as more restaurants take an imaginative approach to cooking by incorporating international influences and taking greater care with presentation.

Cucina gourmet refers to the cuisine found in many internationally recognised restaurants and Michelin-starred establishments. Often located in five-star hotels, these top restaurants have chefs who may be Swiss, French or German and their menus are more continental. After all, Rome is a capital city with local headquarters for major American and European corporations, and there is a steady stream of wealthy gastronomes arriving from abroad. The ordinary Roman will rarely, if ever, frequent these places.

For the average person, pasta and pizza are a big part of their diet. Different types of pasta are used with different sauces, again with accompanying rules to match. British tourists might be surprised to find that *spaghetti bolognese* (often called 'spag bol' in the UK) simply does not exist, either in Rome or elsewhere in Italy. The sauce that is used, *ragù bolognese*, is normally served with *tagliatelle* pasta or *gnocchi*. Spaghetti can be served *alla carbonara* (with a sauce of egg, *pancetta* and parmesan cheese) or *all'amatriciana* (with a sauce of pork cheek, tomato, chilli peppers and *pecorino* cheese).

Pizza is popular in Rome, but it does not have its origins here. Naples has that distinction. Flattened bread dough baked in a wood-fired oven was a peasant food until the 19th century, when a visit by Queen Margherita, wife of King Umberto I, inspired a new creation. The *pizza margherita* was created to correspond with the three colours of the new Italian flag: basil for green, tomato sauce for red and mozzarella for white. Today many Romans still favour their own style of pizza, thinner and flatter than the puffier Neopolitan version which has more cheese. Both kinds are found in Rome.

Usually a Roman restaurant will specialise in either meat or fish. The harbour at Ostia provided ancient Romans with good access to seafood: today there is a thriving fishing port in Fiumicino. Seafood *carpaccio*, commonly served as *antipasti*, consists of a selection of fresh raw fish, sliced very thin and sprinkled with salt and lemon. *Cucina creativa* sometimes has a Japanese influence, where seafood and vegetables are lightly battered and deep-fried in the style of *tempura*.

Many ingredients and dishes originate in Lazio, the region surrounding Rome. Others come from elsewhere in Italy: *bistecca alla fiorentina*, a *chianina* beef steak sliced thick and grilled rare, is from Tuscany; *cinghiale* (wild boar) usually stewed or made into ragù, originates in Umbria.

The Catholic calendar has also influenced Roman eating habits. It was forbidden to have meat on Fridays and on certain Holy days, resulting in a large variety of fish and meatless pasta dishes. The weekly dietary rhythm instituted by the church continues to be followed; many *trattorie* serve fish on Friday, tripe on Saturday and lamb on Sunday.

La Cucina Giudaico Romanesca

Roman Jewish Cooking *by Silvia Nacamulli*

Rome has the oldest Jewish community in the Western world. There has been a Jewish presence in Rome for more than 2,000 years. Throughout the centuries they came from many different regions, melding into a unique Jewish community. The result is one of the most delicious and interesting cuisines in the world.

The presence of Jews in Rome was registered as early as 200 BC, but the Jewish community really began in earnest around AD 70, when Romans brought thousands of Jews back to Rome as slaves after the destruction of the Second Temple in Jerusalem. Many more arrived after the Spanish Inquisition in 1492. With the expulsion edicts, tens of thousands were forced to flee the south of Italy, which was under Spanish rule at the time. At least 30,000 came from Sicily, which is almost the total number of Jews in the whole of Italy today. Others came from Puglia, Sardegna and Calabria. They all brought their own cooking traditions and ingredients.

Exotic flavours found their way into both savoury and sweet dishes. The classic Roman Jewish dish, *spinaci con pinoli e passerine* (sautéed spinach with pine nuts and raisins) is a good example of this (for a recipe, see p.255). Artichokes and aubergines were introduced along with new cooking methods, such as deep-frying. Traditional local dishes were adapted to conform to Jewish dietary rules (*Kasherut*), creating new and original recipes. For example, Roman Jewish cuisine is very famous for beef cold cuts like *coppiette, carne secca* and *salsicce*. These were clearly inspired by the traditional local pork cold cuts, forbidden under Jewish law.

From 1555, Roman Jews were confined in a *ghetto* for over 300 years. In this very small environment people developed a unique style of cooking. The ghetto in Rome was extremely poor, so it became necessary to make the most out of what people had. They used what I call 'inventive thriftiness' – taking parts of foods that others would throw away and making a meal out of them. For example, Jews in the ghetto created a new dish using lettuce stems. Called *testine*, it is made from braised endive stems seasoned with salt, pepper and vinegar.

Another example of creativity combined with necessity was the use of *carne allungata* (stretched meat). This is minced meat with other ingredients added – such as courgettes, carrots, celery and onions – in order to 'stretch it' to feed a larger number of people. A classic dish that is testimony to this is *zucchine ripiene* (courgettes filled with meat). There are also very typical Roman Jewish dishes that are made of fine and delicious cuts of meat such as the *abbacchio* (baby lamb), usually roasted and a real delicacy.

The most famous Roman Jewish dish of all is *carciofi alla giudia*. Made of deep-fried artichokes, each one looks like an open sunflower. It is crispy, light and so delicious that I truly believe it is worth a trip to Rome just for this dish.

Another traditional fried dish is the *fritto misto* (mixed fry). The recipe came from a time when ghetto street vendors known as *friggitori* would batter and fry a variety of vegetables – like artichokes, cauliflower, aubergines, courgettes and courgette flowers – and then mix them with fish, usually *baccalà* (cod) and anchovies.

With time, many of these dishes became an integral part of typical Roman cooking and they can be found today in most restaurants in the capital.

Silvia Nacamulli is an up-and-coming chef and teacher of Italian cooking based in London. She grew up in Rome, where she was taught by three generations of fine Italian Jewish cooks.

To learn more about Silvia visit www.cookingforthesoul.com

Dining in Rome

Romans start the day with a *cappuccino* or a *caffelatte* and a pastry. Italians insist that after about 10am, coffee should be an *espresso*. Those who must have milk can ask for a *macchiato* (espresso with a touch of milk) without embarrassment. Stand at the bar and drink your morning coffee, as it can cost an additional two or three euros to sit at a table. In some bars you pay first and then order.

Lunch can be substantial: a full meal will feature *antipasti* (starter), *primi* (first course) of pasta or rice, *secondi* (second course) of meat or fish, often served with *contorni* (side dish) of vegetables, followed by *dolci* (sweet) or fruit and finally coffee. The trend today is to have only one or two courses. The busy Roman who can't find the time for a traditional long lunch will often stop at a *tavola calda* for a quick meal. These establishments serve ready-cooked food to take away or eat in cafeteria style. Roman bakeries offer another quick lunch alternative.

Romans are very social and they will often stop for an *aperitivo* with friends after work. A glass of beer or wine ordered during the early evening will often be accompanied by a small selection of snacks: tiny pizzas or *bruschetta* with a few nuts and olives. There is no additional charge for the food, but sometimes the drinks may be slightly more expensive.

Dinner is served later at around 9pm. Many restaurants will not seat anyone before 8pm. You won't receive a warm welcome if you arrive early.

Coperto (a cover charge) is no longer allowed in Rome. Some restaurants may circumvent the law by charging a few euros for *pane* (bread). Romans don't tip, especially in family-run establishments. Often the tip is included in the total without being shown as a separate entry and certainly there is no harm in asking. As a rule, five to ten per cent extra is the correct amount to leave for good service.

Types of establishment

Ristorante

At the higher end of the price range and offering an extended menu. It has become popular for restaurants to call themselves *trattorie* to emphasize the fresh, home-cooked nature of their food.

Trattoria

Usually family-run and serving a limited daily selection, often written on a chalk board. In rural areas these may also be called *osteria* or *locanda*. Credit cards may not be accepted in smaller premises.

Tavola Calda

The name literally means 'hot table'. Offering a variety of pre-prepared dishes, these establishments are popular for lunch. Pasta, potatoes, roast chicken and salad are sold by weight. There is often a small seating area or you may eat standing at a bar or counter.

Bakeries

Rome has many good bakeries where you can buy a slice of pizza or a savoury tart to take away. These make for a nice inexpensive lunch, eaten sitting beside a local fountain or in a park.

Enoteca

A place to taste and purchase wine that often serves snacks.

Bar, caffè

An Italian institution that is usually only open during the day, serving coffee and pastries for breakfast, *panini* and sandwiches for lunch. Complimentary food may be offered with an *aperitivo* later in the afternoon. Bars often close at around 8pm.

Hotels

Many of Rome's top hotels have rooftop restaurants and cocktail lounges. The prices may be high but it's worth stopping in just for the view and a glass of wine or prosecco, often served with a selection of finger food, nuts and crisps.

Museums

Cafés and restaurants located in Roman museums are often better value than surrounding restaurants; many offer stunning views.

Coffee

Espresso short and black

Cappuccino espresso with frothed milk

Caffelatte hot milk with espresso added.

Caffè doppio a double measure of espresso

Caffè ristretto extra strong espresso

Caffè alto or *caffè lungo* with a little water added

Caffè macchiato espresso with a dash of milk

Latte macchiato a glass of hot milk with a splash of coffee

Caffè americano espresso with a lot of hot water added

Caffè estivo with whipped cream

Caffè freddo cold, sweetened black coffee

Cappuccino freddo iced coffee with frothed milk

Caffè corretto with a drop of brandy or grappa

Caffè cremina coffee and whipped sugar (tastes like a meringue)

decaffeinato decaffinated

bollente boiling (coffee is often served lukewarm)

Typical Roman Dishes

antipasti and vegetables

carciofi alla giudia whole artichokes, flattened and deep-fried

carciofi alla romana steamed artichokes stuffed with mint and garlic

carciofi fritti fried artichokes

filetti di baccalà salt cod fillets

zucchini con fiori fried courgette flowers stuffed with anchovies and mozzarella

ricotta al forno con fiori di zucchina baked courgette flowers stuffed with ricotta

la sagra del frittello fried cauliflower tops

pesce carpaccio thin slices of raw fish

primi

spaghetti alla carbonara with a sauce of egg, *pancetta* and parmesan cheese

bucatini all'amatriciana pasta tubes with *guanciale* (pork cheek), tomato, hot chillies and pecorino cheese

spaghetti alle vongole spaghetti with clams

rigatoni con la pagliata pasta with young lamb intestine

risotto alle fave risotto with broad beans

cacio e pepe pasta with pecorino cheese and black pepper

pomodori al riso baked whole tomatoes stuffed with rice

secondi

trippa alla romana tripe flavoured with spearmint and strong pecorino

fritta alla romana deep-fried mixed offal with artichokes

saltimbocca alla romana veal escalopes garnished with sage and ham

pollo alla romana chicken with tomatoes and wine

abbacchio alla scottadito grilled lamb chops

coscio di agnello roast leg of lamb

la vignarola artichoke and broad bean stew

spigola al sale salted sea bass

dolci

ciambelle al vino ring-shaped biscuits dipped in sweet wine

millefoglie filo pastry layered with cream and drizzled with chocolate

fragoline di Nemi con zabaglione Nemi strawberries and Marsala cream

Wine

In terms of volume of production, Italy stands beside France as a dominant player in the world wine market. But it has not always exported its best wine in large quantities. Those who have only drunk Italian wine from supermarkets at home are in for a surprise; the wine really is much better in Italy and it is constantly improving. This is partly because of the scale of production. A lot of Italian wine is made on family-run farms producing less than 10,000 bottles per year. Contrast this with Australia where four producers supply 80 per cent of that country's global exports. Mega-growers in France and California make large Italian producers such as Antinori, Farnese, Frescobaldi and Fontana Candida seem small by comparison. This is good news for wine drinkers who grow bored of wine that all tastes the same. The trend today is a return to the use of traditional Italian varietals, grown by small wineries experimenting with different blends.

Be advised that quality ratings are uneven in Italy. *DOC* wines are produced subject to specifications, but the rating does not always signify quality, which *DOCG* guarantees. *IGT* is a more recent classification intended to rate wines from good regions that do not meet DOC and DOCG qualifications. *Vino da tavola* means 'table wine' and these will vary considerably in quality. Some will be good and others should be avoided.

With competition from Piedmont and Tuscany, Lazio is not a wine region famous for its quality, especially with regard to reds. In fact, over 90 per cent of the local production is white wine, with Frascati being the most popular. Made from the *trebbiano* grape with a touch of added *malvasia*, the best Frascati is pale yellow, almost golden in colour, and tastes of whole grapes with a hint of celery. The leading vineyards are in Colli Albani near Grottaferrata, Marino and Frascati. Fontana Candida is a very good producer; try *Conte Zandotti*, *Villa Simone*, or *Santa Teresa*. Frascati is available dry and medium; the sweet version is known as *cannellino*.

Other regions of Italy promote wines that are made locally. Rome is much more liberal; the average list will include wines from all over the country. Remember that Italian wine is made to accompany Italian food. Just as there are rules for creating certain dishes – the correct ingredients and method of preparation, the right pasta for the sauce – there are wines that are better for each dish. Although some *trattorie* offer a limited selection, any restaurant with a good list will have wines that go well with the food they serve; ask your waiter for advice on the best choice.

Vino Santo A sweet wine often served with hard almond biscuits called *cantucci*. The *vino santo* produced in Lazio comes from the *aleatico* grape, a muscat-flavoured variety with a slight bouquet of musky rose. Aleatico di Gradoli is a top producer.

Prosecco A sparkling, dry white wine produced in Veneto, which has become popular throughout Italy. It has a light, fruity bouquet and is often enjoyed as an *aperitivo*. The best ones are *Prosecco di Conegliano-Valdobbiàdene (DOC)*. Prosecco is available in different styles: *secco* (dry), *amabile* (medium-sweet), or *frizzante* (semi-sparkling).

Grappa A strong brandy distilled from grape *pomace* – the skins and seeds of grapes left over after pressing for wine. Juniper berries or plums can also be used to make grappa. The best comes from Piedmont, Tuscany and Sicily. Be careful, grappa is extremely strong.

Limoncello Made with lemon peel and sugar, this is a digestive drink served after meals. A speciality of the south, it has a creamy refreshing taste much like sorbet. Limoncello is usually kept in the freezer and served very cold in specially chilled glasses. Beware, this sorbet has a kick: homemade varieties can be up to 95 proof.

Beer *Chiara* or *bionda* is a pale lager; *rossa* is more like a bitter with a reddish colour; *scura* is a darker beer similar to stout; *malto* is malt beer; *alla spina* is beer from the tap; *in bottiglia* means 'in the bottle'.

There are a lot of good restaurants in Rome but too many mediocre ones that get by on just the tourist trade. To be listed in The Purple Guide, restaurants must be special in some way, with good food and a friendly atmosphere. We don't like arrogant service even if it comes with a Michelin star or two. For this reason you may not find some restaurants that are listed in other guides. All establishments have been tried by the author or a member of our team. Our reviews are completely independent; we do not accept payment or discounts for our recommendations.

Restaurant Listings

Restaurants are listed according to price range, signified by the € symbol. Prices are average per person, for 2-3 courses including a glass of house wine. Listings are by district, in descending order of price. Restaurants and *trattorie* are listed first, followed by *enoteche* (wine bars). Cafés, bakeries and ice cream are next, with bars and nightclubs at the end of each section. Booking is recommended, especially for dinner.

€€€€	€75 and over
€€€	€40 - €75
€€	€20 - €40
€	€20 and under

SMOKING IS BANNED IN ALL BARS AND RESTAURANTS IN ITALY.

Cucina Gourmet

These famous restaurants are in a league of their own. Each one is located in a five-star hotel. Be prepared to spend upwards of €150 per person; the usual credit cards are accepted. Reservations are required, sometimes weeks in advance. Jacket and tie are obligatory. La Pergola, La Terrazza and Il Chiostro all have rooftop views.

La Pergola (Cavalieri Hilton)
Via Alberto Cadlolo 101
06 35091; off map
chef Heinz Beck
Rated as the number one restaurant in Rome and the second best in Italy.

La Terrazza (Hotel Eden)
Via Ludovisi 49
06 478 121; map 5, E1
chef Enrico Derflingher
Also offers a macrobiotic menu.

Le Jardin du Russie
(Hotel de Russie)
Via del Babuino 9
06 328 881; map 1, D5
chef Luigi Sforzellini

Sapori del Lord Byron
(Hotel Lord Byron)
formerly known as Relais le Jardin
Via G. Notaris 5
06 361 3041; off map
chef Michele Sonentino

Il Chiostro (Hotel Raphael)
Largo Febo 2
06 682 831 map 11, D1
chef Jean Francois Daridon

Centro Storico

L'Altro Mastai

Via Giovanni Giraud 53
(off Via dei Banchi Nuovi)
06 683 01296
closed Sun, Mon, closed Aug
credit cards accepted
map 11, B2
€€€€

Chef Fabio Baldassare mastered the art of cooking at *La Pergola.* Fabio's menu is imaginative: for starters he offers cold pea soup with tomato-filled wonton and for primi, spaghetti with rabbit and lobster. Mains cover a range of meats and seafood, all of them tastefully presented. Fabio's wine bar is next door and shares its cellar with the restaurant.

Il Gonfalone

Via del Gonfalone 7
06 688 01269
19.45-23.00 Tues-Fri
12.30-14.45,19.45-23.00 Sat
closed 2 wks Aug, closed Sun
credit cards accepted
map 11, A3
€€€

Marco Castaldo's restaurant is in a nice location at the north end of Via Giulia. The Chilean chef Victor Hugo creates some very delicious dishes: terrine of pistachio and tomato; linguine with scampi and olive; baccalà and spaghetti; lamb Provençal. You can order a *tutti piatti* for a taste of everything.

Santa Lucia

Largo Febo 12
06 688 02427
12.30-15.00, 20.00-midnight daily
credit cards accepted
map 11, D1
€€€

A stylish dining room serving modern cuisine. First courses include pasta with swordfish, mozzarella and figs; followed by sautéed octopus or herb-scented rabbit. Desserts are very good.

Il Buco

Via S. Ignazio 8
06 679 3298
12.00-15.00, 19.30-23.30 Mon-Sat
closed Sun
map 12, G2
€€

This Tuscan restaurant is 103 years old and still serving excellent food. Try *linguine al salmone* for primi and *cinghiale all'agrodolci* (wild boar in a bittersweet sauce) for secondi. A refreshing dolci is the *gelato affogato* (ice cream with liqueur). Service is prompt and friendly. The wine list offers Chianti and Montepulciano.

Vecchia Locanda

Vicolo Sinibaldi 2
06 688 02831
12.00-15.00, 19.00-23.00 Mon-Sat
closed Sun, credit cards accepted
map 12, E3
€€

Owner Giorgio Schicchi is passionate about food. He's been here for 12 years and his restaurant is always full. Be sure to try the *polpetto e patate* (tender baby octopus and spicy potatoes) for *antipasti,* followed by spaghetti with shrimp and courgettes. There is a large, reasonably priced wine list and the house Frascati is good. Tables spread out onto the pavement in summer.

La Reina

Vicolo di Montevecchio 2A
06 6830 9314

19.00-01.00, credit cards accepted
English menu available
map 11, C2
€€
Antonio and Alberto create a friendly ambience and serve an interesting menu: duck carpaccio; *orecchiette* pasta with clams and saffron; gilt bream with spinach and roasted sesame. The divine chocolate cake takes 20 minutes to prepare and is served hot. The décor is stylish with low lighting. Service is excellent.

Evangelista
Via delle Zoccolette 11A
06 687 5810
20.00-midnight Mon-Sat, closed Aug
map 11, D6
€€
A special place near Ponte Sisto serving delicious *carciofo al mattone,* artichoke flattened and cooked between two bricks.

Maccheroni
Piazza delle Coppelle 44
06 683 07895
13.00-15.00, 20.00-24.00 Mon-Sat
credit cards accepted, English menu
map 11-12, E1
€€
A local gathering place that serves good traditional food in a relaxed and cheerful way. Start with *bresaola* (thin slices of dried beef with rocket lettuce, *parmigiano* and walnuts). Pasta is their strength. A good choice is *trofie al tartufo nero* (pasta twists with truffle sauce), or *gricia* (with bacon, wine, and goat's cheese). Grilled steak is recommended. The house wine is adequate.

Taverna del Campo
Via del Pellegrino 163
06 686 1302
12.00-midnight daily, closed Tues
www.pierluigi.it (recipes online)
map 11, B3
€€
A brasserie serving well-prepared French style salads and seafood. Try *insalata catalana* with crab, lobster and *rughetta.* The menu

and wine list are extensive and the service is friendly.

L'Angoletto
Piazza Rondanini 51
06 686 8019
lunch and dinner, closed Mon
map 11-12, E2
€€
The house speciality, *moscardini* (deep-fried baby squid) is very good but the seafood antipasti is heavy on the vinegar.Try *spaghetti alle vongole* or lobster ravioli.

Alfredo e Ada
Via dei Banchi Nuovi 14
06 687 8842
lunch and dinner, closed w'ends
no credit cards
map 11, B2 (no exterior sign)
€
A small trattoria with eight tables. The fixed price menu for three courses changes daily depending on what Ada decides to cook.

Cul de Sac
Piazza Pasquino 73
06 688 01094
12.30-14.30, 19.00-23.00 daily
closed for lunch Mon
map 11, D3
€
This classic Roman *enoteca* is directly across from *Pasquino*. Wine lovers will appreciate the choice of more than 1,400 Italian and foreign wines. The menu offers an excellent selection of meats and cheeses.

Bhagavat Atheneum Cultural Library
Via Celsa 4-5 (Piazza del Gesu)
06 6781 427
12.30-20.00 Mon-Fri
map 12, F4
€
Excellent Indian vegetarian cooking and a quiet atmosphere in a busy part of town near Largo Argentina. You can drop in for buffet lunch or just a cup of tea.

Da Baffetto
Via del Governo Vecchio 114
06 686 1617
06.00-01.00 Mon-Sat, no credit cards
map 11, C3
€
A legendary pizzeria that is often crowded. Arrive before 19.30 to avoid the queue.

L'Insalata Ricca (2 branches)
Largo dei Chiavari 85-86
06 6880 3656
12.00-15.30, 16.30-23.30 daily
credit cards accepted
map 11, D4
€
Popular on a Sunday afternoon. They serve large bowls of salad, with more than 30 varieties. The service is fast and the salads are fresh and tasty. A real treat when you crave healthy vegetables.

L'Angolo Divino
Via dei Balestrari 12-14
06 6864 413
10.00-14.30, 17.00-02.00 daily
map 11, D4
This tiny enoteca just off Campo de'Fiori offers a great choice of wines by the glass. Light meals are available at lunchtime and in the early evening.

Cafés, bakeries & ice cream

Caffè Sant'Eustachio
Piazza di Sant'Eustachio 82
08.30-01.00 daily, closed 1 wk Aug
credit cards accepted
map 11-12, E3
This beautiful art nouveau coffee and pastry bar is tucked away in

a small piazza near the Pantheon. Their coffee is reputed to be the best in Rome, served sweetened unless you request *amaro*. There is an enormous variety of cakes, pastries and ice cream.

Chiostro di Bramante
Via della Pace
06 688 09098
map 11, C2
This museum cafè is on the left of Santa Maria della Pace. Relax in a cool, quiet atmosphere while you sip cocktails or enjoy a light meal.

Bar Tre Scalini
Piazza Navona 30
06 687 9148
12.00-15.00, 19.00-23.00
closed Wed
map 11, D2
Famous for the invention of the *tartufo*, a chocolate-covered ice cream ball with a cherry inside. Tre Scalini also serves standard fare for tourists.

Il Fornaio
Via dei Baullari 5-7
06 6880 3947
07.00-20.00 daily
map 11, D4
A bakery with savoury pastries, pizza and sandwiches. Pay for your selection at the cash before collecting your baked goods.

Il Forno
Campo dei Fiori 22
06 688 06662
08.00-14.00, 16.00-20.00 Mon-Sat
map 11, C4
The wood fires of this bakery turn out a best-selling *pizza rossa*, thin pizza dough covered with fresh tomato puree. *Pizza bianca* is a flat pizza bread with virgin olive oil and salt.

L'Antico Forno
Via della Scrofa 33
06 997 05346
map 11-12, E1
Located between the Pantheon and Piazza Navona this is the place to buy fresh, crusty white bread and a selection of *pizzette*: square sandwiches made with pizza bread and filled with ham and mozzarella. The *cantucci al miele* (honey biscuits) are excellent.

Giolitti Gelateria
Via degli Uffici del Vicario
06 699 1243
map 12, F1
Superior ice cream in a wide variety of flavours.

Mariotti
Via Agonale 5-7
06 681 36084
map 11, D2
This gelateria is popular with Italians who queue for their scoop of *nocciola* (hazelnut) ice cream.

Bars

Caffè della Pace
Via della Pace 3-5
06 686 1216
09.00-03.00 Tues-Sun,
15.00-03.00 Mon
map 11, C2
Tucked away near the church of Santa Maria della Pace, this is an excellent place to sit outside, have an *aperitivo* and watch the world go by. With an art nouveau interior, the bar dates from the early 20th century.

Bar del Fico
Piazza del Fico 26-28
06 686 5205
09.00-02.00 Mon-Sat
12.00-02.00 Sun
map 11,C2

Located in an old dairy that has been redecorated. Sip coffee or designer cocktails and indulge in excellent people-watching at one of Rome's chic hot spots.

Bar Daniele
Piazza Mattei
map 12, F5
The staff are friendly and they make good panini.

Nightclubs, music bars

Anima
Via S. Maria dell'Anima
34 785 09256
22.30-02.00 daily
map 11, D2
Busy cocktail/dance club off Piazza Navona.

Bloom
Via Teatro della Pace 29-30
06 688 02029
19.00-02.00, booking advisable
map 11, C2
'See and be seen' in this cocktail and sushi bar near Piazza Navona.

Jazz Café
Via Zanardelli 12
06 682 10119
12.00-03.00 Mon-Sat
€5-€8 admission Fri-Sat
map 11, D1
Cool modern décor and famous cocktails. Live jazz music.

Fluid
Via del Governo Vecchio 46-47
06 683 2361
18.00-03.00 daily
map 11, C2
This ultra-modern cocktail bar is decorated in a forest theme. Good snacks with your aperitivo and a lively after dinner scene.

Lot 87
Via del Pellegrino 87
06 976 18344
19.00-02.00 daily
map 11, B3
A lively modern bar. At *apertivo* buy cocktails for €5 and enjoy the snack buffet. Wireless internet is also available.

Ghetto

Da Piperno
Via Monte de'Cenci 9
06 688 06629
12.45-16.15, 20.00-22.15 Mon-Sat
closed Aug and Easter
credit cards accepted
map 11-12, E6
€€€
This long-standing restaurant is a bastion of traditional Roman Jewish cooking. For a starter, the *carciofi alla giudia* is perfect, or try the mixed platter with zucchini flowers and salt cod fillets. For *secondi*, a variety of lamb is available including *animelle con i carciofi* (lamb entrails with artichokes) for the more adventurous. Save room for the house dolci: *palle del nonno*, 'grandfather's balls' (pastry filled with ricotta and chocolate).

La Taverna del Ghetto
Via Portico d'Ottavia 8
06 688 09771
12.00-15.00, 19.00-01.00 daily
closed for dinner Fri and lunch Sat
credit cards accepted
www.latavernadelghetto.com
map 12, F6
€€€
Raffaele Fadlun and his wife Miriam Sonnino serve traditional dishes with a creative twist. The homemade pasta is fresh daily. Try *tonnarelli con carciofi romaneschi e bottarga* (pasta with artichoke and mullet roe). The lamb is personally selected by the Rabbi; the *scottadito* (grilled chops) are excellent.

Al Pompiere
Via Santa Maria dei Calderari 38
06 686 8377
12.30-15.00, 19.30-23.00 daily
closed Sun, closed mid Jul-Aug
credit cards accepted, English menu
map 11-12, E5 (no exterior sign)
€€
The restaurant is set on the spacious first floor of an old palazzo. Service can be careless but if you want traditional Jewish cooking at reasonable prices this is a good bet. Ask for a mixed plate of fried artichokes and stuffed zucchini flowers. For a secondi try baked lamb with artichokes, spinach and pinenuts. The homemade desserts are excellent (especially the ricotta and the almond cakes) and it is possible to order a taster plate of cakes to share.

Da Giggetto
Via del Portico d'Ottavia 21A
06 686 1105
12.00-15.30, 19.30-midnight Tues-Sun; closed first two weeks of Aug;
credit cards accepted, English menu
map 12, F6
€€
This family-run restaurant owned by the Catholic Ceccarelli family has been serving authentic Jewish cooking for 80 years. Located next to the ruins of Portico d'Ottavia, the restaurant is popular with tourists. Try the *carciofi alla giudia* for starters, followed by a salad and perhaps *abbacchio* (roast baby lamb). The outdoor terrace is pleasant on warm evenings.

Sora Margherita
Piazza delle Cinque Scole 30
06 687 4216
12.00-15.00 Tues-Fri and Sun
closed August, no credit cards
map 11-12, E6 (no exterior sign)
€

Locals come here for Gianna's fresh homemade *agnolotti* and Lucia's fried artichokes. The *cacio e pepe*, made with ricotta cheese, is excellent, as are the kosher veal sausages with polenta.

Cafés, bakeries & ice cream

Dolceroma
Via Portico d'Ottavia 20B
06 689 2196
08.00-13.30, 15.30-20.00 Tues-Sat
10.00-13.00 Sunday
closed August
map 12, F6

Traditional Jewish ricotta and cherry cheesecakes sit alongside Austrian strudels, Canadian-style muffins and American brownies.

Forno del Ghetto
Via Portico d'Ottavia 2
map 12, F6

This tiny corner bakery is well known for its ricotta and damson tarts.

Zi' Fenizia
Via Santa Maria del Pianto 64
06 689 6976
08.00-20.00 Sun-Thurs
08.00-15.00 Fri
map 11-12, E5

Rome's kosher pizzeria serves over 30 varieties of pizza-by-the-slice, all without cheese. Sandwiches and falafel are also served.

Pasticceria Boccioni
Via Portico d'Ottavia 1
06 687 8637
08.00-20.00 Sun-Thurs
08.00-17.30 Friday, closed Sat
map 12, F6

A cramped bakery with a 90-year tradition of making Jewish pastries and cakes. Especially delicious are the *torta ricotta vicciole* and *torta ricotta cioccolate.*

Capitolino

See Celio & Laterano for restaurants east of the Colosseum.

San Teodoro
Via dei Fienili 49-51
06 678 0933
12.00-15.00,19.00-00.30 daily
credit cards accepted
map 9, B2
€€€

Theo (above) offers a lunchtime *degustazione* menu of either meat or seafood at €45, excellent value with four courses and a glass of wine. Pasta is handmade by Theo's mother and the ravioli is especially tasty. For secondi try *coda di rospo* (angler fish with courgette flowers topped with a spicy sauce). Be sure to save room for *gelato di cassata* (a ricotta ice cream with nuts and dried fruit). The modern décor is cool and restful. A favourite.

Cafés, Bars

Caffè dei Musei Capitolini
Piazza Campidoglio
06 678 2862
09.00-18.00 Tues-Sat
map 12, H6
Pay extra for table service, so you can enjoy the panoramic view over Rome (pictured above). A ticket for the museum is not required.

Bar Ara Coeli
Piazza Venezia
open daily 24 hours
map 12, H4
Useful if you're out late, includes a tobacconist.

Vaticano

Il Simposio
Piazza Cavour 16
06 321 1502
13.00-14.30, 20.00-23.15 Mon-Fri
20.00-23.15 Sat, closed Aug
credit cards accepted
map 4, H2
€€€
This *belle époque* style restaurant specialises in meat dishes. A *foie gras* menu offers interesting choices including pear and fois gras pie. The attached enoteca provides 30 varieties of wine by the glass. Chocoholics will love the molten chocolate cake.

Taverna Angelica
Piazza Capponi 6
06 687 4514
12.00-14.30, 19.30-00.30 Tues-Sat
19.30-00.30 Mon, closed 2 wks Aug
credit cards accepted
booking essential
map 3-4, E2
€€€
With just 20 seats, this lively place offers a creative menu. Share one or two of the antipasti plates followed by a *primo* of risotto or cavatelli pasta with lamb and aubergine. For a main course try *turbot in cartoccio* (cooked in foil). Vintage wine is sold by the glass and there is a superior selection of cheeses. The homemade ice cream is delicious.

Enoteca Costantini
Piazza Cavour 16
06 320 3575
11.30-15.00, 18.30-01.00 Mon-Fri
18.30-01.00 Sat, closed Sun
closed Aug
credit cards accepted
map 4, H2 (connected to Il Simposio)
Piero Costantini selects the wines personally and offers 80 types of cheese as accompaniment.

Dino e Tony
Via Leone IV 60
06 397 33284
12.30-15.30, 19.30-23.00
map 3, C1
€
Two brothers serve classic *cucina romana* including an especially good *spaghetti all'amatriciana,* with *guanciale* made by their parents in Amatrice. Beware you don't fill up on *antipasti della casa* because Dino and Tony will insist you at least try a primo and then a secondo and then a dolce.

Enoteca Borgo Antico
Borgo Pio 21
06 686 5967
12.30-15.00, 20.00-24.00 Mon-Sat
closed 3 wks Aug
credit cards accepted
map 3-4, E2
A typical wood-and-brass style enoteca, offering a fixed price lunch with a primo, salad and glass of wine.

Cafés, bakeries & ice cream

Antonini
Via Sabotino 19-29
06 3751 7845
07.00-21.00 daily
credit cards accepted
map 4 (north of G1)
Posh Romans come here to buy fancy cakes and canapés. Indoor and outdoor seating is available.

Caffe Sant'Angelo
Lungotevere Castello 50
09.00-20.00 Tues-Sun
map 4, G2
This vine-covered restaurant at the top of Castel Sant'Angelo offers great views and good service.

Tridente

Ristorante Nino
Via Borgognana 11
06 679 5676
12.30-15.00, 19.30-22.30 Mon-Sat
closed August
credit cards accepted
map 5, C2
€€€
Serving Tuscan cuisine since 1934, the house specialties include *bistecca alla fiorentina, ribollita* (bread soup) and *pappardelle in sugo di lepre* (pasta with hare sauce). Unsurprisingly, the wine list features a large selection of Chianti and other Tuscan wines.

Il Margutta
Via Margutta 118
06 326 50577
12.30-15.30, 19.30-23.00 daily
credit cards accepted
map 2, D6
€€€
The English chef creates imaginative dishes in this vegetarian restaurant. The tempura is light and the *cannelloni di ricotta* fresh. A fixed price lunch is offered on weekdays and an all-you-can-eat buffet served at Sunday brunch.

La Buca di Ripetta
Via di Ripetta 36
06 321 9391
map 1, D6
€€
One of our favourites, it has a nice atmosphere with muted lighting and relaxed, efficient service. Diners are a mixture of locals and tourists. *Primi* include *risotto con funghi* and *spaghetti alle vongole*. The grilled fillet steak is excellent. For dessert the tiny

fragolini in season are absolutely delicious. Women will be impressed by the spa-like facilities.

Palatium
Via Frattina 94
06 692 02132
10.00-02.00 daily, booking essential
map 5, B2
€€
With a wine bar downstairs and a restaurant upstairs, Palatium is modern and smart, but the friendly staff ensure a relaxed atmosphere. The restaurant promotes products from the Lazio (Latium) region including the local wines. Beer is not served. Antipasti plates are large enough to share, try fresh tomatoes and *bufala* mozzarella. Primi and secondi are tastefully prepared versions of traditional cuisine. One of our editor's favourites.

'Gusto
Piazza Augusto Imperatore 9
06 322 6273
Pizzeria 12.30-15.00, 19.30-01.00
Ristorante 12.45-15.00, 19.45-24.00
brunch 12.00-15.30 Sat/Sun
Enoteca 11.00-02.00
Osteria 12.30-15.00, 18.45-24.00
www.gusto.it
map 5, A1
€€
A complex with a restaurant, pizzeria, wine bar, osteria and cook's shop. We recommend the €8 buffet lunch served on the ground floor. The food is very good and the price includes a beer (a glass of wine is €2 extra). Staff often bring out hot pizza and pies and you are permitted to sample late offerings. Service in the upstairs restaurant is uneven. The wine bar holds impromptu jazz sessions in the evenings.

Il Brillo Parlante
Via della Fontanella 12
06 324 3334
12.30-15.30, 19.30-01.00 Tues-Sun
credit cards accepted
map 1, D6
€
A cavernous cellar restaurant with a wood-burning pizza oven. Choose a light meal of pizza and pear and gorgonzola salad or have a primi of *tagliata di manzo* with rocket and cherry tomatoes. For dessert, try a tasty *tiramisù, millefoglie* or the cheese selection.

Edy
Vicolo del Babuino 4
06 360 01738
12.15-15.30, 18.30-24.00 Mon-Sat
credit cards accepted
map 1-2, E6
€
A family-run trattoria with soft lighting and a warm atmosphere. The house specialties are *spaghetti al cartoccio con frutti di mare* (spaghetti and seafood cooked in foil) and *fettuccine con ricotta e carciofi* (fettuccini with ricotta and artichokes). The pasta can be more *al dente* than you might like.

Al Gran Sasso
Via di Ripetta 32
06 321 4883
closed Sat
map 1, D6
€
The bright lighting is more than compensated for by good home cooking. The service is friendly and attentive and the prices are reasonable. The rabbit and red pepper stew is tasty as is the pumpkin risotto. Leave room for Mama's homemade apple cake, *torta di mela.*

Pizza's House al Corso
Via del Corso 51
06 323 0648
map 5, B1
€
The spelling of the name is not a mistake. This is a busy spot for lunch, offering *tavola calda* and several varieties of pizza piled high with toppings. The food is fresh and tasty and there is a small eating room at the back. Friendly service.

Enoteca Buccone
Via di Ripetta 19
06 361 2154
09.00-20.30 Mon-Thurs
09.00-24.00 Fri-Sat
closed 3 wks Aug
credit cards accepted
map 1, D6
This antique wine bar has authentic marble-topped inlaid wooden counters and an 1896 cash register. The bar belongs to the Association of Historic Shops in Rome (p.160) and is a good place for a light lunch. They offer a meat and cheese sampling platter and staff will gladly match your wine to your food.

Obika
Piazza di Firenze
06 683 2630
10.00-24.00 daily
map 5, A3
A mozzarella bar with Japanese décor. They serve many varieties of cheese in addition to cold meats and primi of pasta or gnocchi. We recommend the tasting plate of four *bufala* cheeses, combined with a glass of wine from an extensive selection.

Caffè Notegen
Via del Babuino 159
06 320 855
map 5, B1
An historic cafè, Notegen has been in business since 1882.

Bars

Hassler Hotel
Piazza Trinità dei Monti 6
06 678 9991
credit cards accepted
map 5, C2
A comfortable piano bar on the ground floor is good for quiet conversation and a light meal. Drinks are served with complimentary snacks.

Hotel d'Inghilterra
Via Bocca di Leone 14
06 699 811
credit cards accepted
map 5, B2
Decorated like a traditional Englishman's club. Voted one of the best bars in Italy by Gambero Rosso.

Rosati
Piazza del Popolo
06 322 5859
07.45-23.30 daily
credit cards accepted
map 1, D5
Rosati's is the place to people watch; we especially enjoyed observing a pretty blonde persuade her much older lover to spend money he clearly didn't want to spend.

Vitti
Piazza di S. Lorenzo in Lucina 33
06 687 6304
07.00-22.00 daily
map 5, B2
This bar is a lovely place to sit outside and relax. Vitti serves a selection of fresh salads for lunch and tasty little snacks for aperitivo. The coffee here is especially good as is the Sicilian *cassatina*, made with marzipan, ricotta and chocolate chips.

Bar Tritone
Via del Tritone 144
map 5, D3
Good sandwiches and a place to sit down with waiter service.

Cafés, bakeries & ice cream

Antico Caffè Greco
Via Condotti 86
06 679 1700
08.00-20.30 daily, closed 1 wk Aug
map 5, C2
This famous café was founded in 1760 and strategies to oppose Napoleon were planned at its tables. At various times Shelley, Byron and Goethe stopped in for coffee. Today occasional literary and musical evenings provide a glimpse of its illustrious past.

Ciampini
Viale Trinità dei Monti
06 678 5678
summer:
08.00-01.00 Tues, Thurs-Sun
winter: 08.00-20.00
map 5, C1
Set in a vine-covered patio with great views towards St Peter's, the atmosphere is pleasantly relaxed. This is a good place to bring children, as there is a small

pond with turtles. The restaurant is *al fresco* at the moment, but there are plans to enclose part of it. Service is friendly and the chips are excellent.

Dolci & Doni
Via delle Carrozze 85A
06 6992 5001
09.00-24.00 daily, closed 2 wks Aug
credit cards accepted
map 5, B2
This is a very expensive *pasticceria* and restaurant but the cakes are stunning, especially the *millefoglie.*

Canova-Tadolini Museum
Via del Babuino 150A
06 321 10702
10.00-19.30, closed Sun
map 5, B1
An elegant coffee bar set in a sculpture studio displaying copies of the great masters. Also serves light meals and desserts in the upstairs seating area.

Le Pain Quotidien
Via Tomacelli 24-25
06 6880 7727
09.00-24.00 Tues-Sun
map 5, A2
A bakery/restaurant with authentic rye bread and moist blueberry muffins. Brunch is served at weekends.

Borghese

Caffè delle Arti
Via Gramsci 73
06 326 51236
12.00-15.00, 19.00-00.30 Tues-Sun
12.00-15.00 Mon
credit cards accepted
map 1-2, E3
The café is located next to the Galleria d'Arte Moderna. In this grand vaulted room, with *putti* floating around the ceiling, you might be forgiven for thinking you have stumbled into an exclusive eatery – until you spot the local on-site workmen waiting for their takeaways. They serve light lunches or full meals in a relaxed and friendly manner.

International Wine Academy of Rome
Vicolo del Bottino 8
06 699 0878
www.wineacademyroma.com
map 5, C1
The only wine academy in all of Italy was established in 2002 by Roberto Wirth, owner of the Hassler Hotel. Tastings of four wines are offered daily in the wine bar from 18.00-19.00 for €20 per person. The academy is located in the Palazzetto, which also contains a hotel and an excellent restaurant.

Il Palazzetto
06 699 341005
12.30-14.30, 19.30-23.00 daily
closed weekends
map 5, C1
€€€
Chef Antonio Martucci creates a seasonal menu with unexpected takes on traditional cooking. Some of the more interesting items include: a starter of rosemary-flavoured salt cod with pistachio bread and truffles; a primo of roasted prawns wrapped in pasta and served with cucumber mint gazpacho; secondo of sautéed veal fillet with black truffle sauce and crunchy bacon and aubergine timbale. Desserts are creative and outstanding.

Quirinale & Esquilino

I rang the bell at Agata e Romeo a full hour early for my lunch booking. I had tried and failed to change hotels because a *manifestation* made it impossible. So there I was, standing at Agata's door with my bags, tripod, pillow and laptop. Agata answered and ushered me into her tiny restaurant, removed my collection of things to a safe place and bid me to return in an hour.

I had to wait a long time for my companion (delayed by the manifestation). Romeo brought me a glass of *prosecco* and we laughed at Roman life, my stress soon evaporating in the presence of his warm hospitality. My companion arrived and we enjoyed a leisurely lunch, stayed past closing and had a long chat with Agata and Romeo.

Agata e Romeo is located in the trattoria that once belonged to Agata's father. Agata grew up in the kitchen and has always loved to cook. She and her husband Romeo took over the family business in 1980. Romeo is a talented host and sommelier who has assembled one of the best wine cellars in Rome. Daughter Maria Antonietta selects the cheeses.

Agata is credited with bringing *haute cuisine* to Rome.

Agata e Romeo
Via Carlo Alberto 45
06 446 6115
13.00-15.00, 20.00-23.00 Mon-Fri
closed Sat, Sun, 2 wks Aug
book well in advance for dinner
credit cards accepted
map 6, H5
€€€€

The menu changes according to what inspires Agata. You might start with a flan of aged *soghano pecorino* with pear sauce and honey, followed by *risotto* with pumpkin and scallops wrapped in *pancetta*. A main course could be lamb fillet with pinenuts, raisins and wild chicory strudel, or pigeon with brandy and *cassis* sauce. Agata's *millefoglie* is so special that the recipe is under copyright protection. There is a *degustazione* menu of two complete meals with wine: *cucina romana* (€85) and *Agata's selection* (€135) or you can order from the menu.

Papok
Salita del Grillo 6B
06 699 22183
12.00-14.30, 19.30-23.00 Tues-Sun
credit cards accepted
booking advisable
map 5, D6
€€
Our Roman correspondent recommends this pretty restaurant. Fish is the house specialty: try squid with courgettes or linguine with swordfish and aubergines. There is also a choice of meat and vegetable dishes. Desserts include tiramisù and good cakes.

Santa Cristina
Via della Cordonata 21-22
06 699 25485
lunch and dinner
closed Sunday
map 5, D5
€€
Hidden away on a tiny street is this restaurant where parents cook and their grown children serve. Specialty primi include: lasagne made with gruyere cheese and onion; penne with vodka sauce; seafood risotto and pepper steak or chicken with gorgonzola for secondi.

Trattoria Monti
Via di San Vito 13
06 446 6573
lunch and dinner daily
closed Mon & Sun eve
closed August
credit cards accepted
map 6, H6
€€
The Camerucci family specialise in dishes from Le Marche with an emphasis on meat. Try the *timballo di coniglio con patate,* rabbit casserole with potatoes. The house white is a good Verdicchio and service is friendly.

Nanà
Via della Panetteria 37
06 691 90750
lunch and dinner
map 5, D3
€
You will receive a warm welcome from the Neopolitan owner of this trattoria near Trevi fountain. Chef Giuseppe Ruotolo creates interesting dishes that have Italian women asking for the recipe. The *tortino di patate* (a variation on lasagne made with potatoes) is a house favourite. Prices are reasonable and the house wine is a bargain.

Vineria Monti DOC
Via Giovanni Lanza 93
06 487 2696
lunch and dinner
map 6, G6
€
Raffaella's trattoria has a convivial atmosphere with good music on the stereo. The simple blackboard menu changes daily and often includes a North African dish. A variety of Tuscan wines are available by the glass to accompany the well-prepared food. Try the warmed apple strudel for dessert.

Enoteca Cavour 313
Via Cavour 313
06 678 5496
12.30-14.30, 19.30-00.30 Mon-Sat
closed Aug
credit cards accepted
map 6, F6
Sample wine, cheeses and meats from all of Italy's regions. Opening hours are unpredictable.

Al Vino al Vino
Via dei Serpenti 19
06 485 803
11.30-13.30, 17.00-24.30 daily
map 5-6, E6
A small wine bar with a friendly atmosphere and a choice of more than 500 wines. The real specialty of the house is a selection of grappa and other distilled spirits. Light meals are served, including a tasty *parmigiana di melanzane,* aubergine with parmesan.

Enoteca Trimani
Via Cernaia 37
06 446 9661
map 6, H2
The Trimani family have been serving wine in these large premises since 1876 and the counter is still the original Carrara marble. They have excellent soups, salads and crostini. Located just north-east of Termini, this enoteca is one of the few places to relax near the train station.

Cafés, bakeries & ice cream

Panella
Via Merulana 54
06 487 2812
map 6, H6
Since 1920, the Panella family has been baking over 80 varieties of bread from regions around Italy.

Regoli
Via Statuto 60
06 487 2812
map 6, H6
Carlo and his wife Laura specialise in cakes made with cream or cheese. Try the *torta ai frutti di bosco,* a ricotta cheesecake with wild strawberries, or indulge in a slice of the delicious chocolate profiterole cake. The *millefoglie* is superb.

Palazzo del Freddo di Giovanni Fassi
Via Principe Eugenio 65-67
06 446 4740
12.00-24.00
map 6, east of I6
Founded in 1880, this parlour has become an institution and some claim it serves the best ice cream in Rome. Try the *ninetto,* a confection of chocolate and cream, or one of the fresh fruit sorbets.

Celio & Laterano

Crab
Via Capo d'Africa 2
06 772 03636
13.00-15.00, 20.00-23.30 daily
closed Sun & Mon lunch
closed 3 wks Aug, 2 wks Dec-Jan
credit cards accepted
map 9-10, E3
€€€
The restaurant is located close to a busy intersection near the Colosseum and it is easy to walk by the plain entrance. Inside is a cool, peaceful haven with a welcoming host, Giuseppe Tontorelli. Popular with oyster lovers, Crab offers a selection of three different varieties served fresh on the half shell. The lobster ravioli is homemade and stuffed full of lobster, served with a chilli sauce and topped with more chunks of tender lobster. Crab is perfect for a long lunch after a morning's sightseeing in the Forum.

Luzzi
Via San Giovanni in Laterano 88
06 709 6332
lunch and dinner
map 10, F3
€€
Located near San Clemente, Luzzi offers a choice of Roman specialties or pizza. For antipasti try the seafood *carpaccio,* perhaps followed by cold pasta with chopped tomatoes, basil and mozzarella. For secondi try *abbacchio al forno* (roast lamb) with potatoes or *scaloppine alla pizzaiola.*

Le Naumachie
Via Celimontana 7
06 700 2764
map 10, F3
€
A reasonably priced trattoria popular with locals. The menu is limited to pasta dishes and grilled meats. House favourites include the *tagliatelle alle naumachie* and *bucatini all'amatriciana.*

GIUSEPPE TONTORELLI AT CRAB

Enoteca Divinare
Via Ostilia 4
06 709 6381
map 9-10, E3
An intimate wine bar serving a vast selection of top-quality wines and a sophisticated array of cold dishes, cheeses and salami. The splendid coffee is made using an antique machine still in excellent working order. The bar also sells delicious pralines.

Enoteca Il Tajut
Via di San Giovanni in Laterano 244
347 883 7574
map 10, G3
Here you may sample products from Fruili including: Pinot Grigio wine; San Daniele *prosciutto;* and Moretti beer.

Cafés, bakeries & ice cream

Caffé Caffé
Via S.S Quattro 44
06 700 8743
10.00-02.00 daily
map 10, F3
A café that is open late and offers something for everyone: the best pastries for breakfast; over 60 varieties of tea; wine by the glass served until 2 am; light meals with a Spanish or Greek influence.

San Crispino
Via Acaia 56
06 704 50412
closed Tuesday
overview map G6
The limited selection of ice cream is made with organic ingredients including one flavour made using Sardinian honey. Ice cream is served in cups because cones contain artificial flavours and preservatives.

Aventino

There are no restaurants on the Aventine.

Testaccio

Checchino dal 1887
Via Monte Testaccio 30
06 574 3816
12.30-15.00, 20.00-23.30
closed Sun, Mon, closed August
credit cards accepted
booking advisable
overview map D6
€€€€
This Testaccio institution is owned by the Mariani family and is located across from the old slaughterhouse. The menu is strictly *cucina romana*, serving traditional specialties (with offal), but there is also *penne arrabiata* and *bucatini all'amatriciana* for the less adventurous. Service is exceptional.

Agustarello
Via Giovanni Branca 100
06 574 6585
12.30-15.00,19.30-23.30
closed Sun
no credit cards, booking advisable
map 8, H6
€€
The décor may be basic but the food is good. Augustarello specialises in *cucina romana* but also offers an excellent *tonnarelli cacio e pepe* (with cheese and pepper) and *involtini con il sedano* (veal rolls stuffed with celery).

Felice
Via Mastro Giorgio 29
06 574 6800
12.15-14.30, 20.00-22.30 daily
closed Sun, closed August, cash only
map 8, H6
€
Felice is like Basil from Fawlty Towers. You must ask nicely to be admitted or he will point to the bogus reserved signs he keeps on the tables. If Felice likes the look of you, he will remove a sign with a flourish and serve you a fantastic meal of authentic *cucina romana* for a bargain price. Felice's is especially popular at lunchtime with shoppers and stallholders from the nearby Testaccio market. The *straccetti* (strips of beef) are highly recommended.

Acqua e Farina
Piazza O. Giustiniani 2
06 574 1382
19.30-23.30 daily
overview map D6
€
Find this modern pizzeria/ ristorante near the cemetery in Testaccio. It specialises in mini-pizzas that you choose like *tapas*. The pizzas are small because yeast is not used; everything is made with flour and water (hence the name). A break from the ordinary with nice bread, good desserts, a friendly staff and lots of young people.

Cafés

Volpetti
Via Volta 8
06 574 4305
map 8, I6
An offshoot of Volpetti's famous delicatessen in Via Marmorata, this small café serves tasty snacks and lunches using ingredients sourced from the deli.

Trastevere

Sabbatini
Piazza Santa Maria in Trastevere 13
06 581 2026
12.30-14.30, 19.45-21.30 daily
closed 2 wks Aug
credit cards accepted
booking advisable
map 8, G2
€€€
Our wine expert recommends this restaurant located on the piazza. House specialties are pasta: *spaghetti alle vongole* or *tagliatelle con porcini*. Be aware that grilled sea bass and *bistecca alla fiorentina* are sold by the gram and can be expensive. Service is attentive and there is a good wine list.

Le Mani in Pasta
Via dei Genovesi 37
06 581 6017
lunch and dinner daily
closed Mon
credit cards accepted
booking is essential
map 8, H3
€€
Locals queue outdoors in the rain for a table in this trattoria specialising in seafood. Start with the super-fresh *antipasto di mare* (seafood *carpaccio*) and you must have *spaghetti alle vongole* – Romans claim this is the best in town. The primi are generally better than secondi but the *tagliate di fileto di manzo* (beef fillet) is very good. Open Sunday lunch.

Osteria della Gensola
Piazza della Gensola15
06 583 32758
12.30-15.00, 19.30-24.00 Mon-Sun
closed Saturday lunch
closed 2 wks Aug
credit cards accepted
map 8, H2
€€
A Sicilian family-run restaurant serving fresh seafood. Try *insalate di mare* (seafood salad delicately flavoured with orange), or *fritti gamberi e calamari* (deep-fried prawns and squid). Other delicacies include *spiedino misto* (mixed seafood kebab) and the *verdure di stagione grigliate* (grilled aubergine and courgette with sautéed *radicchio*). The house Pinot Grigio complements the seafood perfectly. An outdoor eating area is situated on a busy corner with traffic.

Arco di San Calisto
Via Arco di San Calisto 45
06 581 8323
lunch and dinner
credit cards accepted
map 8, G2
€€
Located just off Piazza di Santa Maria in Trastevere, this restaurant has an outdoor garden terrace that offers a pleasant place to sit, with tables that aren't too close together. The cuisine here is fairly standard and secondi are better than primi; the *vitello al limone* was light and delicate. Wine is not sold by the glass.

Antica Pesa
Via Garibaldi 18
06 580 9236
lunch and dinner, closed Sun
map 8, F1
€€
This long-established restaurant was famous in the 60s. It serves traditional Roman fare in a comfortable atmosphere and the word is that Robert De Niro eats here when he's in town.

Alle Fratte di Trastevere
Via delle Fratte di Trastevere 49-50
06 583 5775
12.30-15.00, 18.30-01.30 daily
closed Wed
credit cards accepted
map 8, G3
€€
A good basic trattoria that has something to satisfy everyone: well-prepared pizzas, pasta and steak. Service is friendly and the staff speak English.

da Augusto
Piazza de Renzi 15
12.00-15.00, 20.00-23.00 Mon-Sat
closed mid Aug-mid Sept
map 8, F2
cash only
€
This busy working-class trattoria serves tasty daily specials at reasonable prices. Seating is crowded and the bill is written on the paper table coverings.

L'Insalata Ricca
Via G. C. Santini
06 588 1301
map 8, H3
€
The Trastevere branch of the chain (p.233).

Enoteca Ferrara
Piazza Trilussa 41A
06 583 33920
10.00-15.00, 17.30-02.00
book for dinner
map 8, G1
The Paolillo sisters have a substantial cellar with more than 850 wines and they also serve excellent meals in the back garden. Take home a gift-boxed, 100-year-old bottle of balsamic vinegar or choose from a variety of capers, olives, pesto and

tomato sauces.

Enoteca Trastevere

Via Lungaretta 86
06 588 5659
17.00-02.00 Mon-Sat
16.00-01.00 Sun, closed 3 wks Jan
credit cards accepted
map 8, G2

Stacked floor to ceiling with bottles of wine, including a vintage Barolo, that can be ordered by the glass. This a popular meeting place that sometimes hosts live music. Trays of assorted cheeses and crackers make a nice accompaniment to the wine.

Bars

dell'Arancia

Piazza Santa Maria in Trastevere 2
338 110 8064
credit cards not accepted
10.00-01.00 daily
map 8, F2

The exterior is decorated with mounds of oranges piled high in baskets and terracotta pots. Enjoy an aperitivo while watching the local children play near the fountain. Try the house special: Campari and orange served in a giant crystal flute.

Cafés, bakeries & ice cream

Lettere Caffè

Via S. Francesco a Ripa 100
06 5833 9379
also at:
Via del Moro 40
www.letterecaffe.org
map 8, G4

Known locally as the writer's café, this is a delightful spot, decorated in a beatnik, shabby-chic style. Choose from a wonderful selection of drinks: teas served in miniature teapots on top of their own cups, speciality hot chocolates, or alcoholic beverages. There is free entertainment every evening, ranging from jazz to eastern European folk and poetry readings. Check their website for listings or come along and be surprised. Light meals are served including a fixed price menu on Sunday evening. This includes a choice of three dishes at €7. The polenta with a sauce of porcini mushrooms is delicious.

Caffè di Marzio

Piazza Santa Maria in Trastevere 15
06 581 6095
07.00-02.00 Tues-Sun
map 8, G2

Catch a ray of morning sun at this bar located on the piazza with a view of the fountain and the church. Sitting outside is costly but worth it.

Bibli

Via dei Fienaroli 28
06 588 4097
11.00-24.00 Tues-Sun
17.30-24.00 Mon
www.bibli.it
map 8, G3

Tucked away in the heart of Trastevere this bookshop has a great café that is easy to miss from the outside. Bibli serves lunch and dinner daily and a buffet brunch on Sunday from 12.30-15.00 when you may eat as much as you want for around €16. There is also a pleasant courtyard terrace. Homemade cakes, coffee, tea and drinks are served throughout the day.

Menu reader

Italian-English
con, alla refers to how meals are prepared and/or the type of sauce

A

abbacchio alla scottadito grilled lamb chops
acciughe sott'olio anchovies in oil
aceto vinegar
acqua water
affettato misto cold sliced meats
aglio garlic
agnello lamb
coscio di roast leg of lamb
al forno baked
albicocca apricot
amatriciana guanciale (pig's cheek), tomato and hot chillies
ananas pineapple
anatra duck
anguilla eel
antipasti starters
aragosta lobster
arancia orange
aringa herring
arrosto roast
asparagi asparagus

B

baccalà dried cod
bagnacauda raw vegetables in oil & lemon
basilico basil
baverese ice-cream cake with cream
birra beer
bistecca beef steak
bollito boiled
braciola di maiale pork steak
brodo clear broth
bruschetta bread slices rubbed with oil
burro butter

C

cacciatora with a red wine and mushroom sauce
cacio e pepe pasta with pecorino cheese and black pepper
caffè coffee
calamari squid
calda hot
calzone folded pizza
canella cinnamon
cannelloni stuffed pasta
cappelle di funghi mushroom caps
capretto kid, goat
carbonara with eggs and pancetta
carciofi artichokes
alla giudia flattened and deep-fried
alla romana steamed and stuffed with mint and garlic
fritti *fried*
carne meat
carote carrots
carpaccio sliced raw meat or fish
carré di maiale pork loin
castagne chestnuts
cavoletti di Bruxelles brussels sprouts
cavolfiore cauliflower
cavolo cabbage
cefalo mullet
cernia grouper
cicoria chicory
ciliege cherries
ciambelle al vino ring shaped biscuits
cime di rapa sprouting broccoli
cinghiale wild boar
cioccolata chocolate
cipolle onions
coniglio rabbit
contorni vegetables
coperto cover charge
cotoletta veal, pork or lamb chop
cozze mussels
crema custard
crespelle pancake
crostata tart
crostini bread rounds

D

datteri dates
degustazione tasting
diavola deep fried
digestivo liqueur or grappa

F

fagioli beans
fegato liver
fettuccine pasta
fichi figs
formaggi cheese
fragole strawberries
fragoline di Nemi con zabaglione Nemi strawberries and Marsala cream
frittata omelette
fritta alla romana deep fried mixed offal with artichokes
fritto misto mixed fried seafood
frullato milkshake

frutta fruit
frutti di mare mixed seafood
funghi mushroom

G

gamberetti shrimp
gamberi prawns
gazzosa lemonade
gelato ice cream
gnocchi potato pasta
gnocchi alla romana made with semolina and baked
gorgonzola blue cheese
granchio dressed crab
granita a drink with crushed ice
grigliata grilled

I

indivia endive
insalata salad

L

lasagne layered pasta
latte milk
lattuga lettuce
legumi legumes
lenticchie lentils
lepre hare
limone lemon
lingua tongue

M

maiale pork
mandorla almond
manzo beef
marroni chestnuts
marsala sweet wine
marzapane marzipan
mascarpone cream cheese
mela apple
melanzane aubergine
melone melon
menta mint
meringhe meringue
merluzzo cod
millefoglie al cucchiaio mille feuille, pastry layered with cream
minestrone vegetable soup
mozzarella soft white cheese

N

nocciole hazelnuts
noci walnuts
nodino veal chop

O

olio oil
origano oregano
ostriche oysters

P

pagliata (pajata) young lamb intestine
pancetta bacon
pane bread
panino filled roll
panna cream
pasta noodles
patate potato
pecorino sheep cheese
penne pasta quills
peòci mussels
pepe pepper
peperoni peppers
peperoni ripieni stuffed peppers
pera pear
pesca peach
pesce fish
carpaccio thin slices of raw fish
piselli peas
polenta cornmeal
pollo chicken
alla romana with tomatoes and wine
polpette meatballs
polpettone meatloaf
pompelmo grapefruit
pomodori tomatoes
al riso baked whole tomatoes stuffed with rice
porri leeks
prezzemolo parsley
primi piatti first course
prosciutto cured ham
prugne plums
puré di patate mashed potatoes

Q

quaglie quails

R

radicchio chicory
ragù tomato sauce with meat
rapa white turnip
rapanelli radishes
ravioli stuffed pasta
razza skate
ricotta cottage cheese
ricotta al forno con fiori di zucchina baked courgette flowers stuffed with ricotta
rigatoni ribbed pasta tubes
ripieni stuffed
riso rice
risotto rice dish
alle fave risotto with broad beans
rosmarino rosemary

S

sagra del frittello fried cauliflower tops
salame salami
sale salt

salmone salmon
salsiccia sausage
saltimbocca alla romana veal escalopes stuffed with bacon
salvia sage
sarde sardines
scaloppine veal escalop
sgroppino dessert of lemon sorbet, vodka and prosecco
sedano celery
senape mustard
seppie cuttlefish
servizio service
sogliola sole
speck smoked ham
spezzatino stew
spigola al sale salted sea bass
spinaci spinach
stracchino soft cheese
stracciatella soup with beaten eggs
succo juice

T

tacchino turkey
tagliata finely sliced beef fillet
tagliatelle egg pasta
tagliolini noodles
tartufo truffle
tavola table
tè tea
tonno tuna
torta tart flan
tortellini stuffed pasta
tramezzini triangular filled sandwiches
trippa tripe
alla romana flavoured with spearmint and strong pecorino
trota trout

U

uccelletti small birds wrapped in bacon
uova eggs
uva grapes

V

verdura vegetables
vignarola artichoke and broad bean stew
vino bianco white wine
vino rosso red wine
vitello veal
vongole clams

Z

zafferano saffron
zucca pumpkin
zucchine courgettes
con fiori fried flowers stuffed with anchovies and mozzarella
zuppa soup

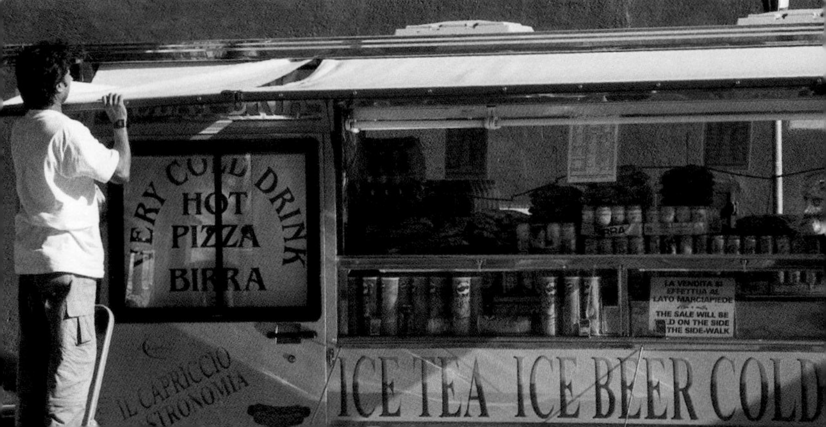

Recipe

This is a traditional and well-known dish in Rome's Jewish community. You can see the *Sephardi* influence in the combination of pine nuts and raisins. These give it a sweet and sour flavour, not common in traditional Italian cooking but widespread in Sephardi cuisine. The recipe was most likely brought to Rome by Jews who came from Sicily during the Spanish Inquisition. A very similar dish is also present in Venetian Jewish cooking – *Silvia Nacamulli*

Spinaci con pinoli e passerine (Sautéed spinach with pine nuts and raisins)
Serves 4-6

1 kg fresh baby spinach leaves
4-5 tablespoons of extra virgin olive oil
½ onion, finely chopped
handful of raisins
handful of pine nut kernels
salt and freshly ground black pepper to taste

Wash the spinach well and put it in a deep saucepan. Cover and let it steam at medium heat. You don't need to add any additional water when steaming the spinach as it releases its own liquid while cooking. By not adding any water, you will allow the spinach to retain all of its vitamins.

Leave the spinach to steam for 5 minutes until the leaves are tender, then drain and squeeze the water out.

Meanwhile, heat the olive oil and the chopped onion in a frying pan with some salt and pepper. Leave to cook, stirring occasionally, for 5 minutes until the onion is soft. Add the steamed spinach to the frying pan and turn the flame up to medium heat. Leave to cook for 10 minutes, adding the raisins and the pine nuts halfway through.

Tip: Soak the raisins in lukewarm water for 5 minutes before adding them to the spinach, so they are soft and juicy.

Serve warm or at room temperature.

Articoli da Regalo
Di Rienzo
caffe

SHOPPING

Even men have fun shopping in the Eternal City. Shops open daily at around 10am (noon on Sunday) and close around 7.30pm (later in summer). A few shops close for lunch but most stay open all day. Many shops close during August. Sales are in January and July.

Designer labels are found in the streets around Piazza di Spagna (p.161) with the best shopping in the streets between Via del Babuino and Via del Corso. Outside of Tridente, good shopping can be found on Via Nazionale, Via Cola di Rienzo and in Trastevere. In Centro Storico, Via dei Cestari is the cleric's Bond Street, where nuns and priests do their shopping. This is the perfect place to buy purple socks fit for a pope or cardinal.

Roman shop assistants are enthusiastic about their clothes. They may insist you try items that are not what you would normally select. As a rule, they have good taste and though they may seem aggressive, their motive is to transform you into *la bella figura.* On returning home, items they have helped you select will often be the ones that receive the most compliments. Roman women tend to favour very high heels and this is reflected in the stock.

Rome is *the* place to purchase accessories: handbags that attract envious glances on the high street, gloves that make for instant chic, scarves that go with all your outfits. Men will appreciate the range of personal grooming items available, from shaving brushes to scissors of every type – all beautifully displayed. A tempting array of pens and leather organisers are available in stationers around the city.

Antiques dealers are to be found on Via Giulia and Via dei Coronari in Centro Storico and in Via del Babuino near the Spanish Steps. Trendy homeware stores are mostly located in Tridente while more unusual hand-made objects are in the small shops of Trastevere.

A designer outlet mall with 95 shops is located 25 km from the city centre (p.265).

Centro Storico

Gifts, toys, handicrafts

Bartolucci
Via dei Pastini 98
06 6919 0894, map 12, F2
www.bartolucci.com
Handmade wooden toys and clocks for children and babies.

Centro Raku
Via dei Pastini 20
06 6787 682, map 12, F2
www.raku.it
Raku clocks and ceramics.

Al Sogno
Piazza Navona 53
06 686 4198, map 11, D2
Pinocchios and Venetian masks displayed in a theatrical setting.

Evo
Via dei Coronari
06 688 01041, map 11, C1
A shop selling unusual household gifts including scale models of cars and motorcycles.

El Patio
Via del Pellegrino 61
06 681 36463, map 11, C3
Pretty handmade ceramics.

Tè e Teiere
Via del Pellegrino 85
06 686 8824, map 11, C3
Delicate porcelain teacups and teapots are displayed alongside manly mugs. Also sells tea.

Books, stationery, art supplies

Papiro
Via del Pantheon 50
06 679 5597, map 12, F2
www.ilpapirofirenze.it
Beautiful handmade paper products from Florence.

Ditta G. Poggi
Via del Gesu 74-75
06 678 4477, map 12, F4
www.poggi1825.it
Good general art supplies shop.

Il Museo del Louvre
Via della Reginella, 28
06 688 07725, map 12, F5
www.casettibooks.com
Part art gallery, part rare book collection with *Belle Epoque* fashion and photography magazines.

Libreria Fanucci
Piazza Madama 8
06 68 61141, map 11, D2
www.libreriafanucci.it
One of the oldest bookshops in Rome stocks English language travel guides, popular fiction and science-fiction. Open late.

Irradazioni
Via di Tor Millina 11
06 681 92989, map 11, C2
wwwirradiazioni.com
Stocks classic English and American authors, from Jane Austen to Hemingway.

Feltrinelli
Largo Argentina, map 12, F4
Large shop with several shelves of books in English.

La Discoteca al Pantheon
Via della Minerva 9-10
06 679 8650, map 12, F2
Good selection of CDs including classical, opera, Italian and popular music.

Grace Gallery
Via della Rotonda 3
06 976 03377, map 12, E3
www.gracegallery.com
Photographer Nancy Robinson displays stunning images available framed or unframed at reasonable prices (from €15 unframed).

Grotta del Libro
Via del Pellegrino 172
06 687 7567, map 11, B3
Old Italian fashion magazines.

Clothing, shoes and accessories

Sirni
Via della Stelletta 33
06 688 05248, map 12, E1
www.sirnipelletteria.it
A stylish boutique selling leather accessories, bags and briefcases.

Brandy
Via dei Giubbonari 40
map 11, D5
Mainstream clothing for men.

Cecilia and Omero
Via del Governo Vecchio
map 11, C2
Stocks vintage 70s clothing, nice sundresses and classic Dior.

NuYorica
Piazza Pollarola 36-37
map 11, D4
Designer shoes from Martin Margiela and Marc Jacobs – also offbeat pieces and handbags.

Ghezzi
Via dei Cestari 32-33
map 12, F3
Suppliers of socks and thermals to cardinals and bishops. Buy your purple socks and ski thermals here.

Camiceria Mattioli
Via della Stelletta 30
06 687 3359, map 12, E1
A small shop selling gorgeous cuff links, designer ties, classic shirts and suits.

Studiomode
Via del Pellegrino 75
map 11, C3
Womenswear by local designers.

Supermarkets, food and drink

Di Meglio
Via Giustiniani 18B
06 683 3166, map 12, E2
A supermarket off Piazza della Rotonda that is a good place to buy bottled water.

Tridente

A 24 hr news kiosk is located at the corner of Via del Tritone and Via del Corso.

Gifts, kitchenware

Michel Harem
Via Sistina 137A
06 474 6466, map 5, D2
Entering the shop is like falling into a boudoir. It is packed full of kitsch gifts but at Christmas, this is the place to come for your tree-top angel and other decorations.

MICHEL HAREM

Recanto do Brasil
Via della Frezza 66
06 4543 2093, map 5, A1
www.recantodobrasil.com
Interesting shop selling Brazilian handicrafts and pottery.

C.U.C.I.N.A
Via Mario de'Fiori 65
06 679 1275, map 5, C2
A modern store full of interesting kitchenware and seasonal items.

Tad
Via del Babuino
06 326 95122, map 5, B1
A chic emporium selling ultra cool home accessories and a large assortment of candles.

Books, stationery, art supplies

Altieri
Via del Leone 20
06 678 0184, map 5, B2
Leather journals and Moleskin notebooks in assorted colours.

The English Bookshop
Via di Ripetta 248
06 320 3301, map 5, A1
This small well-stocked bookshop also sells African textiles, sandals and silk handbags.

The Lion Bookstore
Via dei Greci 33
06 326 54007, map 5, B1
closed during August
Browse through design and style books over a cappuccino and piece of cake in the adjoining café. Excellent kids section.

Anglo American
Via della Vite, 102
06 678 4347, map 5, C2
English literature and biographies with a selection of guide books.

Fabriano
Via del Babuino 173
06 3260 0361, map 5, B1
Stylish modern stationers selling pens, pencils, notepaper and journals in bright colours.

Arion
Via Veneto 42
06 482 5308, map 5, E2
This shop is one of a chain of 12 shops featuring good travel, cuisine, photography and childrens' sections.

Fratelli Alinari
Via Alibert 16A (Via Margutta)
06 679 2923, map 5, C1
The shop displays classic black and white photography of the chic Alinari brothers.

Clothing, shoes and accessories

Settimio Mieli
Via san Claudio 70
06 692 91106, map 5, B3
This family-run glove shop was established in 1924. All colours and sizes at moderate prices.

Artigianato del Cuoio
Via Belsiana 90 (second floor)
06 678 4435, map 5, B2
Handmade leather goods by Giancarlo Breda – bags, briefcases and luggage. Will make to order.

Pratesi
Piazza di Firenze 22
06 688 03720, map 12, E1
A small shop with beautiful handmade leather bags and cases.

Pitran
Via del Gambero, 18
06 6794012, map 12, E1
A good selection of menswear in larger sizes.

Fatto a Mano
Via dell'Oca 34
06 361 2184, map 1, C6
Colourful handmade silk clothing and accessories.

Il Fiocco
Via del Gambero 13
06 679 0625, map 5, B2
Underwear for women and men.

FABRIANO

Maesano
Largo F. di Borghese 80
06 687 1559, map 5, A2
Affordable clothing for men and women.

Tie Shop
Via della Carrozze
map 5, B2
Good selection of ties and gloves. Branches at Via Cola di Rienzo, Via Veneto and Via Ottaviano.

Fabrizio Bulckaen
Via del Babuino, 158A
06 322 2343, map 5, B1
Shoes ranging from classic courts to more frivolous designs – all for under €250.

XCorsi
Via del Corso 348
06 679 1374, map 5, B1
Clothing for the young and trendy.

Perfume and jewellery

L'Olfattorio
Via di Ripetta 34
06 361 2325, map 5, A1
Book here for a guided perfume sampling. Perfumes are not sold here, but you will be directed to the shop selling your chosen scent.

Stefano Fiori
Via Sistina 22
map 5, D2
A tiny jewellery shop selling handmade silver with semi-precious stones.

Quirinale & Esquilino

Jewellery and grooming

Muzio
Via del Tritone 50
06 678 1586, map 5, C3
Hair accessories, combs, brushes, perfume and general toiletries.

Dierre Bijoux
Via Merulana 165
06 704 94695, map 6, H6
Mimmo and Danilo Ranati's costume jewellery business has been here for 36 years, making tiaras for beauty contests and accessorising fashion shows. Buy buttons, beads and sequins to embellish your creations.

Benedetta
Via della Panetteria 7
06 699 22205, map 5, D3
This shop stocks amber and silver

jewellery as well as unusual pieces made with seashells and cameos.

Books and stationery

Feltrinelli International
Via E Orlando 84
map 6, G3
Books in a range of languages geared towards students and teachers of English, as well as fiction and guidebooks.

Clothing and accessories

Valentino Guido
Via Sistina 16/16A
06 448 1619, map 5, D2
Via delle Quattro Fontane 4/4A
06 420 11339, map 6, E3
Well-designed leather bags and luggage at competitive prices.

Altariva
Via del Tritone 31
06 678 5885, map 5, C3
Large selection of shoes and boots including some by local designers.

Califfo Moda
Via Merulana 277
map 6, H6
Inexpensive shoes and bags.

Leather Craftsman
shop: Via del Lavatore 43
06 679 4690
workshop: Vicolo dei Maroniti 27
map 5, D3
Beautiful leather goods handmade by a husband and wife team.

Pitran
Via Merulana 5
06 446 5873, map 6, H6
www.pitran.com
Fashionable womenswear in larger sizes. Menswear at number 30.

Camomilla Italia
Via del Viminale 80
06 481 8024, map 6, G4
Inexpensive clothing for teens.

Zelig
Via Torino 138-139
06 488 1698, map 6, G4
Reasonably priced clothes for teens and young adults.

Galleria Colonna
Via del Corso
map 12, G1
Rome's chic indoor shopping mall.

Supermarkets, food and drink

Il Tino di Vino
Via del Lavatore 31
06 679 2935
Via della Panettaria 42B
06 679 2598, map 12, I1
Wines and delicacies including caviar and assorted preserves.

Panella: L'Arte del Pane
Via Merulana 54/55
06 487 2651, map 6, I6
closed Thursday and Sunday
One of Rome's most celebrated bakeries makes excellent cake. The large bread sculptures are fun.

Trastevere

Elettromania
Via delle Fratte di Trastevere 44D
06 581 8348, map 8, G3
Photographic film and one-hour developing service. They will print from digital memory cards.

Jewellery and accessories

Parentesi
Piazza S G. della Malva 7
06 5812 513, map 8, F1
Clothing and accessories with an ethnic influence.

Tath
Via San Francesco a Ripa 4
06 581 6849, map 8, G3
A small shop packed with a variety of silk and patterned scarves.

Lo Scrigno
Via dei Baullari 145
06 5899 828, map 8, H2
One of two colourful shops that sell a variety of accessories including bags, belts and scarves.

LO SCRIGNO

Pandora
Piazza S. Maria in Trastevere 6
06 581 7145, map 8, G2
Murano glass jewellery, ceramics and accessories vie for space in this small well-stocked shop.

Meteore
Via Natale del Grande 14
06 581 8920, map 8, F3
The shop displays lovely patterned scarves and jewellery with semi-precious stones.

Beauty

Roma-Store
Via della Lungaretta 63
06 581 8789, map 8, G2
This perfumery is packed to the rafters with lotions and potions, including French and English scents: Diptyque, Crabtree & Evelyn, L'Occitane, Creed, Penhaligons and the range of TJ le Clerc cosmetics.

Homeware

Azi
Via S. Francesco a Ripa 170
06 588 3303, map 8, G3
Interesting home accessories for modern interiors.

Gifts

Centro Didatticco Specializzato
Via della Luce 31-32
06 581 79716, map 8, G4
A toyshop in a beautifully restored building with arched ceilings. Well stocked with wooden toys, Lego, Brio, beads, stationery and books.

Polvere di Tempo
Via del Moro 59
06 588 0704, map 8, G2
www.polvereditempo.com
Argentinian born artisan and architect Adrian Rodriguez is the owner of this intriguing shop that is a favourite with men. Dedicated to time and travel, the shop stocks sand-timers, globes, compasses and leather-bound journals. Many pieces are hand-made by Adrian.

POLVERE DI TEMPO

ALMOST CORNER BOOKSHOP

Books and stationery

The Almost Corner Bookshop
Via del Moro 45
06 5836 942, map 8, G2
A very good English bookshop run by Dermott O'Connell.

Food

Amico del Biologico
Via S. Francesco a Ripa 106
06 581 12621, map 8, G3
An organic health food shop selling a good range of products including fruit and vegetables, cosmetics, herbal remedies and beer. Friendly staff.

Valzani
Via del Moro 37
06 5803792, map 8, G2
www.valzani.it
Film director Nanni Moretti frequents this bakery for the sacher torte, and named his cinema after it (p.286). Valzani have been known to make wedding cakes in the shape of the Vittorio Emmanuele Monument.

Department stores

Coin (Vaticano)
Via Cola di Rienzo 173
map 4, F1
Competitive prices, good for homewares and mid-range fashion, in-store coffee bar, supermarket.

La Rinascente (Tridente)
Piazza Colonna
06 679 7691, map 12, G1
One of the most expensive and exclusive department stores in Rome.

Upim (Esquilino)
Piazza S. Maria Maggiore
06 446 5579, map 6, H5
Department store with reasonable prices selling mid-range fashion, accessories, bed linen and kitchenware.

Standa (Trastevere)
Viale Trastevere 62-64, map 8, G3
Cheap and economical with a supermarket in the basement.

Designer outlet

McArthur Glen
Via Ponte di Piscina Cupa 64
Castel Romano (25km from Rome)
06 505 0050
10.00-20.00 daily
www.macarthurglen.com
Factory outlet mall with 95 shops including Dolce and Gabbana, Guess, Diesel and Versace. Shops are situated along stylish avenues and around small piazzas. There are numerous restaurants and bars to refresh you when you need a break from snapping up the bargains. Take exit 26 on the GRA and follow the signs to Castel Romano. Free parking.

CHURCHES, MONUMENTS
MUSEUMS & GALLERIES

CLOISTER OF ST PAUL'S
OUTSIDE THE WALLS

Opening times for churches are generally 8am-12 noon and 3.30pm-7pm daily. Be sure to dress sensibly when visiting. Knees, shoulders and midriffs should be covered. Many churches hold concerts. We have indicated this by the symbol ♪. The website www.roma.katolsk.no has a comprehensive list of Rome's churches.

Centro Storico & Ghetto

Sant'Agnese In Agone ♪
Piazza Navona
06 6819 2134 map 11, D2
Founded on the site of the brothel where, in 304, the young St Agnes was exposed naked to force her to renounce her faith. A bas-relief shows the miraculous growth of her hair, which fell around her body to protect her modesty. Borromini designed the façade facing Bernini's fountains.

Sant'Andrea della Valle
Piazza Sant'Andrea della Valle
06 686 1339 map 11, D/E4
The location of the first act of Puccini's opera *Tosca*. Carlo Maderno's dome is the largest in Rome after St Peter's.

Chiesa del Gesù (Il Gesù)
Piazza del Gesù
06 69 7001 map 12, G4
This was the first Jesuit church and the style is imitated throughout the Catholic world. It has a breathtaking ceiling, with frescoes that contain a clear message pertaining to the reformation: Catholic worshippers are joyfully uplifted into the heavens while Protestants and heretics are flung into hell's fires.

Chiesa Nuova
Piazza della Chiesa Nuova
06 687 5289 map 11, B2
San Filippo Neri set noblemen to work as labourers building this church. There are three paintings by Rubens: *Madonna and Angels* above the altar, *Saints Domitilla Nereus and Achilleus*, and *Saints Gregory, Maurus and Papias* (left).

San Giovanni de'Fiorentini ♪
Via Acciaioli 2
06 6889 2059 map 11, A2
English mass Sunday 18.00
The altar is by Borromini, who is buried here. A charming museum upstairs has an early Michelangelo, *St John the Baptist*, and two busts by Bernini. The church admits animals and at Easter a baby lamb is blessed.

Sant'Ignazio di Loyola ♪
Piazza di Sant'Ignazio
06 679 4406 map 12, G2
Dedicated to Ignatius Loyola (1491-1556) who converted in 1521 after being wounded in battle. He consequently founded the Jesuits. Look for the *tromp l'oeil* cupola and other tricks of perspective.

Sant'Ivo alla Sapienza ♪
Corso del Rinascimento 40
06 686 4987 map 11, D3
Borromini's fanciful church with his trademark combination of concave and convex surfaces.

San Marco
Piazza San Marco 48
06 679 5205 map 12, H4
One of the first churches in central Rome. Founded in 336 by Pope Mark and dedicated to St Mark the Evangelist, patron saint of Venice. This is the church of the Venetian community.

Santa Maria dell'Anima
Via della Pace 20
06 682 8181 map 11, D2
The German church in Rome is now much more lively given the nationality of the new Pope.

Santa Maria della Pace
(St Mary of Peace)
Vicolo dell'Arco della Pace 5
06 686 1156 map 11, C2
The first chapel on the right has Raphael's luminous fresco, *Sibyls and Angels.*

Santa Maria in Campitelli
Piazza di Campitelli 9
06 6880 3978 map 12, F6
The church's icon *Madonna del Portico* is said to have cured the plague outbreak of 1656.

San Nicola in Carcere
Via del Teatro di Marcello 46
06 686 9972 map 9, A1
Medieval church built on the site of three Roman temples dedicated to Juno, Spes and Janus.

San Salvatore in Lauro
Piazzo San Salvatore in Lauro 15
06 687 5187 map 11, C1
A beautiful altarpiece by Pietro da Cortona, *The Birth of Jesus,* is in the first chapel to the right.

Tridente & Borghese

All Saints ♪
Via del Babuino 153B
06 3600 1881 map 1, E6
The Anglican church in Rome has a Victorian interior and a regular programme of concerts.

Sant'Andrea delle Fratte
Via Sant'Andrea delle Fratte 1
06 679 3191 map 5, C3
Has Bernini's two original angels from Ponte Sant'Angelo: *Crown of Thorns* and *Derogatory Inscription.*

ALL SAINTS

Borromini created the fanciful belltower complete with angels, flaming torches and exaggerated scrolls like semi-folded hearts.

San Lorenzo in Lucina
Via in Lucina 16A
06 687 1494 map 5, B3
Built on a well that was sacred to Juno, protecter of women. Above the main altar is the *Crucifixion* by Guido Reni.

Santa Maria della Concezione
Via Veneto 27
06 452 850 map 6, E2
crypt open daily 09.00-12.00, 15.00-18.00, donation expected
Cardinal Barberini, a Capuchin friar and brother to Urban VIII, had this church built in 1626. There is a Caravaggio inside. The most fascinating and macabre aspect of this church is the crypt where you can view the bones of about 4,000 monks who died between 1528 and 1870. These have been ornately displayed throughout this ossuary, creating a kind of Baroque *memento mori*.

Santa Maria della Vittoria
Via XX Settembre 17
06 427 40571 map 6, F2
Bernini's *The Ecstacy of St Theresa* is in the Cornaro Chapel.

Santa Maria in Montesanto
Piazza del Popolo
06 361 0594 map 1, D5
This is one of two neighbouring churches in Piazza del Popolo, along with Santa Maria in Miracoli. The two appear to be identical but because the site on the left was narrower, Miracoli (on the right) has a circular dome and Santa Maria an oval one.

Trinità dei Monti
Piazza della Trinità dei Monti
06 679 4179 map 5, C2
Well located at the top of the Spanish Steps, this church offers grand views over Rome.

Santi Vincenzo e Anastasio
Vicolo dei Modelli 73
06 678 3098 map 5, C4
Now the home of the Bulgarian Orthodox Church in Rome.

Esquilino & Quirinale

Sant'Andrea al Quirinale
Via del Quirinale 29
0 4890 3187 map 6, E4
Bernini considered this church his only perfect work and is reputed to have received no payment for it. As an old man, he often came here for mass.

Santi Apostoli
Piazza dei Santi Apostoli
06 679 4085 map 5, C5
The enormous *Tomb of Pope Clement XIV*, with the figures *Humility and Modesty*, is Canova's first major work in Rome. Above the sanctuary, angels look as if they are falling out of the sky in a 1709 fresco by Giovanni Odazzi: *The Rebel Angels.*

San Carlo alle Quattro Fontane
Via del Quirinale 23
06 488 3261 map 10, F3
Near to Sant'Andrea, but much smaller, this church was built by Borromini. It was both his first and last work in Rome.

Santi Domenico e Sisto
Largo Angelicum 1 (entrance through adjacent university building)
06 670 21 map 5, D5
closed July-Sept
The tall Baroque façade and twin staircases leading towards the entrance make this church highly unique. Bernini decorated the first chapel on right.

Santa Maria dei Monti
Via Madonna dei Monti 41
06 4855 31 map 5, E6
A sweet little church set in a quiet piazza. It was designed by Giacomo della Porta in 1580.

San Martino ai Monti
Viale del Monte Oppio 28
06 487 3166 map 6, G6
Built on the site of a house church belonging to Equitius.

Santa Prassede ♪
Via Santa Prassede 9A
06 488 2456 map 6, H5
In the apse, Santa Prassede and Santa Pudenziana stand on either side of Christ.

Santa Pudenziana
Via Urbana 160
06 481 4622 map 6, G5
This site was once the home of a Roman Senator named Pudens who is mentioned in the Bible, in Paul's greetings to Timothy. Legend says that St Peter was a guest here. Pudenziana was the daughter of Pudens and sister of Prassede.

Santa Susanna
Via XX Settembre 14
06 4201 4554 map 6, F2
The American Catholic Church in Rome. Obtain tickets here for papal audiences (p.284).

Laterano & Celio

Santa Balbina
Piazza di Santa Balbina 8
06 578 0207 map 9, C6
Surrounded by cypresses and dedicated to St Balbina, a 2nd century martyr, the church overlooks the Baths of Caracalla.

Santa Bibiana
Via Giovanni Giolitti 154
06 446 1021 overview map G3
Santa Bibiana is the first fully clothed figure sculpted by Bernini.

Santa Croce in Gerusalemme
P. di Santa Croce in Gerusalemme 12
06 701 4769 overview map H4
A pilgrimage church founded by Emperor Constantine's mother, St Helena, in AD 320.

San Gregorio Magno
Piazza San Gregorio 1
06 700 8227 map 9, D4
An imposing church, long past its days of glory, famous for being the departure point of St Augustine on his mission to evangelise England.

Santi Giovanni e Paolo
Piazza Santi Giovanni e Paolo 13
06 772 711 map 9, D4
The 4th century church was built here following the martyrdom of two Roman officers, Giovanni and Paolo, who lived on this site. The arches beside the church formed part of a street of shops. Roman houses have been discovered beneath the church. (p.182,278)

Santa Maria in Domnica
Piazza della Navicella 12
06 700 1519 map 10, E4
Originally a house church (dominicum), it is worth seeing the splendid 9th century mosaic of the Virgin and Child, surrounded by saints. The portico was added by Sansovino in 1513.

Santa Stefano Rotondo
Via di Santo Stefano Rotondo 7
06 4211 99 map 10, F4
The church is notable for its gory 5th century frescoes of martyrdom. Now the Hungarian church in Rome.

Santi Quattro Coronati
Via dei Santi Quattro Coronati 20
06 7047 5427 map 10, F3
Santi Quattro Coronati means 'four

SAN ANSELMO

crowned saints' and refers to four Christian soldiers who were martyred after refusing to worship a Roman pagan god.

Scala Santa and Sancta Sanctorum
Piazza di San Giovanni in Laterano 14
06 772 6641 map 10, I3
Scala Santa: free , Sanctorum: €3
The 28 steps of the Scala Santa (Holy Staircase) are said to be the very ones that Christ ascended in Pontius Pilate's house before his crucifixion, brought to Rome by St Helena in the 4th century. The steps are covered with wooden planks which can only be ascended on your knees.

Aventino & Testaccio

Sant'Alessio
Piazza di Sant'Alessio 23
06 574 3446 map 8, I5
St Alexis was a hermit who lived here incognito. The church contains a statue of him clutching the letter he held when he died which revealed his true identity.

San Anselmo ♪
Piazza San Anselmo
06 57911 map 8, I5
Monastery and seminary dedicated to St Anselm, Archbishop of Canterbury. Built in 1900, it is known for Gregorian chant on Sunday mornings. The gift shop sells products from monasteries around the world.

Santa Sabina ♪
Piazza Pietro d'Illiria 1
06 579 40600 map 9, A4
The site of the home church of Sabina, a Roman matron converted to Christianity by her Greek slave. The two were subsequently martyred together. Founded in AD 425 to convert patricians living in the villas of the Aventine, the church still looks much as it did in the 5th century.

Trastevere

San Crisogono
Piazza Sonnino 44
06 581 8225 map 8, H3
Mosaics in the apse are by followers of Pietro Cavallini.

San Francesco a Ripa
Piazza San Francesco d'Assisi 88
06 581 9020 map 8, G4
St Francis of Assisi stayed here in 1219. His stone pillow and crucifix are preserved in his cell. *The Blessed Ludovica Albertoni* is one of Bernini's better pieces.

Out of the Centre

Sant'Agnese Fuori le Mura
(St. Agnes Outside the Walls)
Via Nomentana 349
06 861 0840 overview map G/H1
admission charge for catacombs
Sant'Agnese includes the ruins of a covered cemetery with catacombs containing the remains of St Agnes. Inside are mosaic portraits of the popes. It is said that the world will end when there's no more room for portraits. Behind the church is **Santa Costanza**, a mausoleum for Constantia and Helena, daughters of Constantine.

San Lorenzo Fuori le Mura
(St. Lawrence Outside the Walls)
Piazzale del Verano 3
06 4915 11 overview map I3
San Lorenzo was martyred at the Forum (p.86) for donating tax money to the poor. His remains are under the altar together with the bones of St Stephen. San Lorenzo is Rome's patron saint (and the patron saint of chefs).

San Sebastiano & Catacombs
Via Appia Antica 136
06 788 7035 off map
closed mid Nov-mid Dec
admission charge for catacombs
A pilgrimage church with frescoes by Perugino. It houses one of the arrows that killed St Sebastian, together with the column to which he was tied.

Monuments & Galleries

The following sights are not found in the main body of the book. Opening hours may be subject to change without notice. It is advisable to check opening hours by calling directly. As a rule, ticket offices close 30 to 60 minutes before the actual closing times and most do not accept credit cards. Some archaeological sites require prior permission to visit.
Phone/fax: 06 671 03819

Museums and galleries are free to EU citizens aged over 65 and under 18. Passports must be shown as identification. Art history and fine art students are usually admitted free with student ID.

MANY MUSEUMS AND GALLERIES ARE CLOSED ON MONDAYS. ALL ARE CLOSED ON 1 JANUARY, 25 APRIL, 1 MAY, 1 NOVEMBER AND 25 DECEMBER.

Museum cards (valid for seven days), can be purchased at participating museums.

• **Roma Archaeologia Card** €20
allows one admission to each of these museums/sights:
Colosseo - Palatino - Palazzo Altemps - Palazzo Massimo - Terme di Diocleziano - Crypta Balbi - Terme di Caracalla - Cecilia Metella - Villa dei Quintili

• **Museum card** €7
allows one admission to sights of the Museo Nazionale Romano:
Palazzo Altemps - Palazzo Massimo - Terme di Diocleziano - Crypta Balbi

www.pierreci.it is a good site for information on museums, monuments and current exhibitions. Purchase tickets and tourist passes in advance by clicking through to Omniticket Network **www.ticketclic.it**

Centro Storico

Chiostro del Bramante
Via della Pace
06 680 9098 map 11, C2
Built by Bramante for the church of Santa Maria della Pace, these cloisters are used for exhibitions and there is a peaceful café.

Column of Marcus Aurelius
Piazza Colonna
Map 12, G1
The 30-foot marble column was erected after the death of Marcus Aurelius in AD 180. A chronicle of the Emperor's battles in Germany, it was restored and Christianised in 1589 on the orders of Sixtus V. The statue on top is a bronze of *St Paul.*

Crypta Balbi
Via delle Botteghe Oscure 31
06 399 67700 map 12, F5
09.00-19.45 Tues-Sun
admission €4
A new addition to the Museo Nazionale Romano, designed to illustrate Rome's changes through the ages. It includes the ruins of the 1st century BC Theatre of Balbus. The guided tour is recommended.

Museo Napoleonico
Piazza di Ponte Umberto I
06 6880 6286 map 11, D1
09.00-19.00 Tues-Sat (until 13.00 Sun)
admission €2.60
After Napoleon's death in 1821, Pius VII (Chiaramonte) allowed many of the Bonaparte family to settle in Rome. The museum has the collections of Count Giuseppe Primoli, great-grandson of Joseph Bonaparte.

Palazzo Altemps
Piazza Sant' Apollinare 44
06 399 67700 map 11, D1
09.00-19.45 Tues-Sun, €5
This spacious 15th century palace holds a collection of classical sculpture collected by the Altemps family.

Palazzo Braschi (Museo di Roma)
Via di San Pantaleo 10
06 671 08346 map 11, D3
09.00-19.00 Tues-Sun €6.20
see Piazza Navona (p.50)

Palazzo Giustiniani
Via Giustiniani 11
06 399 67350 map 11-12, E2
This 16th century palazzo now belongs to the Italian Senate and is used for special exhibitions.

Palazzo Madama
Corso del Rinascimento
06 670 61 map 11, E2
guided visits in Italian 10.00-18.00 first Sat of each month
Cardinals Giovanni and Giuliano de'Medici lived here and so did Caravaggio. It has been the seat of the Upper House of the Italian parliament since 1871.

Palazzo Venezia
(Museum of Decorative Arts)
Via del Plebiscito 118
06 699 941 map 12, G4
09.30-19.00 Tues-Sun €4
www.galleriaborghese.it
Built in 1455 for Venetian Pope Paul II, this was the location of the Venetian Embassy until the fall of Venice in 1797. The sumptuous interior contains Renaissance paintings by Starnina and Giovanni da Modena. Terracotta models for Bernini's *Fontana del Tritone* (Piazza Navona) are found in rooms 18-26. It was Mussolini's headquarters and he addressed the crowds in the piazza from the central balcony. The mosaic-floored Sala del Mappamondo was once his office. He would intimidate visitors by making them

walk 60 feet to his desk in silence.

Piazza di Montecitorio

• Palazzo di Montecitorio
06 676 01 map 12, F1
guided visits 10.00-18.00 first Sun of each month excluding August
admission free, www.camera.it
Commissioned by Innocent X, designed by Bernini and expanded by Carlo Fontana, the art nouveau façade was added in 1918 by Ernesto Brasile. Initially the Papal Tribunal of Justice, the palazzo is now the seat of the Lower House of Italy's parliament.

• Obelisco di Montecitorio
Built in 10 BC for the Emperor Augustus and brought to Rome from Heliopolis in Egypt. Once part of an enormous sundial, the obelisk was discovered lying under medieval houses in the early 1500s and installed in its present location in 1792.

Piccola Farnesina
(Museo Barracco)
Corso Vittorio Emanuele II 166
06 6880 6848 map 11, D3
09.00-19.00 Tues-Sat, until 13.30 Sun
admission €2.60
A museum of ancient sculpture, with a fine assembly of Greek and Egyptian works, Assyrian and Etruscan artefacts, and a small but high-quality collection of ancient Greek ceramics.

Vaticano

Castel Sant'Angelo
Lungotevere Castello 50
06 399 67600
09.00-20.00 Tue-Sun, €5
map 4, G3
Hadrian's mausoleum, later the pope's armoury. Walk up the ramp to the top for good views.

Tridente & Borghese

Ara Pacis Augustae
Lungotevere in Augusta
06 688 06848 map 5, A1
due to re-open autumn 2005
Erected in 13-19 BC, the 'altar of peace' celebrated the *pax romana* established by Augustus.

Casa-Museo Giorgio de Chirico
Piazza di Spagna 31
06 679 6546 map 5, C1
book visits in advance by phone mornings Tues-Sat and 1st Sun of each month, €5.00
www.fondazionedechirico.it
A museum located in de Chirico's home where he lived from 1948 to his death in 1978. The paintings, terracotta articles, casts and artist's tools on display create the feel of a working environment.

Explora
(Children's Museum of Rome)
Via Flaminia 82-86
06 361 3776 map 1, C3
1 hr 45 min sessions, 09.30-17.00 Tues-Fri; 10.00-17.00 Sat, Sun
advance booking necessary, especially at weekends, €7 children, €6 adults
www.mdbr.it
Children are allowed to touch and play with everything on display in a miniature play town.

Galleria Nazionale d'Arte Moderna
Viale delle Belle Arti 131
06 322 981 map 2, F3
08.30-19.30 Tues-Sun €6.50
One of Italy's most important modern collections is housed in a palace built for the 1911 Rome International Exhibition. There are works by the *macchiaoli* (Tuscan Impressionists) as well as Cezanne, Van Gogh, Monet and Degas. Other big names of 20th century

international art are here: Klimt, Mondrian, Duchamp, Kandinsky, Mirò, Klee, Arp and Ernst. To the left of the entrance there is a sculpture gallery with Canova's *Hercules*.

Mausoleo di Augusto
Piazza Augusto Imperatore
06 671 03819 map 5, A1
open by appointment only
This grassy knoll is the unlikely tomb of Emperor Augustus and his family. Inside is the urn containing his ashes.

Villa Giulia (Etruscan Museum)
Piazzale di Villa Giulia 9
06 322 6571 map 1, D2
8.30-19.30 Tues-Sun €4
Opened in 1889, this is the home of pre-Roman works found outside the city in excavations around Lazio, Tuscany and Umbria. The palazzo was built between 1551-55, with Giacomo da Vignola, Bartolomeo Ammannati, Giorgio Vasari and Michelangelo all making contributions. To the right of the main entrance, the garden has a 20th century reconstruction of an Etruscan temple. The collection is organised chronologically over two floors. As well as sculpture and ceramics, there are gold objects and bronze devotional figures. In the **Cerveteri** room, look for the *Sarcofago degli sposi* – a terracotta sarcophagus depicting a married couple lying down as if at a banquet.

Villa Medici
(Accademia di Francia a Roma)
Viale Trinità dei Monti 1
06 676 11 map 5, C1
guided tours of the gardens, phone to check times
Bought by Cardinal Ferdinando de'Medici in 1576, this 16th century villa has a beautiful Renaissance garden and views across the city to Castel Sant'Angelo. It is home to the French Academy. Former students are Fragonard and Boucher. Nicolas Poussin and Ingres were adviser and director respectively.

Quirinale & Esquilino

Domus Aurea (Golden House)
Viale Domus Aurea
06 3996 7700 map 10, E2
09.00-19.00 Wed-Mon
advance booking required €5
visits by 45 minute guided tour, maximum 25 people
Nero built the Domus Aurea on parts of the Esquiline, Celio and Palatine after the fire. Following his suicide in AD 68, his successors attempted to erase all traces of the palace. Parts of one wing escaped destruction and these underground rooms are on display. In winter the temperature is very cold.

Museo Nazional d'Arte Orientale
Via Merulana 248
06 487 4415 map 6 H6
08.30-14.00 Mon, Wed, Fri, Sat
08.30-19.30 Tue, Thur, Sun
closed 1st & 3rd Mon of month, €4
The collection includes pre-historic Iranian ceramics, Tibetan paintings, Japanese painted screens, Chinese jade and sculpture from Afghanistan, Nepal and Kashmir.

Museo Nazionale delle Paste Alimentari (Pasta Museum)
Piazza Scanderbeg 117
06 699 1119 1120 map 12, I1
09.30-17.30 daily €10
A museum dedicated exclusively to pasta, with a gift shop selling pasta-making tools.

TRAJAN'S MARKET

Palazzo Colonna
(Galleria Colonna)
Via della Pilotta 17
06 678 4350 map 5, C5
09.00-13.00 Sat only, closed Aug
free guided tours in English at 11.45
book in advance €7
www.galleriacolonna.it
Pictures are not labelled so use a reference guide to match numbers with art works. Famous paintings include *Assumption of the Virgin* by Rubens, Annibale Carracci's *The Bean Eater* and Titian's portrait of *Onofrio Panvini.*

Palazzo delle Esposizioni
Via Nazionale 194
06 474 5903 map 5-6, E4
closed for renovation until spring 2006
Built by the city of Rome in 1882 as an exhibition centre. Now hosts contemporary art and photography exhibitions, as well as live performances, films and lectures.

Palazzo Massimo alle Terme
(Museo Nazionale Romano)
Largo di Villa Peretti 1
06 399 67700 map 6, H3
09.00-19.00 Tue-Sun €7
A light and airy palazzo housing a collection dating from 300 BC to AD 400. Classical sculpture is found on the lower floors but the highlight is the second floor with entire painted rooms brought from ancient Roman villas. The frescoed dining room from Livia's villa is particularly outstanding: a painted garden with trees and birds that are almost oriental in their grace and simplicity.

Trajan's Market
Via IV Novembre
06 679 0048 map 5, D6
admission charge
Part of Trajan's Imperial Forum, this was one of the first shopping malls: a bustling centre of activity with 150 shops and offices spread over six floors. In AD 107, Trajan tore down a slum to build the complex, which was considered a wonder of the classical world. Each floor was dedicated to selling specific products, with offices for distribution of the corn dole (a social programme for the poor) on the upper storey. Fish were kept alive in ponds fed by fresh water from a dedicated

acqueduct and salt water piped in from Ostia. At time of writing, the Markets are closed temporarily but it is possible to visit Foro di Traiano (Trajan's Forum) at the reduced price of €3.20. Entrance is from Trajan's Column.

Trajan's Column
map 5, C6
Completed in AD 113 the column depicts Trajan's successful campaigns in Dacia (now Romania). Carvings spiral upwards from the base to illustrate events from preparation to victory. The monument is built of marble drums with the joints cleverly concealed. Windows illuminate the interior spiral staircase (closed to the public) which leads to a viewing platform on top, where a statue of St Peter has been standing since 1597.

Laterano & Celio

Museo degli Strumenti Musicali
(Museum of Musical Instruments)
P. de Santa Croce in Gerusalemme
06 701 4796 overview map H4
08.30-19.30 Tue-Sun €2
www.galleriaborghese.it
With more than 3,000 pieces, there is an excellent collection of Baroque instruments. One section is devoted to ancient cultures and another to non-European countries. The museum also has one of the first pianos ever made, dating from 1722, as well as spinets, harpsichords and clavichords.

The Roman Houses (p.182)
enter from Clivo Scauro
06 7045 4544 map 9, D4
10.00-13.00; 15.00-18.00 daily €6
closed Tues, Wed

Trastevere

Museo di Roma in Trastevere
Piazza Sant'Egidio 1
06 581 6563 map 8, F2
10.00-20.00 Tue-Sun €2.60
A small museum with exhibits relating to Roman life and popular culture in the 18th and 19th centuries, with a reconstruction of shops and a tavern.

Out of the Centre

Museo d'Arte Contemporanea Romano (MACRO)
Via Reggio Emilia 54
06 671 070400 overview map G1
09.00-19.00 Tue-Sun, public hols
10.00-14.00, €5.20
www.macro.roma.museum
There are two MACROs. Similar in concept to the Tate Modern, this one is located in a restored Peroni beer factory and is home to the permanent collection and administrative offices. The second (below) is in Testaccio, with temporary exhibitions held at hours to suit the local nightlife.

MACRO al Mattatoio
Piazza Orazio Giustiniani 4 (off map)
16.00-24.00 Tue-Sun

EUR
Located south of the centre, the name is an acronym for *Esposizione Universale di Roma*, a world fair planned by Mussolini before the war to glorify Fascism. The event never took place but the area was made into a model city with glass and steel buildings laid out on a grid. As well as the museum below, there is an old-fashioned amusement park called *LunEur* (Via delle Tre Fontane, open late afternoon/evenings) and Rome's

largest outdoor swimming pool is found here. Take the Metro to EUR Fermi or EUR Palasport

• Piscine delle Rose
Viale della America 20
06 592 717
09.00 19.00 June-Sept.
€10 full day, €8 half day

Museo della Civiltà Romana
Piazza Giovanni Agnelli 10
06 592 6041 off map
09.00-18.15 Tue-Sat; 09.00-13.00 Sun & public hols, €6.20

Opened by Mussolini in 1937 to mark the bi-millennium of the Emperor Augustus. The giant model of 4th century Rome is no longer completely accurate, but it gives a good impression of the city in Constantine's time. Also displayed are casts of the relief carvings from Trajan's Column.

Roman type

The typeface you are now reading (Palatino) has its historical roots in ancient Rome. This is true for all modern Western typefaces. Though the history of writing itself can be traced back to 3000 BC, all modern letterforms have their most immediate heritage in Roman inscriptions.

The language of type hints at this architectural connection: *Roman* means upright as opposed to italic, *capital* is also the term used for the uppermost part of a stone column and we habitually refer to *columns* of type on a page.

Early Latin writing was heavily influenced by these chiselled-in-stone letterforms

but it evolved over the centuries into a variety of other shapes. These include the lower case letter and the introduction of sans serif typefaces (letterforms without additional decorative strokes). The other typeface in this book (Gill Sans) is one such typeface. Many people still regard serif typefaces as the easiest to read, the serifs leading your eye smoothly from one letter to the next.

TRAVEL BASICS

Climate

Spring and autumn are the best times to visit, with warm temperatures (14-22°C) and many sunny days. The summers can be extremely hot and humid (frequently above 30°C) and prone to intense thunderstorms. Romans desert the city in August and many businesses close. Winter weather (5-17°C) is more unpredictable with bursts of heavy rain and icy winds, but snow is rare.

Documents

A visa is not necessary for British and EU passport holders. Non-EU citizens should ask their own consulate or the Italian Embassy.
• Passport Agency 0870 521 0410 www.passport.gov.uk
• Foreign & Commonwealth Office 020 7008 1500 www.fco.gov.uk
• Italian Embassy 020 7312 2200 www.embitaly.org.uk

E111 form (changes)
The E111 form entitles UK residents to free medical and dental treatment and to pay local rates for prescriptions. It is available at UK post offices and must be carried with you. New European Health Insurance cards will replace existing forms. If your certificate is pre-2005, you must obtain a transitional form.

Arriving and departing

By air

For up-to-the-minute flight arrival and departure information for both Fiumicino and Ciampino, log on to the airports of Rome website: www.adr.it 06 65951

Leonardo da Vinci (Fiumicino) airport

Cashpoint
A cashpoint is located in the arrivals baggage claim near carousel 8. Another machine is situated at the train station in terminal B and there is one in the lobby of the Hilton (a 10 minute walk from the car hire hub at terminal C).

Trains to Rome
Trains depart from terminal B. Purchase a ticket before boarding (cash queue is quickest).
Express to Termini: €9.50 one way, journey time 20 minutes.
Stopping train to Trastevere, Ostiense, Tuscolana and Tiburtina: €5.00 one way, 30 minutes to Trastevere.
Tickets must be stamped on the platform before boarding.

The Termini train requires lifting luggage up steps into the train and again into the overhead compartment. The Trastevere train doors are level with the platform allowing luggage to be wheeled onboard. Trains to Trastevere are recommended if your hotel is in Trastevere or on the west side of Centro Storico. There is a taxi rank outside the station or catch the No. 8 tram to Largo Argentina.

At Termini, airport trains arrive and depart at the far end of the train station. It is a 15 minute walk from the main ticket office to the platforms. On departure you can order a taxi to drop you at the entrance nearer the platforms. Tickets can be purchased on the platform before departure.

Nightbus to Rome
A night service departs from Terminal C to Tiburtina station. Tickets cost €3.60 at the automatic machine, or €5 on the bus. Taxis depart from Termini or Tiburtina to your final destination.

A taxi into Rome will cost around €40 and may take longer than the train due to traffic.

Ciampino airport

Ten miles south-east of Rome, this airport is currently used by Ryanair and easyJet.
The COTRAL bus service departs every 30-40 mins to Anagnina metro station (end of line A). Tickets cost €1 from machines in the arrivals hall.

By train (www.trenitalia.it)

Main line trains arrive at Termini.

By bus (www.cotralspa.it)

Tiburtina (metro line B) is the terminus for long distance buses.

Driving

Non-residents are not allowed to drive in the historical centre. It is recommended that you park either in the Termini or Vatican areas.

Parking

• Terminal Park (Stazione Termini)
Via Marsala 30-32
06 4454694
• Terminal Gianicolo (Vaticano)
Via di Porta Cavalleggeri
06 68 40 331
Additional car parks are located by metro stations away from the centre (Anagnina, Cinecittà on line A, or Ponte Mammolo on line B). Fees are economical (some as low as €1.50 per day) but car parks are unattended.

Getting around

Essential information is found on pages 14-37 of this book. Our transport map on page 310 shows principal routes around the city.

Rome's public transport system is run by ATAC. Collect a free transport map *(Mappa dei Trasporti Pubblici)* at their information office in Piazza dei Cinquecento, near Termini (open 07.30-19.00). Download maps from:
www.atac.roma.it

Tourist buses

Two services start from Termini. Buy tickets on board. You can get on and off at any of the stops.
• 110 City Tour Bus, €13
09.00-20.00 daily (every 15 mins)
Open-topped buses make a round trip taking in principal sights.
• Archeobus, €8
09.45-16.45 daily (hourly departures)
Tour of central historical sights and those along Via Appia.

Tourist information

Rome's Tourist Board (APT) has two information offices.
• Fiumicino Airport
International arrivals-terminal B
06 659 56074
08.15-19.00 Mon-Sun
• Visitor Centre, Via Parigi 5
09.00-19.00 Mon-Sat
www.romaturismo.it
In addition, The Comune di Roma (Council of Rome) run the green information kiosks. These are marked on our maps. APT offices also cover the region of Lazio.

Enjoy Rome is an independent tourist office near Termini with a friendly English-speaking staff. Services include free accomodation booking, how to see the city for

less, and walking tours. They even offer a late-night shuttle service to Fiumicino. www.enjoyrome.com
Via Marghera 8A
08.30-19.00 Mon-Fri, 08.30-14.00 Sat

Museum cards

For entrance to museums and monuments.(p.273)

Mondays and holidays

Galleries, museums, shops and restaurants are often closed on Monday. On April 25th (Independence Day) and November 1st (All Saints Day) the above applies and even the Vatican is closed.

Papal Audiences

Anyone can attend, but you need to obtain tickets in advance. Write or fax (less than a month ahead) to:

• Prefettura della Casa Ponteficia, 00120 Città del Vaticano
09.00-13.00 Mon-Sat
15.00-20.00 Tues
06 698 83273, fax 06 698 85863

Indicate your language, the dates of your visit, the number of people in your party, and your address in Rome. You should then collect the tickets the day before, or on the same day, by presenting yourself at the specific window. This is past the 'Bronze door' (Piazza San Pietro at the basilica end of the right arm of the colonnade).

Alternatively, you can complete a form online through the American Catholic Church in Rome, and collect tickets from Santa Susanna near Termini.

• www.santasusanna.org
Via XX Settembre 15, map 6, F2

Disabled travellers

Efforts are being made to broaden accessibility. Stations on metro line B have lifts and adapted toilets and more buses have disabled access. When booking a taxi, ask for a *sedia a rotelle* (wheelchair). There are free parking spaces for disabled visitors with an official placard.

CO.IN and A.N.T.H.A.I are two non-profit associations offering the following services:

Roma per Tutti is a telephone helpline in English to answer queries on accessibility in the city.
06 716 23919, 09.00-17.00 Mon-Fri

Roma Accessibile is a multilingual guide for disabled visitors. To get a free copy, phone or write to:

• CO.IN Via Enrici Giglioli 54A
06 232 67504
www.coinsociale/tourism/services
email: turismo@coinsociale.it

• A.N.T.H.A.I. (Associazione Nazionale Tutela Handicappati e Invalidi)
Corso Vittorio Emanuele 154
06 682 19168, fax 06 688 92684
09.00-13.00, 14.00-20.00 Mon-Fri
General information and assistance.

Medical and dental

Medical treatment

• call **118** for an emergency
• 24 hour English-speaking Medline 06 808 0995

Hospitals (Ospedale)

You can obtain treatment at any of the casualty departments (*pronto soccorso)* of the hospitals marked on our maps.

• Ospedale Fatebenefratelli Isola Tiberina, Piazza Fatebenefratelli 2 06 68371
• Ospedale Pediatrico Bambino Gesù (children only), Piazza S. Onofrio 4 06 68591
• Salvator Mundi Hospital (private) Viale delle Mura Gianicolensi 67 06 588 961
• Ospedale George Eastman Viale Regina Elena 287, 06 844 831 24 hr dental hospital

Chemists (Farmacia)

Many pharmacists speak English and can assist with minor ailments. In Italy, medicine is often given by suppository (*supposta*) to avoid harming the digestion. Be sure to ask the chemist. Usual hours: 8.30-13.00, 16.00-20.00 Mon-Sat

Three central 24 hour chemists:

• Farmacia Internazionale Piazza Barberini 49
• Farmacia della Stazione Piazza dei Cinquecento (Termini).
• Farmacia del Vaticano Porta Sant'Anna entrance (Stocks British/American products)

Embassies

• **UK** Via XX Settembre 80A 06 422 00001
• **Ireland** Piazza Campitelli 3 06 697 9121
• **USA** Via Vittorio Veneto 119A 06 46 741
• **Canada** Via G.B de Rossi 27 06 445 981
• **Australia** Via Alessandria 215 06 445 981
• **New Zealand** Via Zara 28 06 441 7171

Police and emergencies

There are three types of police in Rome and it's important to contact the correct one – do not approach a Carabiniere to report a petty theft or traffic incident.

• *Polizia*, state police dealing with general crime, particularly theft
• *Carabinieri*, military police dealing with serious crime and state security
• *Vigili Urbani*, traffic police

Emergency numbers

• **112** Police (English-speaking)
• **115** Fire Brigade, *Vigili d. Fuoco*
• **118** Ambulance, *Ambulanza*

Thefts and losses

In the event of a theft, a police report will be required if you are going to make an insurance claim. Report to the Polizia station at Termini. If a passport was lost or stolen, contact your embassy. If only credit cards were stolen, and these have been cancelled, it may not be necessary to make a police report – credit card companies are often satisfied with a telephone report.

Communication

Postage

Stamps to the UK cost 41c for letters or postcards and are for sale at post offices or tobacconists. Post letters within the Vatican for speedier delivery: their postal service is run by the Swiss.

Telephones

Dial the city code 06 for all numbers in Rome.

Useful numbers

• 12 Italian directory enquiries
• 170 International operator
• 176 International enquiries

To reach a UK operator dial 172 followed by country code 0044. To call UK mobiles from abroad, dial 0044 and drop the first zero from the number. To ring a local number from a UK mobile within

Rome, dial 06 followed by the number.

Internet cafés

• Internet Café
Via della Pelliccia 21, in Trastevere
Via S. Elena 1, near Largo Argentina
• Easy Internet
Via Barberini 2-16, 06 429 03388
open 24/7 – 250 PCs
• The Netgate
Piazza Firenze 25, 06 689 9098
10.30-21.00 daily – 28 PCs

Money

Banking hours

08:30-13.30, 15.00-16.00 Mon-Fri
Some banks in tourist areas stay open all day. Most banks close on weekends and national holidays.

Cashpoints

Roman *bancomats* vary and some do not accept international transactions from smaller banks. Look for the *Cirrus* symbol and be sure to bring one card from a globally recognized bank. Cards from internet banks may not work in some machines.

Practical

Tobacconists (Tabacchi)

Purchase cigarettes from licensed tobacconists identified by a white T on a black background. These shops often close by 8pm. Some bars will sell cigarettes after hours and there are vending machines tucked into doorways, but these often charge premium prices.

SMOKING IS BANNED IN ALL PUBLIC PLACES, BARS AND RESTAURANTS.

Toilets

Public toilets in Rome are rare and locals rely on bars. It is best to purchase something before availing yourself of the facilities. Toilets are often unisex as many bars have only one small cubicle.

Tipping

Tipping is left to your discretion but, as a guide, approximately €5 per week for hotel maids and €6 per week for breakfast in the hotel restaurant.

Entertainment

What's on

Events listings on the web:
• www.whatsoninrome.com
Events listed in publications:
• Wanted in Rome
a monthly English magazine
• Roma C'e
a weekly listing in English

Tickets

Book in advance for concerts and other cultural events from agencies in Rome (booking fee).
•Orbis, Piazza Esquilino 37
06 482 7403
• Ricordi, Via del Corso 506
06 320 2790
• www.ticketone.it

English language cinema

• Pasquino, Piazza Sant'Egidio 10
06 581 5208, no credit cards
This cinema screens only English language films. Daily showings on three screens.
•Nuovo Sacher, Largo Ascianghi 1
06 581 8116, no credit cards
Owned by actor and director Nanni Moretti. The cinema is named after Moretti's favourite sacher torte from Valzani. *Versione originale* film screenings Mon-Tues. Films screened outdoors in summer.

Other cinemas show films in the original language at designated times. Check film listings on www.whatsoninrome.com

Music

Contemporary

• Alexanderplatz, Via Ostia 9
06 367 42171, monthly pass €7
21.00-01.30 Mon-Sat
Legendary jazz club near Ottaviano. Dinner served from 9pm, concerts start at 10.30pm. They host outdoor concerts at Villa Celimontana in summer.

• Big Mama
Vicolo San Francesco a Ripa 18
06 581 2551, monthly pass €7
21.30-01.30 Tues-Sat
Small 20-year-old blues club in Trastevere. Hosts Italian and international bands.

• Fonclea, Via Crescenzio 82
06 689 6302, map 3-4, E1
12.00-15.00, 20.30-02.00 daily
free except Sat, €5
This club, pub and restaurant has been hosting blues, jazz and rock since the 1970s.

Classical, Opera and Ballet

Rome finally got its new major auditorium, **Parco della Musica**, in 2002. (see panel)
Other venues are:

• Teatro dell'Opera
Piazza Gigli 1, map 6, G4
06 481 601, summer programme at Terme di Caracalla

• Accademia Filamonica Romana
Via Flaminia 118 (Flaminio metro)
06 320 1752

• Oratorio del Gonfalone
Via del Gonfalone 32A, map 11, A3
06 687 5952

• Accademia Nazionale di Santa Cecilia
06 808 2058, www.santacecilia.it
various locations around the city

Many churches in the city host concerts. We have indicated this in our book by the symbol ♪.

Parco della Musica

Via P. de Coubertin 15
06 808 2058, www.auditorium.com
10.00-18.00 daily, admission free
Designed by Renzo Piano, the three concert halls that make up this complex in the north of the city have more than lived up to expectations. Large bug-like structures surround a spacious outdoor venue, complete with an area of Roman ruins uncovered during construction. The complex also contains a bookshop, restaurant and bar.

Theatre

For current information about English language theatre, go to www.whatsoninrome.com
There is often something taking place in the Forum during the summer to interest all ages.
Rome's most beautiful theatre is:

• Teatro Argentina, Largo di Torre Argentina 52, map 11-12, E4
06 688 04601, museum open by appt

Sport

The following is a list of activities in the central area of Rome.

Gym/Swimming

• Roman Sport Center
Viale del Galoppatoio 33
(entrance in Via Veneto) map 2, G6
06 320 1667
June-Oct 09.00-22.00 daily
Nov-May 09.00-22.00 Mon-Sat
daily pass €26
Two Olympic sized swimming pools, aerobics studios, a gym, dry and steam saunas, squash courts and sunbeds.

Jogging

Villa Borghese and Villa Doria Pamphilj have running paths.

Football (spectating)
Romans are passionate and political about their teams: Roma and Lazio. Roma supporters are left-wing, Lazio supporters lean to the right. Teams play Sundays, September-June at Stadio Olimpico. Purchase tickets from the clubs' own stores (cash only).
• AS Roma Store, Piazza Colonna 360
•Lazio Point, Via Farini 34

Cycle Hire
Occasional car-free days make cycling in Rome a pleasant option. Bikes can be hired from:
•Collalti Bici, Via del Pellegrino 82
06 688 01084, 09.00-13.00, 15.30-19.30 Tues-Sat
• in the Pincio Gardens
• Appia Antica Visitors Centre
Via Appia Antica 42

Children

Most children will have some knowledge about ancient Rome, either from school or from reading *Asterix*, but pick up the English version of *Conosci Roma* when you arrive. This free children's guide to Rome is available from the information kiosks around the city.

• The Colosseum – Always a winner, as costumed gladiators usually lurk around willing to be photographed.
•The Forum – Purchase one of the overlay guidebooks to see how it all once looked.
•The Palatine – A green picnic spot, with orange trees and great views.
• Villa Borghese – Many activities for children (p.162)
• Explora – Hands-on museum for children (p.275)
• Appia Antica – The Appian Way National Park. Hire bikes

Annual Events and Festivals
(including public holidays)

Spring
Festa di Santa Francesca Romana 9 March
Motor vehicles of any kind are taken to the church of Santa Francesca Romana to be blessed.
Maratona della Città di Roma
3rd Sunday in March
www.maratonadiroma.it
Rome's annual marathon begins and ends at the Via dei Fori Imperiali. Sign up online.
Settimana Santa e Pasqua
(Holy Week and Easter) March/April
• Good Friday, Colosseum
The Pope leads an outdoor mass followed by the Procession of the Cross at 9pm.
• Easter Sunday (public holiday)
St Peter's Square
The Pope leads Easter mass and gives blessings.
• Easter Monday (public holiday)
Festa della Primavera
March/April
Azaleas on the Spanish Steps.
Natale di Roma 21 April
Rome's birthday celebrated at the Campidoglio with fireworks.
La Festa della Liberazione
25 April (public holiday)
Everything in Rome is closed.
Settimana dei Beni Culturali
late April/May www.beniculturali.it
Culture week. Museums and monuments offer free admission and have longer opening hours. Special art collections normally closed to the public are open.
Primo Maggio (Labour Day)
1 May (public holiday)
Bus services suspended. Free concert in Piazza San Giovanni.

Summer

Republic Day
2 June (public holiday)
Anniversary of the Republic.

Festa di San Giovanni
23-24 June
Piazza di Porta San Giovanni
Celebrated with fireworks, food and a candlelit procession.

Festa di San Pietro e Paolo
29 June, St Peter's & San Paolo
St Peter's holds a mass, St Paul's has an all night street-fair.

Festa delle Catene
1 August, San Pietro in Vincoli
St Peter's chains on display in a special mass.

Festa della Madonna della Neve
5 August, Santa Maria Maggiore
Flower petals are released onto the congregation during mass.

Ferragosto (Assumption)
15 August (public holiday)
Virtually everything is closed.

Autumn

La Notte Bianca
September/October
www.lanottebianca.it
'The White Night', when most attractions are open all night.

RomaEuropa
September-November
www.romaeuropa.net
Based at the Villa Medici, one of Rome's major arts festivals.

Tutti Santi (All Saints)
1 November (public holiday)
Absolutely everything is closed.

Vino Novello Tasting
late November
Celebration of the year's new wine in Campo de' Fiori.

Winter

Festa dell'Immacolata Concezione
December 8 (public holiday)
Piazza di Spagna
Feast of the Immaculate Conception celebrated around a statue of the Madonna.

Midnight Mass
December 24, St Peter's
Service held by the Pope. Book months in advance. Call Prefettura office: 066 988 3273/ 3114

Natale and Santo Stefano
(Christmas Day and Boxing Day)
25, 26 December (Public Holidays)
Piazza San Pietro
Christmas message and blessing.

San Silvestro and Capodanno
(New Year's Eve and New Year's Day)
31 December
1 January (Public Holiday)
Piazza del Popolo
Welcome the new year with a free concert, disco, and fireworks. Some elderly residents still honour the tradition of throwing unwanted furniture from their balconies. A few brave souls dive from Ponte Cavour into the Tiber.

Christmas market and Epifania
mid-December-mid-January
Piazza Navona
A traditional Christmas market with children's events, culminates at Epiphany (6 January, public holiday) with the arrival of Befana, a good witch bringing more presents.

Index

T

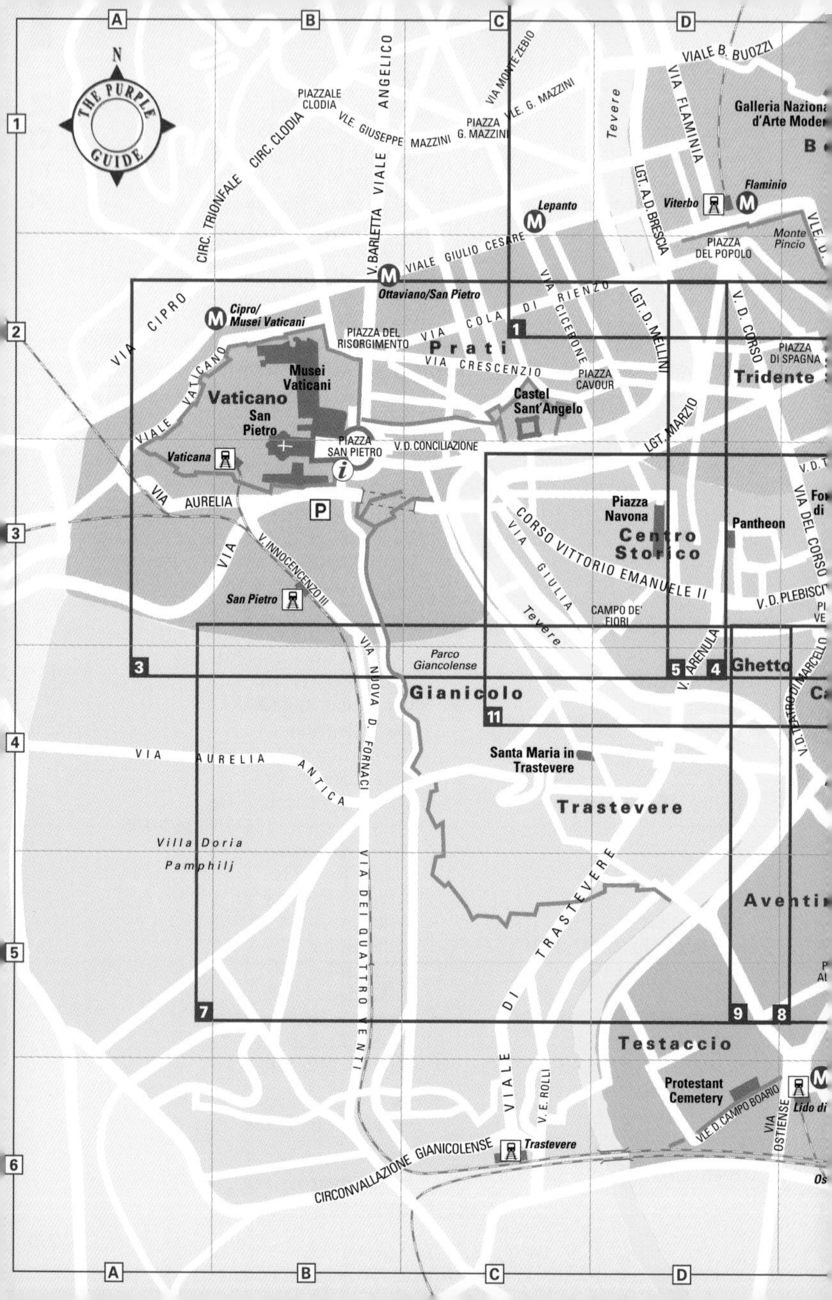

THE PURPLE GUIDE
N
A
B
C
D
1
2
3
4
5
6
PIAZZALE CLODIA
CIRC. CLODIA
CIRC. TRIONFALE
VLE. GIUSEPPE MAZZINI
PIAZZA G. MAZZINI
VLE. G. MAZZINI
VIA MONTE ZEBIO
VIALE ANGELICO
V. BARLETTA
VIALE B. BUOZZI
VIA FLAMINIA
Tevere
LGT. A.D. BRESCIA
Galleria Nazionale d'Arte Moderna
Viterbo
Flaminio
Lepanto
VIALE GIULIO CESARE
PIAZZA DEL POPOLO
Monte Pincio
Ottaviano/San Pietro
VIA CIPRO
Cipro/ Musei Vaticani
VIA COLA DI RIENZO
VIA CICERONE
LGT. D. MELLINI
V. D. CORSO
PIAZZA DI SPAGNA
Tridente
PIAZZA DEL RISORGIMENTO
Prati
VIA CRESCENZIO
PIAZZA CAVOUR
VIALE VATICANO
Musei Vaticani
Vaticano
San Pietro
Castel Sant'Angelo
LGT. MARZIO
PIAZZA SAN PIETRO
V. D. CONCILIAZIONE
Vaticana
VIA AURELIA
P
Piazza Navona
Pantheon
VIA DEL CORSO
CORSO VITTORIO EMANUELE II
VIA GIULIA
Centro Storico
V.INNOCENCENZO III
San Pietro
V. D. PLEBISCITO
CAMPO DE' FIORI
Tevere
Parco Giancolense
VIA NUOVA D. FORNACI
V. ARENULA
Ghetto
Gianicolo
V. D. TEATRO DI MARCELLO
VIA AURELIA ANTICA
Santa Maria in Trastevere
Trastevere
Villa Doria Pamphilj
VIA DEI QUATTRO VENTI
VIALE DI TRASTEVERE
Aventino
Testaccio
Protestant Cemetery
VLE. D. CAMPO BOARIO
VIA OSTIENSE
VIALE
V. E. ROLLI
Trastevere
CIRCONVALLAZIONE GIANICOLENSE
1
3
4
5
7
8
9
11

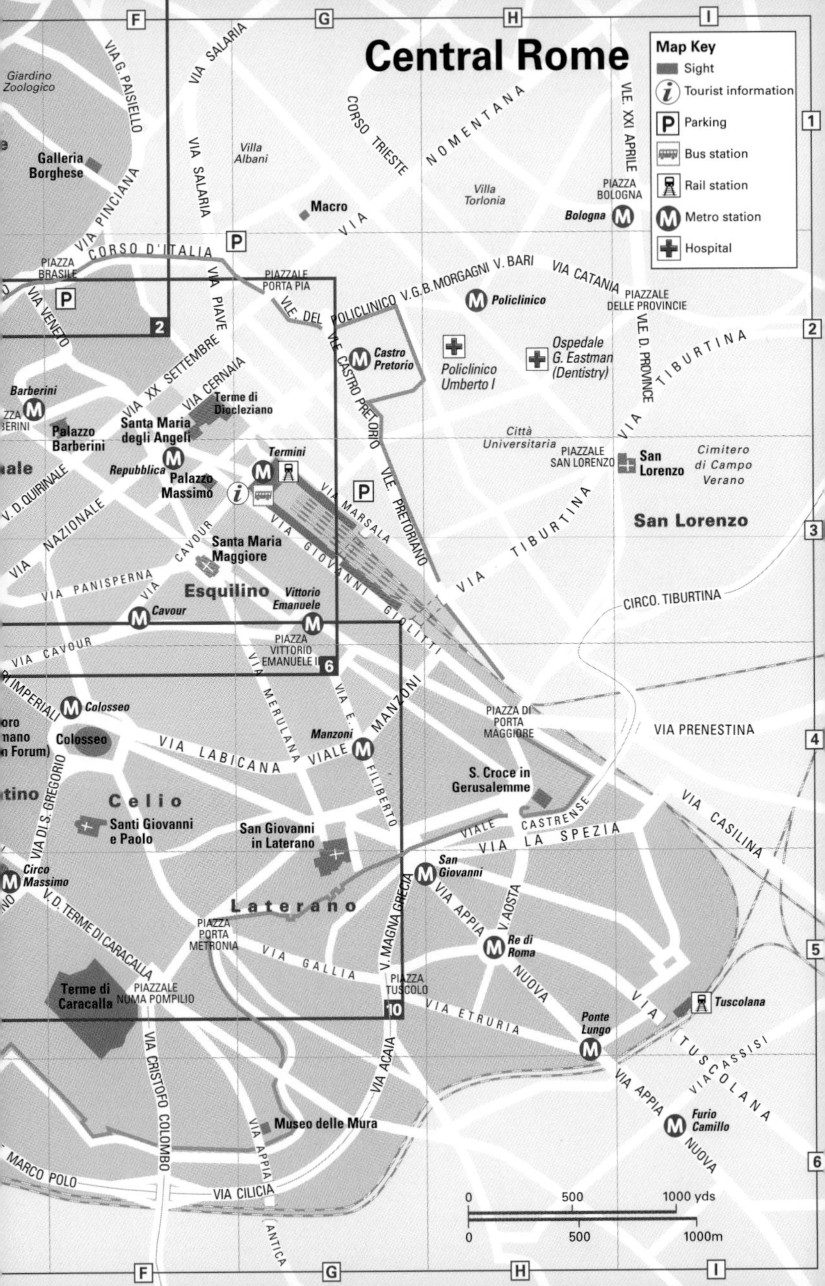

Central Rome
Map Key
Sight
Tourist information
Parking
Bus station
Rail station
Metro station
Hospital
F
G
H
I
1
2
3
4
5
6
Giardino Zoologico
Galleria Borghese
Villa Albani
Macro
Villa Torlonia
Policlinico Umberto I
Ospedale G. Eastman (Dentistry)
Città Universitaria
San Lorenzo
Cimitero di Campo Verano
Barberini
Palazzo Barberini
Santa Maria degli Angeli
Terme di Diocleziano
Repubblica
Palazzo Massimo
Termini
Castro Pretorio
Policlinico
Bologna
Santa Maria Maggiore
Esquilino
Cavour
Vittorio Emanuele
Colosseo
Celio
Santi Giovanni e Paolo
San Giovanni in Laterano
Manzoni
S. Croce in Gerusalemme
San Giovanni
Laterano
Circo Massimo
Re di Roma
Terme di Caracalla
Museo delle Mura
Ponte Lungo
Tuscolana
Furio Camillo
VIA G. PAISIELLO
VIA SALARIA
CORSO TRIESTE
NOMENTANA
VLE. XXI APRILE
PIAZZA BOLOGNA
VIA PINCIANA
CORSO D'ITALIA
PIAZZA BRASILE
VIA VENETO
VIA PIAVE
PIAZZALE PORTA PIA
VLE. DEL POLICLINICO
V.G.B. MORGAGNI
V. BARI
VIA CATANIA
PIAZZALE DELLE PROVINCIE
VLE. D. PROVINCE
VIA TIBURTINA
VIA XX SETTEMBRE
VIA CERNAIA
VLE CASTRO PRETORIO
PIAZZALE SAN LORENZO
V. D. QUIRINALE
VIA NAZIONALE
VIA MARSALA
VLE. PRETORIANO
VIA CAVOUR
VIA GIOVANNI GIOLITTI
VIA PANISPERNA
CIRCO. TIBURTINA
PIAZZA VITTORIO EMANUELE II
VIA MERULANA
VIA E. FILIBERTO
VIALE MANZONI
PIAZZA DI PORTA MAGGIORE
VIA PRENESTINA
VIA LABICANA
VIA DI S. GREGORIO
VIALE CASTRENSE
VIA LA SPEZIA
VIA CASILINA
VIA APPIA NUOVA
V. AOSTA
V. MAGNA GRECIA
PIAZZA PORTA METRONIA
V. D. TERME DI CARACALLA
VIA GALLIA
PIAZZA TUSCOLO
VIA ETRURIA
PIAZZALE NUMA POMPILIO
VIA TUSCOLANA
VIA CASSISI
VIA CRISTOFO COLOMBO
VIA ACAIA
VIA APPIA
VIA MARCO POLO
VIA CILICIA
ANTICA
2
6
10
0
500
1000 yds
0
500
1000m

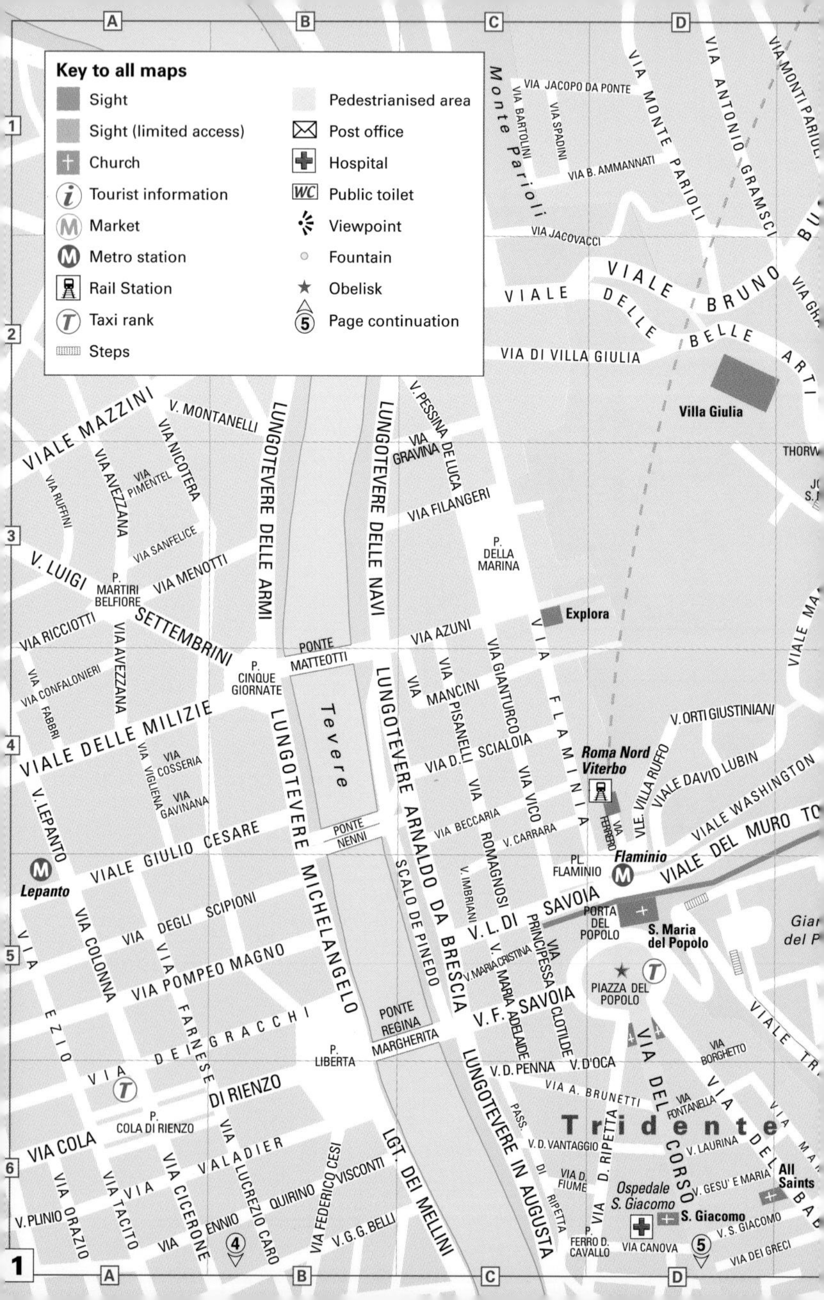

Key to all maps
Sight
Sight (limited access)
Church
Tourist information
Market
Metro station
Rail Station
Taxi rank
Steps
Pedestrianised area
Post office
Hospital
Public toilet
Viewpoint
Fountain
Obelisk
Page continuation
Monte Parioli
VIA JACOPO DA PONTE
VIA BARTOLINI
VIA SPADINI
VIA B. AMMANNATI
VIA MONTE PARIOLI
VIA ANTONIO GRAMSCI
VIA MONTI PARIOLI
VIA JACOVACCI
VIALE DELLE BELLE ARTI
VIALE BRUNO BUOZZI
VIA DI VILLA GIULIA
Villa Giulia
VIALE MAZZINI
V. MONTANELLI
VIA NICOTERA
VIA PIMENTEL
VIA RUFFINI
VIA AVEZZANA
VIA SANFELICE
VIA MENOTTI
V. LUIGI SETTEMBRINI
P. MARTIRI BELFIORE
LUNGOTEVERE DELLE ARMI
LUNGOTEVERE DELLE NAVI
V. PESSINA
VIA GRAVINA
DE LUCA
VIA FILANGERI
P. DELLA MARINA
Explora
VIA RICCIOTTI
VIA CONFALONIERI
VIA FABBRI
PONTE MATTEOTTI
P. CINQUE GIORNATE
VIA AZUNI
VIA MANCINI
VIA PISANELLI
VIA GIANTURCO
VIA FLAMINIA
Tevere
VIALE DELLE MILIZIE
VIA VIGLIENA
VIA COSSERIA
VIA GAVINANA
V. LEPANTO
LUNGOTEVERE MICHELANGELO
LUNGOTEVERE ARNALDO DA BRESCIA
VIA D. SCIALOIA
VIA VICO
VIA BECCARIA
VIA ROMAGNOSI
V. CARRARA
V. ORTI GIUSTINIANI
VLE. VILLA RUFFO
VIALE DAVID LUBIN
VIALE WASHINGTON
VIALE DEL MURO TORTO
Roma Nord Viterbo
VIA FERRERO
PONTE NENNI
VIALE GIULIO CESARE
Lepanto
SCALO DE PINEDO
V. IMBRIANI
PL. FLAMINIO
Flaminio
V. L. DI SAVOIA
PORTA DEL POPOLO
S. Maria del Popolo
VIA COLONNA
VIA DEGLI SCIPIONI
VIA POMPEO MAGNO
VIA EZIO
V. MARIA CRISTINA
V. MARIA ADELAIDE
VIA PRINCIPESSA CLOTILDE
PIAZZA DEL POPOLO
V. F. SAVOIA
VIA DEI GRACCHI
VIA FARNESE
PONTE REGINA MARGHERITA
P. LIBERTA
V. D. PENNA
V. D'OCA
VIA DEL CORSO
VIA BORGHETTO
VIALE TRINITÀ
DI RIENZO
P. COLA DI RIENZO
VIA COLA
VIA VALADIER
VIA LUCREZIO CARO
VIA FEDERICO CESI
VISCONTI
QUIRINO
LGT. DEI MELLINI
LUNGOTEVERE IN AUGUSTA
VIA A. BRUNETTI
PASS. DI RIPETTA
V. D. VANTAGGIO
VIA D. RIPETTA
VIA FONTANELLA
V. LAURINA
VIA DEL BABUINO
Tridente
VIA ORAZIO
VIA TACITO
VIA CICERONE
VIA ENNIO
V. G. G. BELLI
V. PLINIO
VIA D. FIUME
Ospedale S. Giacomo
S. Giacomo
V. GESU' E MARIA
All Saints
V. S. GIACOMO
VIA DEI GRECI
P. FERRO D. CAVALLO
VIA CANOVA
Giardino del Pincio

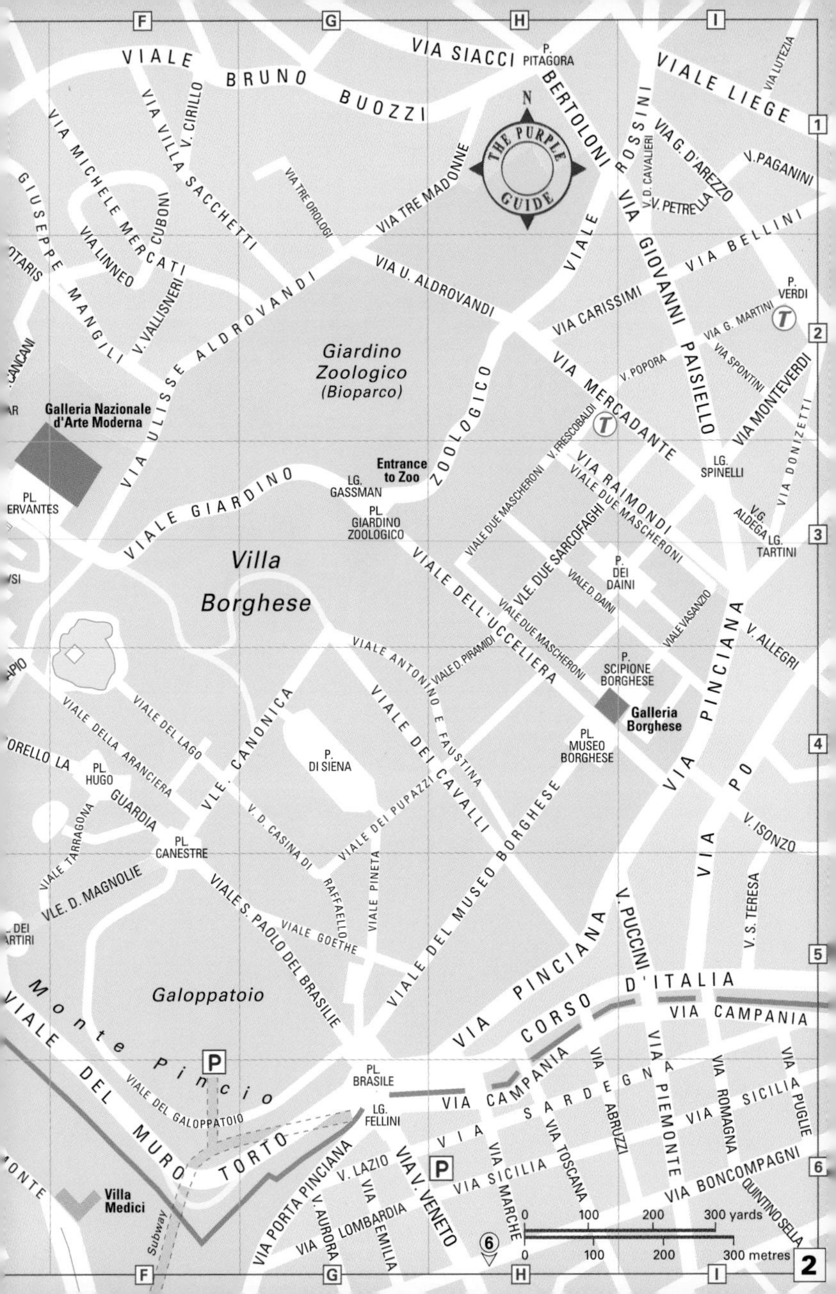

VIALE BRUNO BUOZZI
VIA SIACCI
P. PITAGORA
VIALE LIEGI
VIA LUTEZIA
BERTOLONI
VIA GIOVANNI PAISIELLO
ROSSINI
V. PAGANINI
VIA G. D'AREZZO
V. D. CAVALIERI
V. PETRELLA
VIA BELLINI
P. VERDI
VIA CARISSIMI
VIA G. MARTINI
VIA SPONTINI
VIA MONTEVERDI
V. POPORA
VIA MERCADANTE
V. FRESCOBALDI
LG. SPINELLI
VIA DONIZETTI
VIA RAIMONDI
V.G. ALDEGA
LG. TARTINI
THE PURPLE GUIDE
N
VIA CIRILLO
VIA VILLA SACCHETTI
VIA MICHELE MERCATI
CUBONI
GIUSEPPE
NOTARIS
VIA LINNEO
MANGILI
V. VALLISNERI
VIA TRE OROLOGI
VIA TRE MADONNE
VIA U. ALDROVANDI
VIALE
VIA ULISSE ALDROVANDI
Giardino Zoologico (Bioparco)
VIALE ZOOLOGICO
Galleria Nazionale d'Arte Moderna
PL. CERVANTES
Entrance to Zoo
LG. GASSMAN
PL. GIARDINO ZOOLOGICO
VIALE GIARDINO
Villa Borghese
VIALE DUE MASCHERONI
VLE. DUE SARCOFAGHI
P. DEI DAINI
VIALE D. DAINI
VIALE VASANZIO
VIALE DELL'UCCELIERA
P. SCIPIONE BORGHESE
Galleria Borghese
VIA PINCIANA
V. ALLEGRI
VIALE ANTONINO E FAUSTINA
VIALE D. PIRAMIDI
VIALE DEI CAVALLI
PL. MUSEO BORGHESE
VIA PO
V. ISONZO
VIALE DEL LAGO
VIALE DELLA ARANCIERA
PL. HUGO
GUARDIA
VLE. CANONICA
P. DI SIENA
VIALE DEI PUPAZZI
V. D. CASINA DI RAFFAELLO
VIALE PINETA
VIALE DEL MUSEO BORGHESE
VIALE TARRAGONA
PL. CANESTRE
VLE. D. MAGNOLIE
VIALE S. PAOLO DEL BRASILIE
VIALE GOETHE
V. PUCCINI
V.S. TERESA
CORSO D'ITALIA
VIA CAMPANIA
Galoppatoio
Monte Pincio
VIALE DEL MURO TORTO
VIALE DEL GALOPPATOIO
P
PL. BRASILE
LG. FELLINI
VIA SARDEGNA
VIA ABRUZZI
VIA PIEMONTE
VIA ROMAGNA
VIA SICILIA
VIA PUGLIE
VIA TOSCANA
VIA MARCHE
VIA BONCOMPAGNI
QUINTINO SELLA
VIA V. VENETO
V. LAZIO
VIA PORTA PINCIANA
V. AURORA
VIA EMILIA
VIA LOMBARDIA
Villa Medici
Subway
6
0 100 200 300 yards
0 100 200 300 metres
F G H I
1 2 3 4 5 6
2

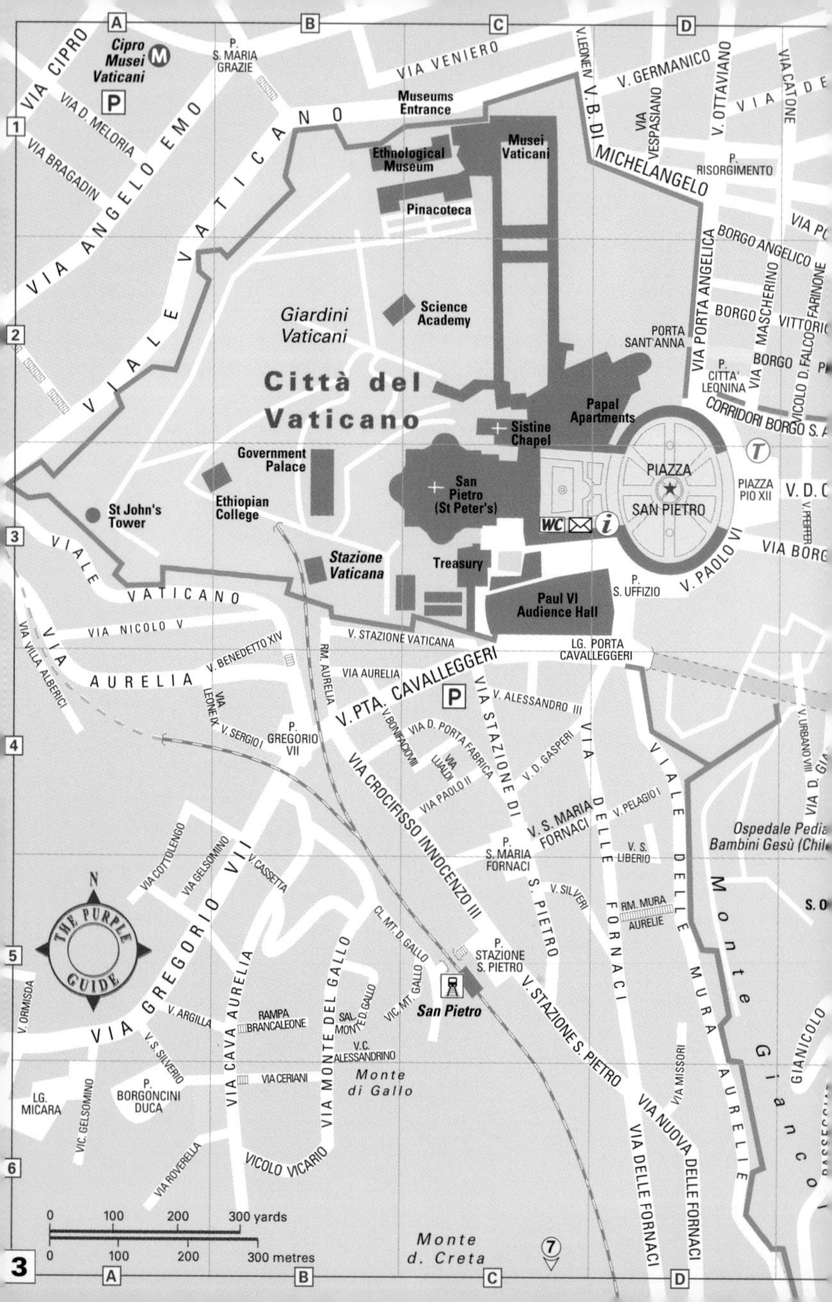

Città del Vaticano
Giardini Vaticani
Museums Entrance
Musei Vaticani
Ethnological Museum
Pinacoteca
Science Academy
Sistine Chapel
Papal Apartments
Government Palace
Ethiopian College
St John's Tower
San Pietro (St Peter's)
Stazione Vaticana
Treasury
Paul VI Audience Hall
PIAZZA SAN PIETRO
Cipro Musei Vaticani
San Pietro
Monte di Gallo
Monte d. Creta
Monte Gianicolo
Ospedale Pedia
Bambini Gesù (Chile
VIALE VATICANO
VIA ANGELO EMO
VIA CIPRO
VIA VENIERO
V. GERMANICO
VIA CATONE
V. OTTAVIANO
V.B. DI MICHELANGELO
VIA PORTA ANGELICA
BORGO ANGELICO
CORRIDORI BORGO S. A
VIA AURELIA
V. PTA. CAVALLEGGERI
VIA STAZIONE DI S. PIETRO
VIA CROCIFISSO INNOCENZO III
VIA GREGORIO VII
VIA CAVA AURELIA
VIA MONTE DEL GALLO
V. STAZIONE S. PIETRO
VIA DELLE FORNACI
VIALE DELLE MURA AURELIE
VIA NUOVA DELLE FORNACI
V. STAZIONE VATICANA
LG. PORTA CAVALLEGGERI
P. GREGORIO VII
P. S. MARIA FORNACI
P. STAZIONE S. PIETRO
PIAZZA PIO XII
P. S. UFFIZIO
PORTA SANT'ANNA
P. RISORGIMENTO
P. S. MARIA GRAZIE
P. BORGONCINI DUCA
LG. MICARA
0 100 200 300 yards
0 100 200 300 metres
THE PURPLE GUIDE

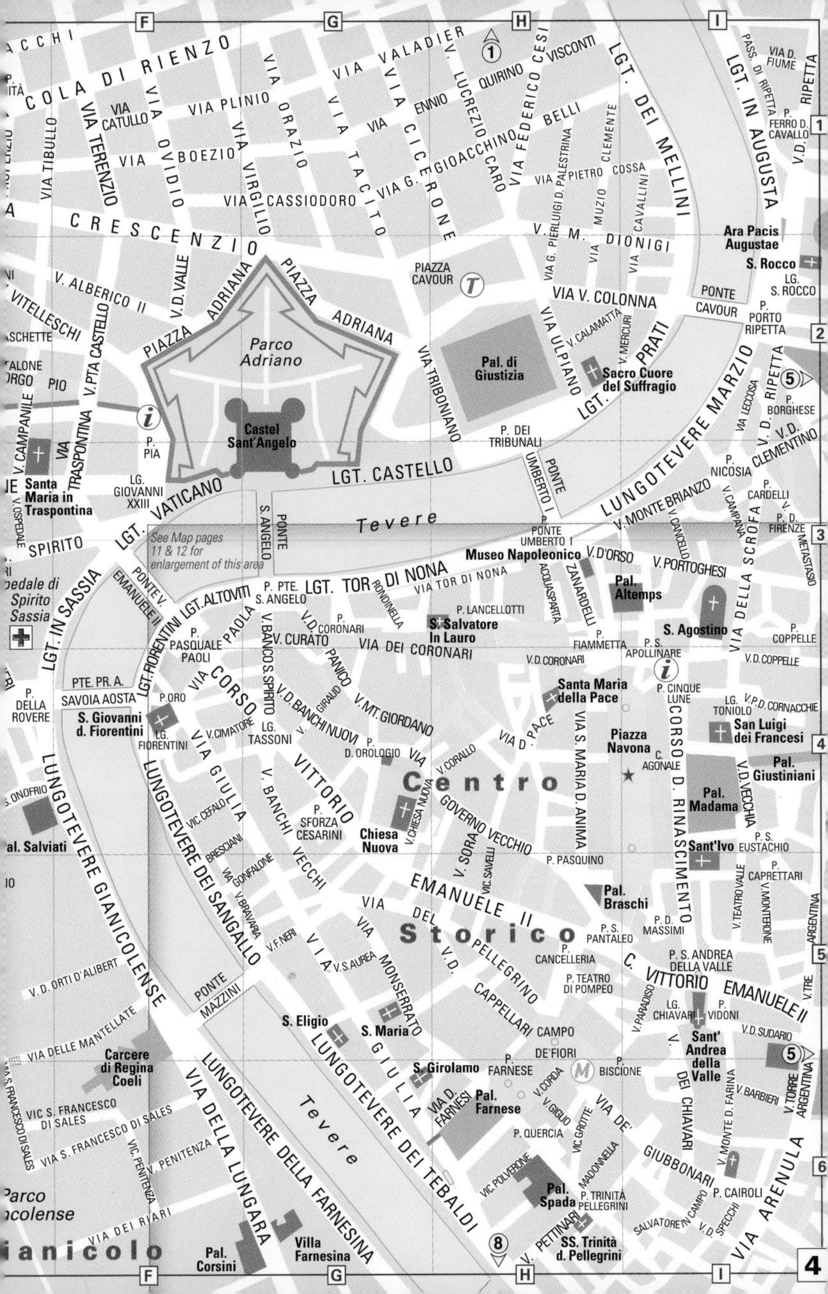
F
G
H
I
1
2
3
4
5
6
COLA DI RIENZO
VIA VALADIER
VIA TERENZIO
VIA CATULLO
VIA OVIDIO
VIA PLINIO
VIA BOEZIO
VIA TIBULLO
VIA VIRGILIO
VIA ORAZIO
VIA TACITO
VIA CICERONE
VIA CASSIODORO
V. LUCREZIO CARO
VIA ENNIO QUIRINO VISCONTI
VIA G. GIOACCHINO BELLI
VIA FEDERICO CESI
VIA PIETRO COSSA
VIA G. PIERLUIGI D. PALESTRINA
VIA MUZIO CLEMENTE
VIA CAVALLINI
V. M. DIONIGI
LGT. DEI MELLINI
LGT. IN AUGUSTA
PASS. DI RIPETTA
VIA D. FIUME
RIPETTA
P. FERRO D. CAVALLO
V.D.
CRESCENZIO
V. ALBERICO II
V.D. VALLE
VITELLESCHI
PIAZZA ADRIANA
Parco Adriano
Castel Sant'Angelo
PIAZZA CAVOUR
VIA V. COLONNA
VIA ULPIANO
V. CALAMATTA
V. MERCURI
PONTE CAVOUR
Ara Pacis Augustae
S. Rocco
LG. S. ROCCO
P. PORTO RIPETTA
LGT. PRATI
Pal. di Giustizia
Sacro Cuore del Suffragio
VIA TRIBONIANO
V.PTA CASTELLO
BORGO PIO
VIA TRASPONTINA
V. CAMPANILE
Santa Maria in Traspontina
P. PIA
LG. GIOVANNI XXIII
LGT. VATICANO
LGT. CASTELLO
P. DEI TRIBUNALI
PONTE UMBERTO I
LUNGOTEVERE MARZIO
VIA LECCOSA
P. BORGHESE
V.D. CLEMENTINO
P. NICOSIA
V. MONTE BRIANZO
V. CAMPANA
P. CARDELLI
P. D. FIRENZE
METASTASIO
Tevere
S. ANGELO PONTE
SPIRITO
V. OSPEDALE
LGT.
See Map pages 11 & 12 for enlargement of this area
Ospedale di Spirito Sassia
LGT. IN SASSIA
PONTE V. EMANUELE II
P. PTE. S. ANGELO
LGT. TOR DI NONA
VIA TOR DI NONA
RONDINELLA
P. PONTE UMBERTO I
Museo Napoleonico
V. D'ORSO
V. CANCELLO
V. PORTOGHESI
VIA DELLA SCROFA
ACQUASPARTA
ZANARDELLI
Pal. Altemps
S. Agostino
P. COPPELLE
V.D. COPPELLE
LGT. ALTOVITI
LGT. FIORENTINI
P. PASQUALE PAOLI
PAOLA
V. BANCO S. SPIRITO
V.D. CORONARI
P. CORONARI
P. LANCELLOTTI
S. Salvatore In Lauro
V. CURATO
VIA DEI CORONARI
P. FIAMMETTA
P. S. APOLLINARE
V.D. CORONARI
PTE. PR. A.
SAVOIA AOSTA
P. DELLA ROVERE
VIA CORSO
PANICO
GIRAUD
V.D. BANCHI NUOVI
V. MT. GIORDANO
Santa Maria della Pace
P. CINQUE LUNE
LG. TONIOLO
V.P.D. CORNACCHIE
S. Giovanni d. Fiorentini
P. ORO
LG. FIORENTINI
V. CIMATORE
LG. TASSONI
P. D. OROLOGIO
VIA D. PACE
VIA S. MARIA D. ANIMA
Piazza Navona
C. AGONALE
CORSO D. RINASCIMENTO
San Luigi dei Francesi
Pal. Giustiniani
LUNGOTEVERE GIANICOLENSE
S. ONOFRIO
Pal. Salviati
LUNGOTEVERE DEI SANGALLO
VIA GIULIA
VIC. CEFALO
BRESCIANI
VIA GONFALONE
V. BRAVARIA
V. BANCHI VECCHI
VITTORIO
P. SFORZA CESARINI
V. CORALLO
Centro
Chiesa Nuova
V. CHIESA NUOVA
GOVERNO VECCHIO
V. SORA
VIC. SAVELLI
Pal. Madama
V.D. VECCHIA
Sant'Ivo
P. S. EUSTACHIO
P. CAPRETTARI
V. TEATRO VALLE
V. MONTERONE
ARGENTINA
P. PASQUINO
Pal. Braschi
EMANUELE II
VIA DEL PELLEGRINO
Storico
P. S. PANTALEO
P. D. MASSIMI
P. S. ANDREA DELLA VALLE
V. F. NERI
VIA MONSERRATO
V. S. AUREA
P. CANCELLERIA
P. TEATRO DI POMPEO
C. VITTORIO EMANUELE II
V. TRE
V.D. ORTI D'ALIBERT
PONTE MAZZINI
V.D. CAPPELLARI
V. PARADISO
LG. CHIAVARI
P. VIDONI
V.D. SUDARIO
VIA DELLE MANTELLATE
Carcere di Regina Coeli
S. Eligio
S. Maria
CAMPO DE' FIORI
Sant' Andrea della Valle
S. Girolamo
P. FARNESE
BISCIONE
V. CORDA
V. BARBIERI
V. TORRE ARGENTINA
VIA GIULIA
VIA D. FARNESI
Pal. Farnese
V. GIGLIO
VIA DE' GIUBBONARI
V. DEI CHIAVARI
V. MONTE D. FARINA
VIC S. FRANCESCO DI SALES
VIA S. FRANCESCO DI SALES
VIC. PENITENZA
V. PENITENZA
VIA DELLA LUNGARA
LUNGOTEVERE DELLA FARNESINA
LUNGOTEVERE DEI TEBALDI
P. QUERCIA
VIC. GROTTE
MADONNELLA
VIC. POLVERONE
Pal. Spada
P. TRINITÀ PELLEGRINI
P. CAIROLI
VIA ARENULA
Parco Gianicolense
VIA DEI RIARI
Gianicolo
Pal. Corsini
Villa Farnesina
V. PETTINARI
SS. Trinità d. Pellegrini
SALVATORE IN CAMPO
V.D. SPECCHI
1
5
8
4

A
B
C
D
1
2
3
4
5
6
Tridente
V. D. VANTAGGIO
LGT. IN AUGUSTA
PASS. DI RIPETTA
VIA D. FIUME
VIA D. RIPETTA
Ospedale S. Giacomo
S. Giacomo
V. GESU' E MARIA
V. S. GIACOMO
VIA DEL BABUINO
VIA MARGUTTA
VLE. TRINITÀ DEI MONTE
V. SEBASTIANELLO
Villa Medici
VLE D. MURO TORTO
Subway
VIA PORTA PINCIANA
V. LAZIO
VIA LOMBARDIA
VIA AURORA
VIA EMILIA
VIA LUDOVISI
VIA CADORE
P. FERRO D. CAVALLO
VIA CANOVA
VIA DEI GRECI
VIA ORSOLINE
V. ALIBERT
VIA D. FREZZA
P. AUGUSTO IMPERATORE
VIA DEL CORSO
VIA VITTORIA
Spagna
WC
Trinità dei Monti
Mausoleo di Augusto
Ara Pacis Augustae
VIA BELSIANA
V. BOCCA DI LEONE
VIA D. CROCE
P. DI SPAGNA
Scalinata di Spagna (Spanish Steps)
S. Rocco
S. Carlo
LG. S. ROCCO
LG. S. CARLO AL CORSO
VIA D. CARROZZE
Museo Keats-Shelley
VIA CRISPI
VIA D. ARTISTI
V. S. ISIDORO
VIA VITTORIA
PONTE CAVOUR
P. PORTO RIPETTA
P. AUGUSTO IMPERATORE
VIA TOMACELLI
VIA CONDOTTI
VIA MARIO DE' FIORI
VIA GREGORIANA
VIA SISTINA
VIA PURIFICAZIONE
Santa Conce
VIA DELL'ARANCIO
LG. GOLDONI
VIA BORGOGNONA
P. MIGNANELLI
V. LEONCINO
Pal. Borghese
V. F. BORGHESE
V. BORGHESE
LG. F. BORGHESE
VIA FRATTINA
V. PROPAGANDA
VIA DUE MACELLI
V. CAPPUCCINI
VIA DI RIPETTA
VIA LECCOSA
P. BORGHESE
V. D. CLEMENTINO
V. D. LEONE
P. S. LORENZO IN LUCINA
VIA D. VITE
VIA MORETTO
LE CASE
V. ZUCCHELLI
Fontana del Tritone
BARB
P. NICOSIA
BIAGIO
P. TORRETTA
VIC. DEL DIVINO AMORE
V. D. LUPA
V. CPO. MARZIO
S. Lorenzo in Lucina
V. D. GAMBERO
VIA D. MERCEDE
V. CAPO
V. S. D. FRATTE
S. Andrea delle Fratte
VIA DEL TRITONE
P. CARDELLI
V. IN LUCINA
VIA CONVERTITE
P. S. SILVESTRO
LG. NAZERENO
LG. TRITONE
V. D. AVIGNONESI
V. BOCCACCIO
V. RASELLA
V. CAMPANA
VIA DELLA SCROFA
V. METASTASIO
P. D. FIRENZE
V. D. PREFETTI
P. DEL PARLAMENTO
V. POZZETTO
VIA DEL TRAFORO
VIA DEI GIARDINI
VIC VALDINA
Pal. Montecitorio
VIA S. CLAUDIO
VIA DEL
V. D. PANETTERIA
V. MARONITI
P. CAMPO MARZIO
V. CAMPO MARZIO
P. S. CLAUDIO
P. POLI
V. STAMPERIA
V. IN ARCIONE
V. D. SCUDERIE
Pal. Chigi
V. POLI
SCAVOLINO
S. Agostino
P. COPPELLE
V. UFFICI D. VICARIO
P. COLONNA
V. S. MARIA IN VIA
Fontana di Trevi
V. D. LAVATORE
VIA D. SCALONE
Quirinal
V. D. COPPELLE
P. D. MONTECITORIO
VIA CROCIFERI
V. MADDALENA
VIA BERGAMASCHI
Pal. del Quirinale
LG. TONIOLO
V. P. D. CORNACCHIE
P. MADDALENA
V. D. MURATTE
V. VERGINI
VIA DEL QUIRINALE
P. CAPRANICA
V. MINGHETTI
San Luigi dei Francesi
P. DELLA ROTONDA
VIA D. PASTINI
Hadrian's Temple
LG. PIETRA D. BRAZZA
VIA DELLA DATARIA
Giardino del Quirinale
V. D. VECCHIA
Pal. Giustiniani
P. D. ORATORIO
UMILTÀ
VIA SEMINARIO
P. S. MACUTO
V. COLLEGIO ROMANO
VIA D. ARCHETTO
MONTICELLO
LUCCHESI
P. DEL QUIRINALE
Pal. Madama
Pantheon
V. S. IGNAZIO
Sant' Ignazio di Loyola
V. S. MARCELLO
VIC. MAZZARINO
VIA PIACENZA
V. D. CONSULTA
VIA XXIV MAGGIO
P. S. EUSTACHIO
Santa Maria Sopra Minerva
V. D. VACCARO
Sant'Ivo
P. CAPRETTARI
P. D. MINERVA
SS. Apostoli
VIA D. PILOTTA
See Map pages 11 & 12 for enlargement of this area
V. TEATRO VALLE
V. MONTERONE
P. S. CHIARA
P. COLLEGIO ROMANO
P. S.S. APOSTOLI
V. TRE ARGENTINA
V. D. CESTARI
Pal. Doria Pamphilj
Pal. Colonna
V. PIOMBO
VIA MANCINO
P. S. ANDREA D. VALLE
P. PIGNA
P. GRAZIOLI
V. D. GATTA
VIC. DORIA
VIA DEL GESÙ
VIA IV NOVEMBRE
VIA MAZZARINO
P. VIDONI
C. VITTORIO EMANUELE II
LG. DI TORRE ARGENTINA
VIA BATTISTI
V. FORNARI
V. S. EUFEMIA
V. TRE CANNELLE
VIA CORDONATA
LG. MAGNANAPOLI
Villa Aldobrandini
Sant'Andrea della Valle
V. D. SUDARIO
VIA PLEBISCITO
PIAZZA VENEZIA
Pal. Venezia
V. D. ASTALLI
P. MADONNA DI LORETO
FORO TRAIANO
LG. ANGELICUM
Teatro Argentina
Area Sacra
Chiesa del Gesù
Trajan's Column
Trajan's Market
Santi Domenico e Sisto
V. BARBIERI
V. TORRE ARGENTINA
V. CELSA
P. S. MARCO
Foro di Traiano
SAL. D. GRILLO
V. MONTE D. FARINA
V. FLORIDA
V. B. OSCURE
V. D. ARACOELI
V. S. MARCO
Monumento Vittorio Emanuele II
Entrance to Museo di Risorgimento
V. ALESSANDRINA
P. D. GRILLO
V. IBERNESI
V. TOR D. CONTI
V. CAETANI
Crypta Balbi
V. POLACCHI
P. D. ARACOELI
V. D. FORI IMPERIALI
V. BACCINA
P. CAIROLI
V. ARENULA
V. FALEGNAMI
P. MATTEI
V. MARGANA
Santa Maria in Aracoeli
V. S. PIETRO IN CARCERE
Foro di Cesare
Foro di Augusto
V. MADONNA D. MONTI
SPECCHI
P. COSTAGUTI
V. REGINELLA
V. D. DELFINI
P. MARGANA
Pal. Nuovo
P. LOVATELLI
P. CAPIZUCCHI
Capitolino
Ghetto
P. CAMPIDOGLIO
Curia
V. CAVOUR

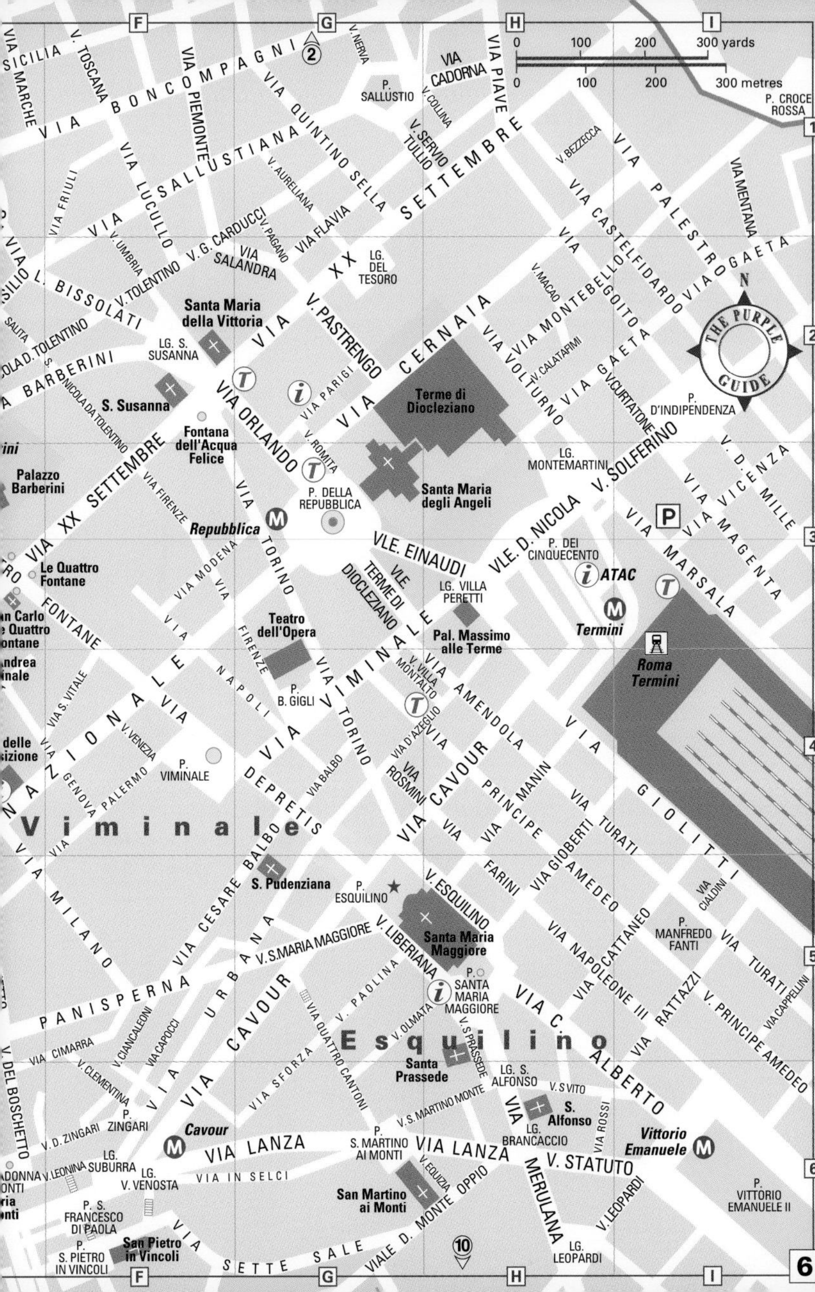

F
G
H
I
1
2
3
4
5
6
300 yards
300 metres
THE PURPLE GUIDE
N
Viminale
Esquilino
Santa Maria della Vittoria
S. Susanna
Fontana dell'Acqua Felice
Palazzo Barberini
Le Quattro Fontane
Terme di Diocleziano
Santa Maria degli Angeli
P. DELLA REPUBBLICA
Repubblica
Teatro dell'Opera
Pal. Massimo alle Terme
Termini
Roma Termini
ATAC
P. D'INDIPENDENZA
P. DEI CINQUECENTO
LG. MONTEMARTINI
LG. VILLA PERETTI
P. SALLUSTIO
LG. DEL TESORO
LG. S. SUSANNA
P. CROCE ROSSA
P. B. GIGLI
P. VIMINALE
S. Pudenziana
P. ESQUILINO
Santa Maria Maggiore
P. SANTA MARIA MAGGIORE
Santa Prassede
LG. S. ALFONSO
S. Alfonso
LG. BRANCACCIO
Vittorio Emanuele
P. VITTORIO EMANUELE II
P. MANFREDO FANTI
Cavour
P. ZINGARI
LG. SUBURRA
LG. V. VENOSTA
P. S. MARTINO AI MONTI
San Martino ai Monti
P. S. FRANCESCO DI PAOLA
P. S. PIETRO IN VINCOLI
San Pietro in Vincoli
LG. LEOPARDI
VIA XX SETTEMBRE
VIA BONCOMPAGNI
VIA SALLUSTIANA
VIA PIEMONTE
VIA LUCULLO
VIA QUINTINO SELLA
VIA CADORNA
VIA PIAVE
VIA PALESTRO
VIA CASTELFIDARDO
VIA GAETA
VIA MENTANA
VIA CERNAIA
VIA VOLTURNO
VIA MONTEBELLO
V. GOITO
V. SOLFERINO
VIA MARSALA
VIA MAGENTA
VIA VICENZA
V. D. MILLE
VIA ORLANDO
V. PASTRENGO
VIA TORINO
VIA NAZIONALE
VIA FIRENZE
VIA MODENA
VIA NAPOLI
VIA VIMINALE
VIA AMENDOLA
VIA CAVOUR
VIA DEPRETIS
VIA GIOLITTI
VIA TURATI
VIA PRINCIPE AMEDEO
VIA GIOBERTI
VIA FARINI
VIA MANIN
VIA ROSMINI
V. ESQUILINO
V. LIBERIANA
V.S.MARIA MAGGIORE
VIA URBANA
VIA PANISPERNA
VIA CESARE BALBO
VIA MILANO
VIA NAPOLEONE III
VIA CATTANEO
VIA C. ALBERTO
VIA RATTAZZI
VIA MERULANA
V. STATUTO
VIA LANZA
VIA IN SELCI
VIA SETTE SALE
VIALE D. MONTE OPPIO
VIA QUATTRO CANTONI
VIA SFORZA
V. PAOLINA
V. OLMATA
V.S.PRASSEDE
V. S. MARTINO MONTE
V. S VITO
VIA ROSSI
V. LEOPARDI
V. EQUIZIA
V. D. ZINGARI
V. LEONINA
V. DEL BOSCHETTO
VIA CIMARRA
V. CIANCALEONI
VIA CAPOCCI
V. CLEMENTINA
VIA BARBERINI
L. BISSOLATI
V. TOLENTINO
V. G. CARDUCCI
VIA SALANDRA
VIA FLAVIA
V. PAGANO
V. AURELIANA
V. UMBRIA
VIA FRIULI
VIA SICILIA
V. TOSCANA
VIA MARCHE
V. NERVIA
V. COLLINA
V. SERVIO TULLIO
V. BEZZECCA
V. MACAO
V. CALATAFIMI
V. CURTATONE
VLE. EINAUDI
VLE. TERME DI DIOCLEZIANO
VLE. D. NICOLA
VIA PARIGI
V. ROMITA
V. VILLA MONTALTO
VIA D'AZEGLIO
VIA BALBO
VIA S. VITALE
V. VENEZIA
VIA GENOVA
VIA PALERMO
VIA CIALDINI
VIA CAPPELLINI
S. NICOLA DA TOLENTINO
SALITA
FONTANE
2
10
6

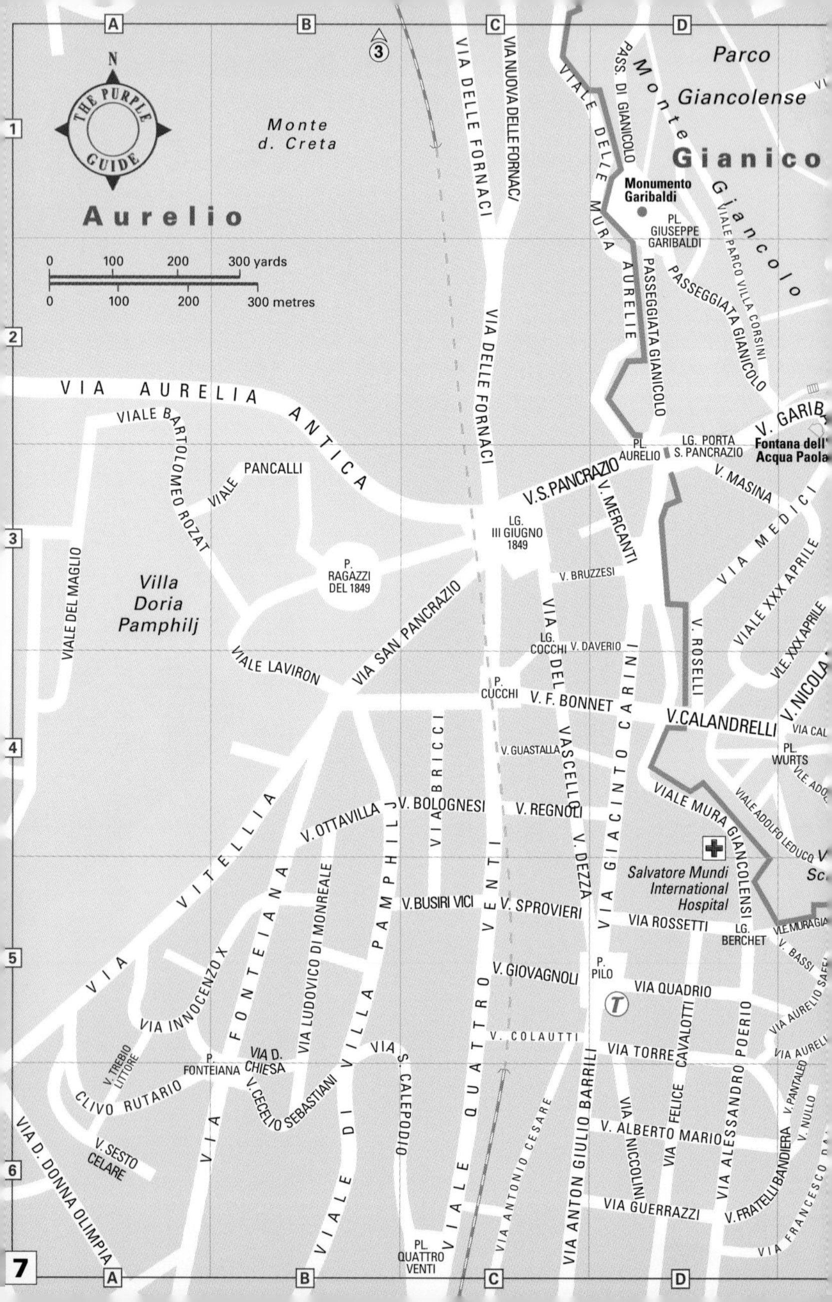

A B C D

THE PURPLE GUIDE

N

Monte d. Creta

Aurelio

0 100 200 300 yards

0 100 200 300 metres

Parco Giancolense

Monte Gianicolo

Monumento Garibaldi

PL. GIUSEPPE GARIBALDI

VIA DELLE FORNACI

VIA NUOVA DELLE FORNACI

VIALE DELLE MURA AURELIE

PASS. DI GIANICOLO

PASSEGGIATA GIANICOLO

PASSEGGIATA GIANICOLO

VIALE PARCO VILLA CORSINI

VIA AURELIA ANTICA

VIALE BARTOLOMEO ROZAT

VIALE PANCALLI

V. GARIB

PL. AURELIO

LG. PORTA S. PANCRAZIO

Fontana dell' Acqua Paola

V.S.PANCRAZIO

V. MERCANTI

V. MASINA

VIA MEDICI

LG. III GIUGNO 1849

P. RAGAZZI DEL 1849

V. BRUZZESI

VIALE XXX APRILE

VLE. XXX APRILE

VIALE DEL MAGLIO

Villa Doria Pamphilj

VIALE LAVIRON

VIA SAN PANCRAZIO

LG. COCCHI

V. DAVERIO

VIA DEL VASCELLO

V. ROSELLI

V. NICOLA

P. CUCCHI

V. F. BONNET

VIA GIACINTO CARINI

V.CALANDRELLI

VIA CAL

V. GUASTALLA

PL. WURTS

VLE. ADO

VIA VITELLIA

VIA BRICCI

V. BOLOGNESI

V. REGNOLI

V. OTTAVILLA

VIALE MURA GIANCOLENSI

VIALE ADOLFO LEDUCQ

V. DEZZA

Salvatore Mundi International Hospital

VIA FONTEIANA

VIA LUDOVICO DI MONREALE

VIA VILLA PAMPHILJ

V. BUSIRI VICI

V. SPROVIERI

VIA ROSSETTI

VLE.MURA GIA

LG. BERCHET

V. BASSI

VIA INNOCENZO X

V. GIOVAGNOLI

P. PILO

VIA QUADRIO

VIA AURELIO SAFFI

VIA AURELIO

VIA QUATTRO VENTI

V. COLAUTTI

VIA TORRE

VIA D. CHIESA

V. TREBIO LITTORE

P. FONTEIANA

VIA S. CALEPODIO

VIA ANTON GIULIO BARRILI

VIA FELICE CAVALOTTI

VIA ALESSANDRO POERIO

V. PANTALEO

CLIVO RUTARIO

V. CECELIO

V. SEBASTIANI

VIA ANTONIO CESARE

VIA NICCOLINI

V. ALBERTO MARIO

V. NULLO

V. SESTO CELARE

VIA D. DONNA OLIMPIA

VIALE DI VILLA PAMPHILJ

VIALE QUATTRO VENTI

VIA GUERRAZZI

V. FRATELLI BANDIERA

VIA FRANCESCO

PL. QUATTRO VENTI

A B C D

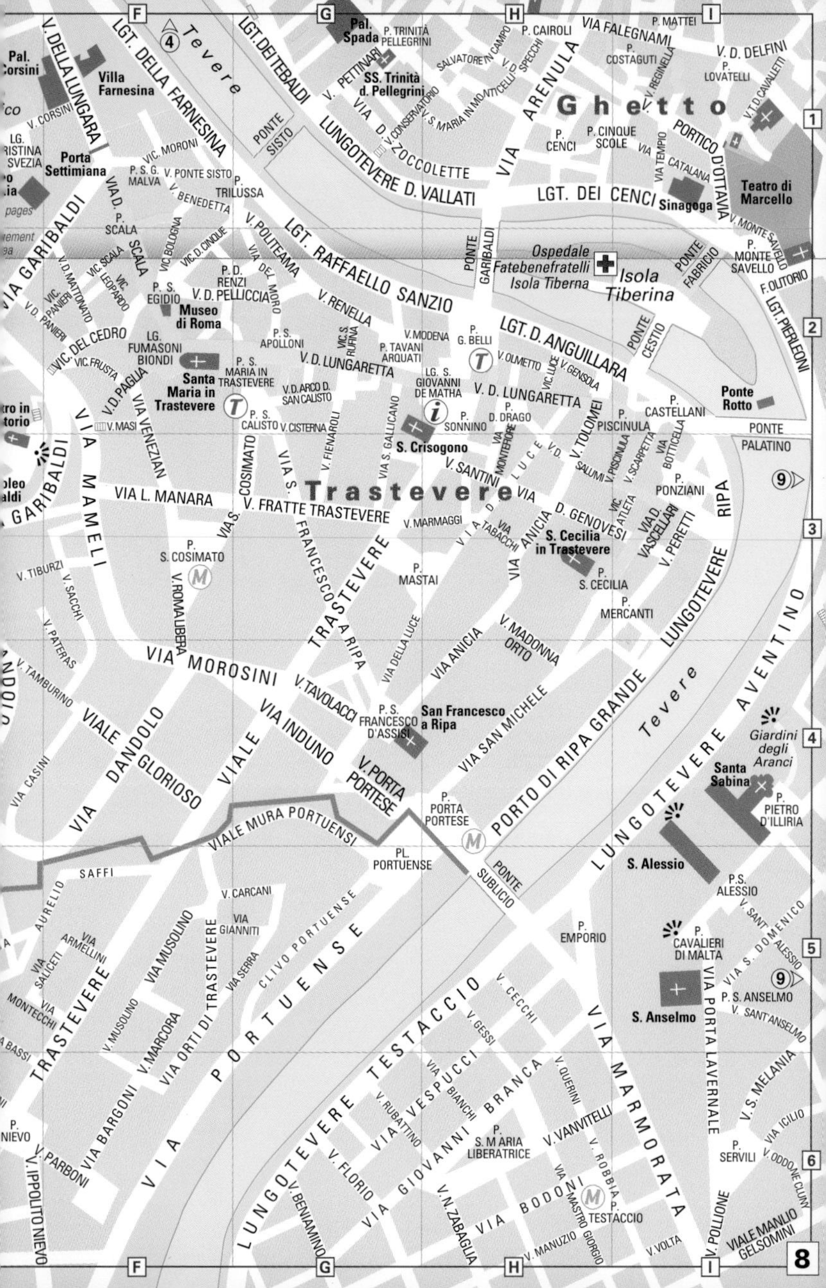

F
G
H
I
1
2
3
4
5
6
8
Pal. Corsini
Villa Farnesina
V. DELLA LUNGARA
LGT. DELLA FARNESINA
Tevere
LGT. DEI TEBALDI
Pal. Spada
P. TRINITÀ PELLEGRINI
SS. Trinità d. Pellegrini
V. PETTINARI
P. CAIROLI
VIA FALEGNAMI
P. MATTEI
P. COSTAGUTI
V. D. DELFINI
P. LOVATELLI
Ghetto
VIA ARENULA
P. CENCI
P. CINQUE SCOLE
VIA TEMPIO
VIA CATALANA
PORTICO D'OTTAVIA
Teatro di Marcello
Sinagoga
LGT. DEI CENCI
LUNGOTEVERE D. VALLATI
V. ZOCCOLETTE
PONTE SISTO
Porta Settimiana
V. CORSINI
VIC. MORONI
P. S. G. MALVA
V. PONTE SISTO
P. TRILUSSA
V. BENEDETTA
VIA GARIBALDI
P. SCALA
V. POLITEAMA
LGT. RAFFAELLO SANZIO
PONTE GARIBALDI
Ospedale Fatebenefratelli
Isola Tiberina
PONTE FABRICIO
P. MONTE SAVELLO
V. MONTE SAVELLO
F. OLITORIO
LGT. PIERLEONI
P. D. RENZI
V. D. PELLICCIA
P. S. EGIDIO
Museo di Roma
V. RENELLA
VIC. DEL CEDRO
LG. FUMASONI BIONDI
P. S. APOLLONI
V. D. LUNGARETTA
P. TAVANI ARQUATI
V. MODENA
P. G. BELLI
LGT. D. ANGUILLARA
PONTE CESTIO
P. S. MARIA IN TRASTEVERE
Santa Maria in Trastevere
V.D. ARCO D. SAN CALISTO
LG. S. GIOVANNI DE MATHA
V. D. LUNGARETTA
Ponte Rotto
P. S. CALISTO
V. CISTERNA
V. D. PAGLIA
VIA VENEZIAN
V. MASI
P. SONNINO
P. D. DRAGO
P. PISCINULA
P. CASTELLANI
PONTE PALATINO
S. Crisogono
V. SANTINI
V. TOLOMEI
VIA MAMELI
VIA L. MANARA
V. FRATTE TRASTEVERE
Trastevere
VIA ANICIA
V. D. GENOVESI
P. PONZIANI
RIPA
P. S. COSIMATO
V. MARMAGGI
S. Cecilia in Trastevere
V. PERETTI
P. S. CECILIA
P. MASTAI
P. MERCANTI
V. TIBURZI
V. SACCHI
V. ROMA LIBERA
VIA MOROSINI
VIA S. FRANCESCO A RIPA
TRASTEVERE
VIA DELLA LUCE
VIA ANICIA
V. MADONNA ORTO
LUNGOTEVERE
AVENTINO
V. TAVOLACCI
P. S. FRANCESCO D'ASSISI
San Francesco a Ripa
VIA SAN MICHELE
PORTO DI RIPA GRANDE
Tevere
Giardini degli Aranci
VIALE GLORIOSO
VIA DANDOLO
VIALE
VIA INDUNO
V. PORTA PORTESE
P. PORTA PORTESE
Santa Sabina
P. PIETRO D'ILLIRIA
VIALE MURA PORTUENSI
PL. PORTUENSE
PONTE SUBLICIO
LUNGOTEVERE
S. Alessio
P.S. ALESSIO
VIA CASINI
V. TAMBURINO
SAFFI
AURELIO
V. CARCANI
VIA GIANNITI
CLIVO PORTUENSE
P. EMPORIO
P. CAVALIERI DI MALTA
V. SANT'ALESSIO
VIA S. DOMENICO
VIA MUSOLINO
VIA ORTI DI TRASTEVERE
VIA SERRA
VIA PORTUENSE
LUNGOTEVERE TESTACCIO
V. CECCHI
V. GESSI
VIA MARMORATA
VIA PORTA LAVERNALE
P. S. ANSELMO
V. SANT'ANSELMO
S. Anselmo
VIA ARMELLINI
VIA SALICETI
VIA MONTECCHI
TRASTEVERE
V. MUSOLINO
V. MARCORA
VIA BARGONI
VIA VESPUCCI
VIA BIANCHI
V. RUBATTINO
VIA GIOVANNI BRANCA
V. QUERINI
P. S. MARIA LIBERATRICE
V. VANVITELLI
V. ROBBIA
V. S. MELANIA
VIA ICILIO
P. SERVILI
V. ODDONE CLUNY
P. NIEVO
V. PARBONI
V. IPPOLITO NIEVO
VIA
V. FLORIO
V. BENIAMINO
V. N. ZABAGLIA
VIA BODONI
VIA MASTRO GIORGIO
P. TESTACCIO
V. MANUZIO
V. VOLTA
V. POLLIONE
VIALE MANLIO GELSOMINI

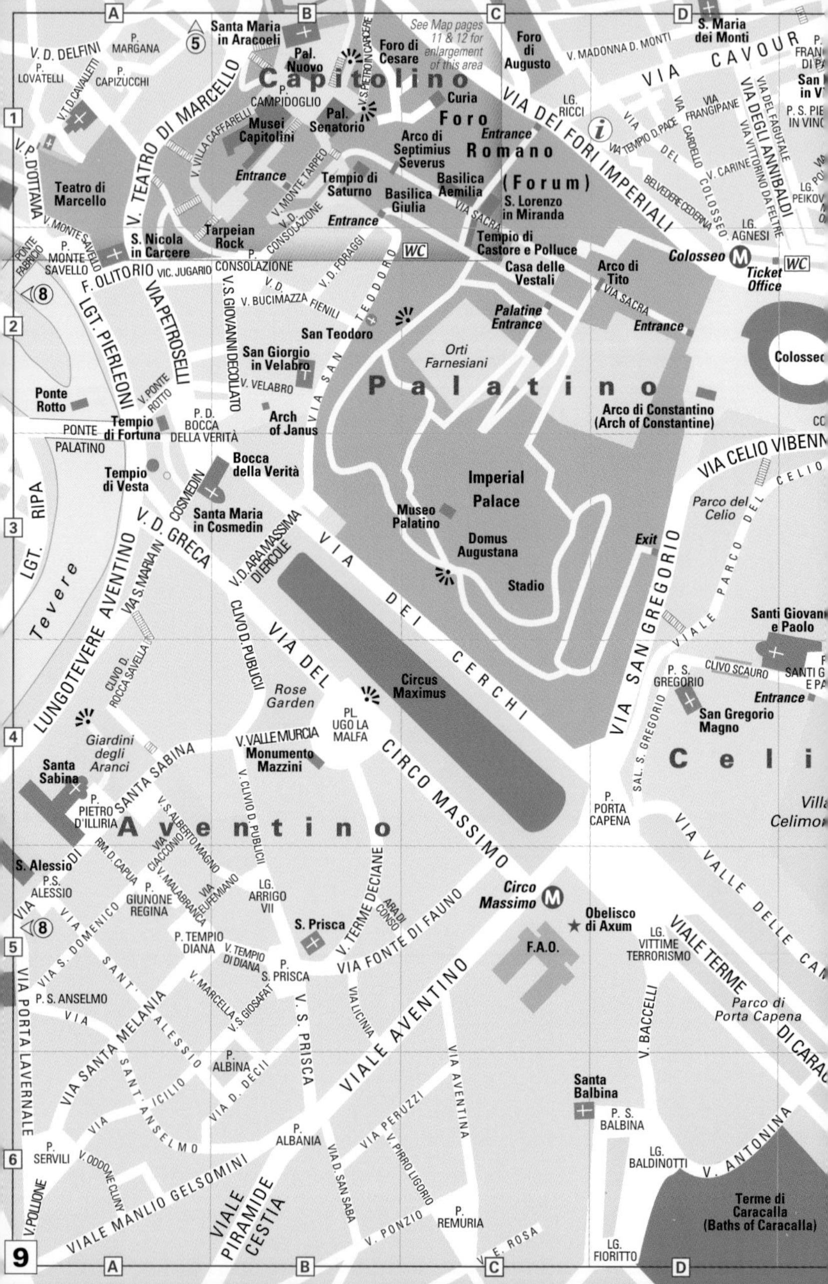

A
B
C
D
1
2
3
4
5
6
9
Santa Maria in Aracoeli
See Map pages 11 & 12 for enlargement of this area
Foro di Augusto
S. Maria dei Monti
V. D. DELFINI
P. MARGANA
Pal. Nuovo
Foro di Cesare
V. MADONNA D. MONTI
VIA CAVOUR
P. LOVATELLI
P. CAPIZUCCHI
Capitolino
P. CAMPIDOGLIO
Curia
VIA DEI FORI IMPERIALI
Foro Romano (Forum)
V. TEATRO DI MARCELLO
Musei Capitolini
Pal. Senatorio
Entrance
LG. RICCI
V.T.D. CAVALLETTI
V. VILLA CAFFARELLI
Arco di Septimius Severus
VIA FRANGIPANE
VIA DEGLI ANNIBALDI
V.P. D'OTTAVIA
V. MONTE TARPEO
Tempio di Saturno
Basilica Aemilia
V. CARINE
VIA VITTORINO DA FELTRE
Teatro di Marcello
Basilica Giulia
S. Lorenzo in Miranda
BELVEDERE CEDERNA
V. COLOSSEO
V. MONTE SAVELLO
V. D. CONSOLAZIONE
VIA SACRA
Tempio di Castore e Polluce
LG. AGNESI
S. Nicola in Carcere
Tarpeian Rock
WC
Colosseo
Casa delle Vestali
Arco di Tito
Ticket Office
PONTE FABRICIO
P. MONTE SAVELLO
F. OLITORIO
VIC. JUGARIO
P. CONSOLAZIONE
V. D. FORAGGI
V. D. FIENILI
V. BUCIMAZZA
VIA SAN TEODORO
Palatine Entrance
LGT. PIERLEONI
VIA PETROSELLI
V.S. GIOVANNI DECOLLATO
San Teodoro
Orti Farnesiani
San Giorgio in Velabro
V. VELABRO
Colosseo
Palatino
Ponte Rotto
V. PONTE ROTTO
Arch of Janus
Arco di Constantino (Arch of Constantine)
PONTE PALATINO
Tempio di Fortuna
P. D. BOCCA DELLA VERITÀ
VIA CELIO VIBENNA
Bocca della Verità
Imperial Palace
Tempio di Vesta
COSMEDIN
Parco del Celio
LGT. RIPA
V. D. GRECA
Santa Maria in Cosmedin
Museo Palatino
Domus Augustana
VIA DEI CERCHI
Exit
V.D. ARA MASSIMA DI ERCOLE
Stadio
VIA SAN GREGORIO
VIALE PARCO DEL CELIO
Tevere
LUNGOTEVERE AVENTINO
VIA S. MARIA IN
CLIVO D. PUBLICII
VIA DEL CIRCO MASSIMO
Santi Giovanni e Paolo
CLIVO D. ROCCA SAVELLA
Rose Garden
Circus Maximus
P. S. GREGORIO
CLIVO SCAURO
Entrance
PL. UGO LA MALFA
San Gregorio Magno
Giardini degli Aranci
V. VALLE MURCIA
Monumento Mazzini
Celio
SAL. S. GREGORIO
Santa Sabina
SANTA SABINA
V. CLIVIO D. PUBLICII
P. PORTA CAPENA
P. PIETRO D'ILLIRIA
Aventino
V.S. ALBERTO MAGNO
VIA VALLE DELLE CAMENE
S. Alessio
RM. D. CAPUA
VIA CIACCONIO
V. MALABRANCA
VIA EUFEMIANO
V. TERME DECIANE
ARA DI CONSO
P. S. ALESSIO
P. GIUNONE REGINA
LG. ARRIGO VII
Circo Massimo
Obelisco di Axum
VIA DI S. DOMENICO
VIA FONTE DI FAUNO
S. Prisca
LG. VITTIME TERRORISMO
P. TEMPIO DIANA
V. TEMPIO DI DIANA
F.A.O.
VIALE TERME DI CARACALLA
VIA PORTA LAVERNALE
P. S. PRISCA
VIA S. ANSELMO
V. MARCELLA
V.S. GIOSAFAT
VIA LICINIA
P. S. ANSELMO
V. S. PRISCA
VIALE AVENTINO
Parco di Porta Capena
VIA SANTA MELANIA
VIA S. ALESSIO
V. BACCELLI
P. ALBINA
VIA AVENTINA
VIA ICILIO
VIA D. DECII
Santa Balbina
P. S. BALBINA
P. ALBANIA
VIA PERUZZI
V. PIRRO LIGORIO
V. ANTONINA
P. SERVILI
V. ODDONE CLUNY
VIA D. SAN SABA
LG. BALDINOTTI
V. POLLIONE
VIALE MANLIO GELSOMINI
VIALE PIRAMIDE CESTIA
Terme di Caracalla (Baths of Caracalla)
V. PONZIO
P. REMURIA
V. E. ROSA
LG. FIORITTO

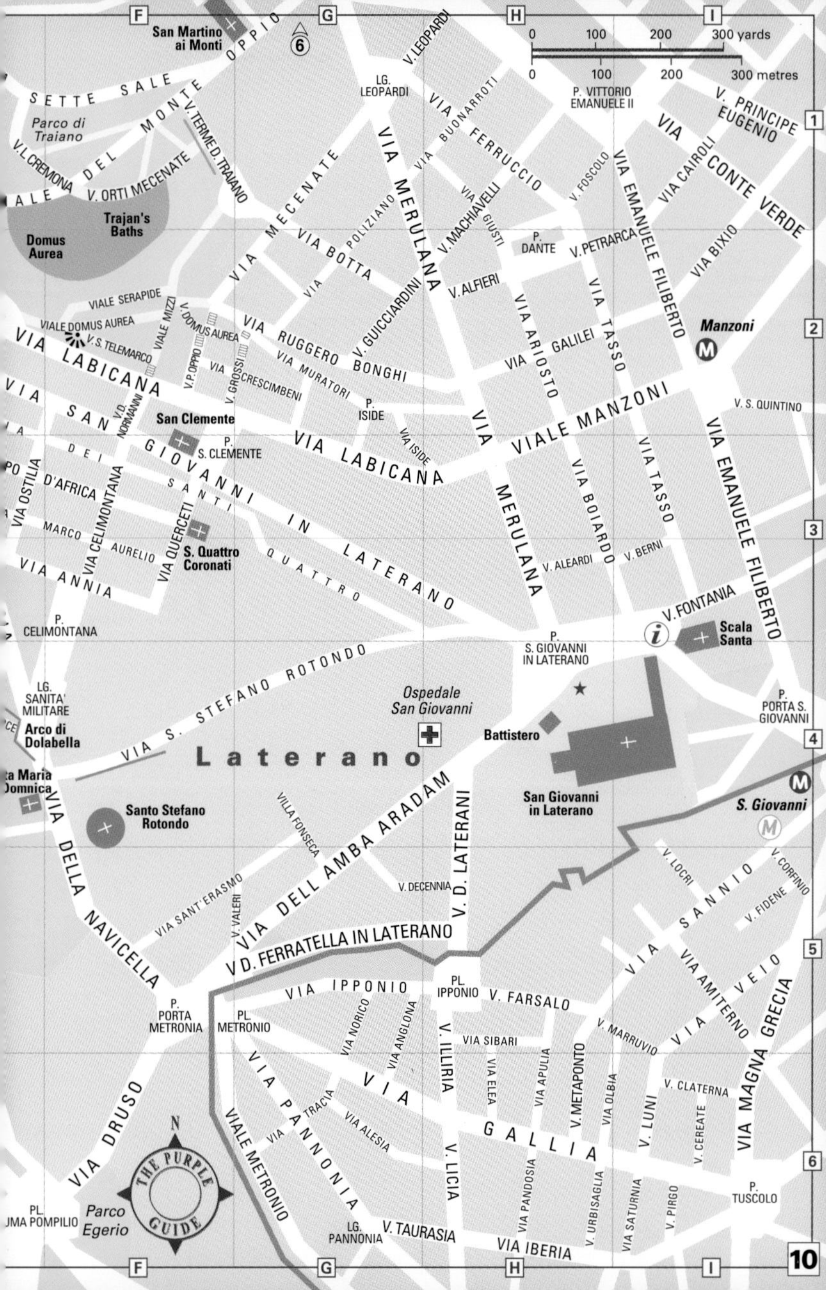
F
G
H
I
1
2
3
4
5
6
10
0
100
200
300 yards
300 metres
San Martino ai Monti
6
Sette Sale
Oppio
Parco di Traiano
Viale del Monte Oppio
V. L. Cremona
V. Terme D. Traiano
V. Orti Mecenate
Trajan's Baths
Domus Aurea
V. Leopardi
LG. Leopardi
P. Vittorio Emanuele II
Via Buonarroti
Via Ferruccio
V. Principe Eugenio
Via Conte Verde
Via Cairoli
V. Foscolo
Via Emanuele Filiberto
Via Merulana
Via Mecenate
Via Poliziano
V. Machiavelli
Via Giusti
P. Dante
V. Petrarca
Via Bixio
Via Botta
V. Alfieri
V. Guicciardini
Via Ariosto
Via Tasso
Viale Serapide
Viale Domus Aurea
V. S. Telemarco
Viale Mizzi
V. Domus Aurea
Via Ruggero Bonghi
Via Galilei
Manzoni
Via Labicana
V. P. Oppio
Via Crescimbeni
V. Grossi
Via Muratori
P. Iside
Viale Manzoni
V. S. Quintino
Via San Giovanni in Laterano
V. D. Normanni
San Clemente
P. S. Clemente
Via Iside
Via dei Santi Quattro
Via Ostilia
D'Africa
Via Celimontana
Via Querceti
S. Quattro Coronati
Marco Aurelio
Via Annia
Via Boiardo
V. Aleardi
V. Berni
V. Fontania
Scala Santa
P. Celimontana
P. S. Giovanni in Laterano
Via S. Stefano Rotondo
LG. Sanita' Militare
Arco di Dolabella
Ospedale San Giovanni
Battistero
P. Porta S. Giovanni
Laterano
San Giovanni in Laterano
S. Giovanni
Santo Stefano Rotondo
Via della Navicella
Villa Fonseca
Via dell Amba Aradam
V. D. Laterani
V. Decennia
V. Locri
V. Corfinio
Via Sannio
V. Fidene
Via Sant'Erasmo
V. Valeri
V D. Ferratella in Laterano
Via Amiterno
Via Veio
PL. Ipponio
Via Ipponio
V. Farsalo
P. Porta Metronia
PL. Metronio
Via Norico
Via Anglona
V. Illiria
Via Sibari
V. Marruvio
Via Magna Grecia
Via Druso
Via Pannonia
Via Tracia
Via Alesia
Via Elea
Via Apulia
V. Metaponto
Via Olbia
V. Luni
V. Claterna
V. Cereate
Via Gallia
Viale Metronio
V. Licia
Via Pandosia
V. Urbisaglia
Via Saturnia
V. Pirgo
P. Tuscolo
The Purple Guide
N
PL. Numa Pompilio
Parco Egerio
LG. Pannonia
V. Taurasia
Via Iberia

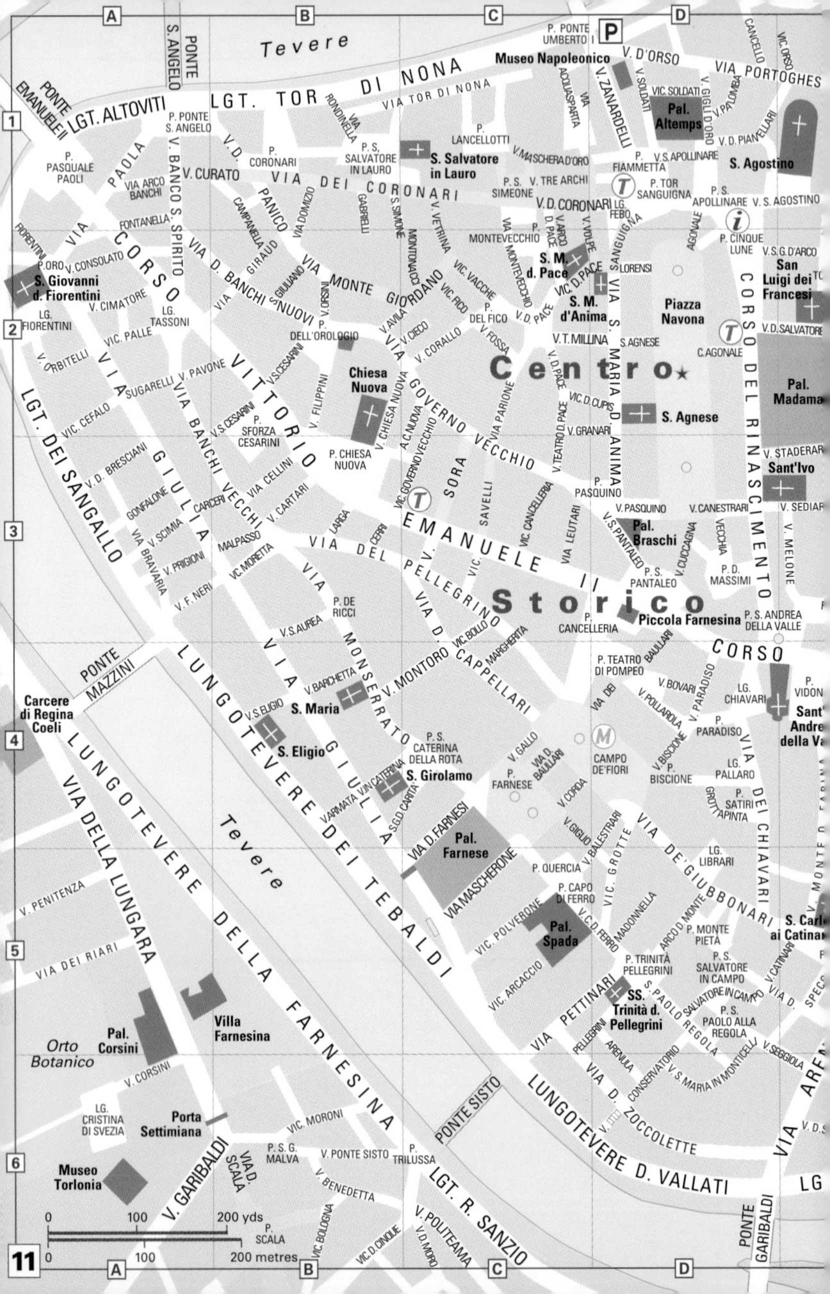

A
B
C
D
1
2
3
4
5
6
Tevere
PONTE S. ANGELO
PONTE EMANUELE II
LGT. ALTOVITI
LGT. TOR DI NONA
VIA TOR DI NONA
P. PONTE UMBERTO I
P
Museo Napoleonico
V. D'ORSO
VIA PORTOGHESI
V. ZANARDELLI
Pal. Altemps
S. Agostino
V. D. PIANELLARI
P. PONTE S. ANGELO
P. PASQUALE PAOLI
PAOLA
V. BANCO S. SPIRITO
V. CURATO
P. CORONARI
VIA DEI CORONARI
P. S. SALVATORE IN LAURO
S. Salvatore in Lauro
P. LANCELLOTTI
V. MASCHERA D'ORO
P. FIAMMETTA
V. S. APOLLINARE
P. S. SIMEONE
V. TRE ARCHI
P. TOR SANGUIGNA
P. S. APOLLINARE
V. S. AGOSTINO
V. D. CORONARI
LG. FEBO
VIA ARCO BANCHI
FONTANELLA
PANICO
CAMPANELLA
VIA DOMIZIO
GABRIELLI
V. VETRINA
MONTEVECCHIO
P. CINQUE LUNE
V. S. G. D'ARCO
San Luigi dei Francesi
VIA CORSO
VIA D. BANCHI NUOVI
VIA MONTE GIORDANO
S. M. d. Pace
VIC. D. PACE
S. M. d'Anima
VIA S. MARIA D. ANIMA
Piazza Navona
CORSO DEL RINASCIMENTO
P. ORO
V. CONSOLATO
S. Giovanni d. Fiorentini
V. CIMATORE
LG. FIORENTINI
LG. TASSONI
VIC. PALLE
P. DELL'OROLOGIO
P. DEL FICO
V. D. PACE
V. T. MILLINA
S. AGNESE
C. AGONALE
V. D. SALVATORE
V. ORBITELLI
SUGARELLI
V. PAVONE
VITTORIO
Chiesa Nuova
VIA GOVERNO VECCHIO
Centro
Pal. Madama
LGT. DEI SANGALLO
VIC. CEFALO
VIA BANCHI VECCHI
V. S. CESARINI
P. SFORZA CESARINI
V. FILIPPINI
V. CHIESA NUOVA
VIA PARIONE
VIC. D. CUPIS
S. Agnese
V. D. BRESCIANI
VIA GIULIA
VIA CELLINI
P. CHIESA NUOVA
SORA
V. GRANARI
V. STADERARI
Sant'Ivo
GONFALONE
CARCERI
V. CARTARI
SAVELLI
VIC. CANCELLERIA
P. PASQUINO
V. PASQUINO
V. CANESTRARI
V. SEDIARI
VIA BRAVARIA
V. SCIMIA
V. PRIGIONI
MALPASSO
LARGA
CERRI
EMANUELE II
Pal. Braschi
V. S. PANTALEO
V. CUCCAGNA
VECCHIA
V. MELONE
VIC. MORETTA
VIA DEL PELLEGRINO
VIA LEUTARI
P. S. PANTALEO
P. D. MASSIMI
V. F. NERI
P. DE RICCI
Storico
P. CANCELLERIA
Piccola Farnesina
P. S. ANDREA DELLA VALLE
V. S. AUREA
VIA MONSERRATO
VIA D. CAPPELLARI
VIC. BOLLO
MARGHERITA
CORSO
P. TEATRO DI POMPEO
BAULLARI
PONTE MAZZINI
LUNGOTEVERE DEI TEBALDI
V. BARCHETTA
V. MONTORO
V. BOVARI
V. PARADISO
LG. CHIAVARI
P. VIDONI
Carcere di Regina Coeli
V. S. ELIGIO
S. Maria
VIA DEI
V. POLLAROLA
Sant'Andrea della Valle
P. S. CATERINA DELLA ROTA
V. GALLO
CAMPO DE' FIORI
P. PARADISO
LUNGOTEVERE
VIA DELLA LUNGARA
S. Eligio
P. FARNESE
VIA D. BAULLARI
V. BISCIONE
P. BISCIONE
LG. PALLARO
S. Girolamo
V. CORDA
GROTTAPINTA
P. SATIRI
VIA DEI CHIAVARI
V. ARMATA
V. IN CATERINA
S. G. D. CARITÀ
VIA D. FARNESI
Pal. Farnese
V. GIGLIO
V. BALESTRARI
VIA DE' GIUBBONARI
LG. LIBRARI
P. QUERCIA
VIA MASCHERONE
VIC. GROTTE
P. CAPO DI FERRO
V. PENITENZA
VIC. POLVERONE
Pal. Spada
V. C. D. FERRO
MADONNELLA
ARCO D. MONTE
P. MONTE PIETÀ
S. Carlo ai Catinari
VIA DEI RIARI
LUNGOTEVERE DELLA FARNESINA
VIC. ARCACCIO
P. TRINITÀ PELLEGRINI
P. S. SALVATORE IN CAMPO
V. CATINARI
VIA PETTINARI
SS. Trinità d. Pellegrini
S. PAOLO REGOLA
SALVATORE IN CAMPO
P. S. PAOLO ALLA REGOLA
Villa Farnesina
Pal. Corsini
Orto Botanico
PELLEGRINI
ARENULA
CONSERVATORIO
V. S. MARIA IN MONTICELLI
V. SEGGIOLA
V. CORSINI
PONTE SISTO
LUNGOTEVERE D. VALLATI
VIA D. ZOCCOLETTE
VIA ARENULA
LG. CRISTINA DI SVEZIA
Porta Settimiana
VIC. MORONI
P. S. G. MALVA
V. PONTE SISTO
P. TRILUSSA
V. GARIBALDI
VIA D. SCALA
Museo Torlonia
V. BENEDETTA
LGT. R. SANZIO
PONTE GARIBALDI
0
100
200 yds
200 metres
P. SCALA
VIC. BOLOGNA
VIC. D. CINQUE
V. POLITEAMA
V. D. MORO
11

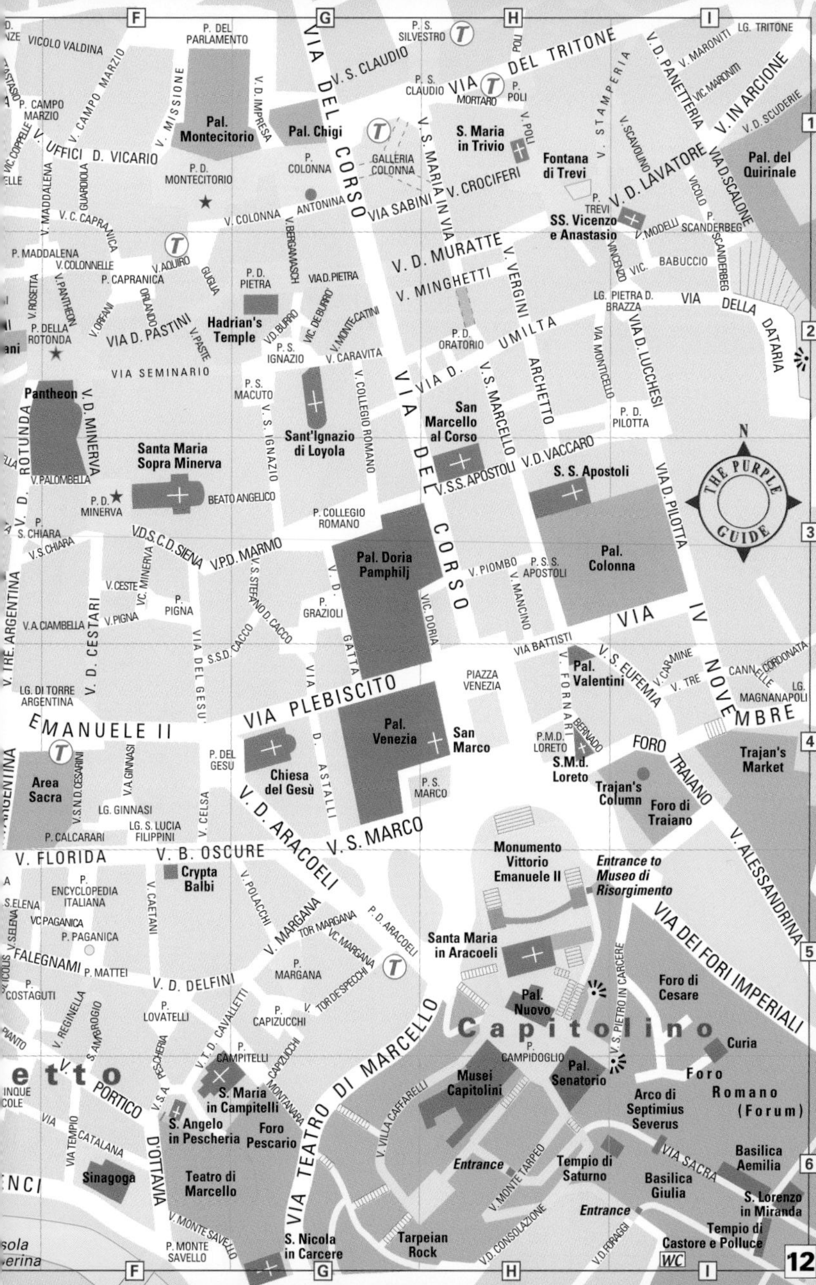
Pal. Montecitorio
Pal. Chigi
Galleria Colonna
S. Maria in Trivio
Fontana di Trevi
SS. Vicenzo e Anastasio
Pal. del Quirinale
Hadrian's Temple
Pantheon
Santa Maria Sopra Minerva
Sant'Ignazio di Loyola
San Marcello al Corso
S. S. Apostoli
Pal. Colonna
Pal. Doria Pamphilj
Piazza Venezia
Pal. Valentini
Pal. Venezia
San Marco
Chiesa del Gesù
Area Sacra
Crypta Balbi
S.M.d. Loreto
Trajan's Column
Foro di Traiano
Trajan's Market
Monumento Vittorio Emanuele II
Entrance to Museo di Risorgimento
Santa Maria in Aracoeli
Pal. Nuovo
Capitolino
Musei Capitolini
Pal. Senatorio
Foro di Cesare
Curia
Foro Romano (Forum)
Arco di Septimius Severus
Tempio di Saturno
Basilica Giulia
Basilica Aemilia
S. Lorenzo in Miranda
Tempio di Castore e Polluce
Tarpeian Rock
S. Nicola in Carcere
Teatro di Marcello
Foro Pescario
S. Maria in Campitelli
S. Angelo in Pescheria
Sinagoga
Via del Corso
Via del Tritone
Via Plebiscito
Emanuele II
Via dei Fori Imperiali
Via Teatro di Marcello
V. D. Aracoeli
V. S. Marco
V. Florida
V. B. Oscure
Via IV Novembre
Via della Dataria
V. D. Muratte
Foro Traiano
V. Alessandrina
Via Sacra
THE PURPLE GUIDE
N

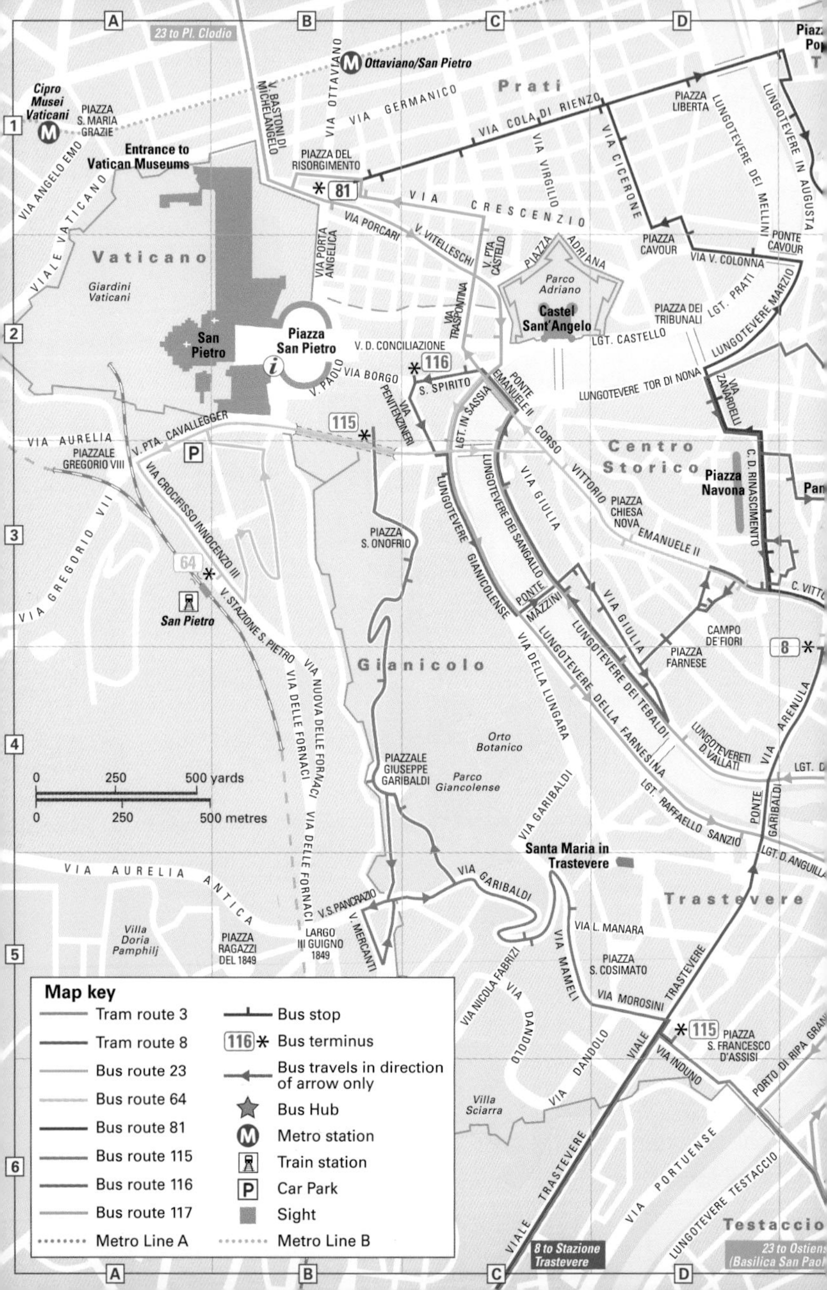

23 to Pl. Clodio
Ottaviano/San Pietro
Prati
Cipro Musei Vaticani
PIAZZA S. MARIA GRAZIE
Entrance to Vatican Museums
PIAZZA DEL RISORGIMENTO
PIAZZA LIBERTA
Vaticano
Giardini Vaticani
San Pietro
Piazza San Pietro
PIAZZA CAVOUR
PONTE CAVOUR
Parco Adriano
Castel Sant'Angelo
PIAZZA DEI TRIBUNALI
Centro Storico
Piazza Navona
PIAZZA CHIESA NOVA
PIAZZALE GREGORIO VIII
PIAZZA S. ONOFRIO
San Pietro
CAMPO DE' FIORI
PIAZZA FARNESE
Gianicolo
Orto Botanico
PIAZZALE GIUSEPPE GARIBALDI
Parco Giancolense
Santa Maria in Trastevere
Trastevere
Villa Doria Pamphilj
PIAZZA RAGAZZI DEL 1849
LARGO III GUIGNO 1849
PIAZZA S. COSIMATO
PIAZZA S. FRANCESCO D'ASSISI
Villa Sciarra
Testaccio
8 to Stazione Trastevere
23 to Ostiense (Basilica San Paolo)
0 250 500 yards
0 250 500 metres
Map key
Tram route 3
Tram route 8
Bus route 23
Bus route 64
Bus route 81
Bus route 115
Bus route 116
Bus route 117
Metro Line A
Bus stop
Bus terminus
Bus travels in direction of arrow only
Bus Hub
Metro station
Train station
Car Park
Sight
Metro Line B

Transport Map
F
G
H
I
1
2
3
4
5
6
116 to Galleria Borghese
Galoppatoio
VIALE DEL MURO TORTO
116
PIAZZALE BRASILE
VIA CAMPANIA
VIA PIEMONTE
VIA PIAVE
VIA BONCOMPAGNI
PIAZZA SALLUSTIO
PIAZZA CROCE ROSSA
BABUINO
VIA PORTA PINCIANA
VIA V. VENETO
VIA LUDOVISI
VIA SALLUSTIANA
VIA XX SETTEMBRE
VIA PALESTRO
Spagna
PIAZZA DI SPAGNA
Spanish Steps
VIA CRISPI
VIA VITTORIO VENETO
VIA SAN BASILIO
VIA L. BISSOLATI
Castro Pretorio
PIAZZA MIGNANELLI
LARGO S. SUSANNA
VIA BARBERINI
VIA CERNAIA
Terme di Diocleziano
V.S.MARTINO D.BATT.
PIAZZA D'INDEPENDENZA
VIA DUE MACELLI
Barberini
VIA ORLANDO
VIA XX SETTEMBRE
PIAZZA DELLA REPUBBLICA
Repubblica
VLE. EINAUDI
VLE. D. NICOLA
PIAZZA S. SILVESTRO
VIA DEL TRITONE
VIA DEL TRAFORO
VIA QUATTRO FONTANE
VIA DEL CORSO
VLE. TERME DI DIOCLEZIANO
PIAZZA DEI CINQUECENTO
VIA MARSALA
Fontana di Trevi
Quirinale
Termini
Termini
64
V. DEL QUIRINALE
VIA NAZIONALE
VIA VIMINALE
VIA DEPRETIS
VIA CAVOUR
PIAZZA QUIRINALE
PIAZZA D. PILOTTA
VIA XXIV MAGGIO
Viminale
PIAZZA DELL' ESQUILINO
Santa Maria Maggiore
VIA GIOLITTI
PIAZZA MANFREDO FANTI
VIA MILANO
VIA IV NOVEMBRE
PIAZZA SANTA MARIA MAGGIORE
PLEBISCITO
LARGO MAGNANAPOLI
VIA PANISPERNA
PIAZZA VENEZIA
V. S. MARCO
VIA MERULANA
Vittorio Emanuele
Cavour
VIA LANZA
V. STATUTO
PIAZZA VITTORIO EMANUELE II
ARACOELI
VIA DEI FORI IMPERIALI
VIA CAVOUR
Esquilino
V. PRINCIPE EUGENIO
MARCELLO
Musei Capitolini
Capitolino
VIA DEGLI ANNIBALDI
VIA C.
3 to Villa Borghese
Foro Romano (Roman Forum)
Parco di Traiano
VIA MERULANA
PIAZZA DANTE
VERDE
VIA PETROSELLI
Colosseo
VIA N. SALVI
Parco Oppio
VIA EMANUELE FILBERTO
Manzoni
Colosseo
VIA LABICANA
VIALE MANZONI
Palatino
VIA CELIO VIBENNA
V. S. GIOVANNI IN LATERANO
S. Clemente
VIA MERULANA
VIA DEI CERCHI
VIA DEL CIRCO MASSIMO
VIA SAN GREGORIO
VIA PARCO CELIO
Celio
VIA CLAUDIA
V. FONTANIA
VIA EMANUELE FILBERTO
117
San Giovanni in Laterano
PIAZZALE UGO LA MALFA
S. Giovanni
entino
Laterano
VIA DELL AMBA ARADAM
Villa Celimontana
VIA DELLA NAVICELLA
Circo Massimo
N
VIALE AVENTINO
VIALE TERME DI CARACALLA
PIAZZA PORTA METRONIA
VIA PANNONIA
V. ILLIRIA
THE PURPLE GUIDE
VIA MAGNA GRECIA
VIA DRUSO
VIA GALLIA
Terme di Caracalla (Baths of Caracalla)
to Stazione Trastevere
to Anagnina

Essential Shopping Italian

Open	**Aperto**	*ah*-**pehr**-*toh*
Closed	**Chiuso**	*kee*-**oo**-*soh*
How much is this?	**Quanto costa questo?**	**kwan**-*toh* **koh**-*sta* **kwes**-*toh?*
Can you write down the price?	**Puo scrivere il prezzo?**	*pwo skree*-**veh**-*reh eel* **preh**-*tso?*
Do you take credit cards?	**Prendete carte di credito?**	*pren*-**deh**-*teh* **kar**-*teh dee* **kreh**-*dee-toh?*
I'd like to buy . . .	**Vorrei comprare . . .**	*voh*-**ray** *kom*-**prah**-*reh*
Do you have anything . . .?	**Avete qualcosa . . .?**	*ah*-**veh**-*teh kwahl*-**koh**-*sah*
larger	**piu grande**	*pyoo* **grahn**-*deh*
smaller	**piu piccolo**	*pyoo* **pee**-*kohl-oh*
Do you have any others?	**Ne avete altri?**	*neh ah*-**veh**-*teh* **ahl**-*tree*
I'm just looking.	**Sto solo guardando.**	*sto* **soh**-*loh gwar*-**dan**-*doh*

Size Chart

Women's dresses, coats and skirts

Italian	40	42	44	46	48	50	52
British	8	10	12	14	16	18	20
American	6	8	10	12	14	16	18

Women's shoes

Italian	36	37	38	39	40	41
British	3	4	5	6	7	8
American	5	6	7	8	9	10

Men's suits

Italian	44	46	48	50	52	54	56	58 (size)
British	34	36	38	40	42	44	46	48 (inches)
American	34	36	38	40	42	44	46	48 (inches)

Men's shirts (collar size)

Italian	36	38	39	41	42	44	46	48 (cm)
British	14	15	15½	16	16½	17	17½	18 (inches)
American	14	15	15½	16	16½	17	17½	18 (inches)

Men's shoes

Italian	39	40	41	42	43	44	45	46
British	6	7	7½	8	9	10	11	12
American	7	7½	8	8½	9½	10½	11	11½